COMPETITIVE INNOVATION MANAGEMENT

Competitive Innovation Management

Techniques to improve innovation performance

James A. Christiansen

First published 2000 by
MACMILLAN PRESS LTD
Houndmills, Basingstoke, Hampshire RG21 6XS
and London
Companies and representatives
throughout the world

ISBN 0–333–80052–4 hardcover

A catalogue record for this book is available
from the British Library.

This book is printed on paper suitable for recycling and
made from fully managed and sustained forest sources.

10 9   8   7   6 5   4   3   2   1
09 08 07 06 05 04 03 02 01 00

Editing and origination by
Aardvark Editorial, Mendham, Suffolk

Printed and bound in Great Britain by
Creative Print & Design (Wales), Ebbw Vale

to
Gwen

Contents

List of Figures   xiii

List of Tables   xvi

Preface   xvii

Acknowledgements   xxi

1 Introduction   **1**

Two companies   1
   The topic of this book   2
   The purpose of this book   4
   Methodology   5
   Introduction to the companies   6
   Outline of the book   10

**Part I A Wide Range of Management Systems and
Practices Impact Innovation Performance**   **15**

2 The Chemical Residues Story   **17**

The mother company: MGE   18
The Chemical Residues project and the Industrial
   Chemicals division   19
   A chemist discovers an idea   20
   Hunting for help and for money   24
   Corporate begins supporting innovation   33
   Reforming project funding and management systems   39
   Changing the organization   48
   Epilog   51

3 Interpreting the Chemical Residues Story   **53**

Roadblocks encountered and management tools used
   during the CR project   53
   Different types of intervention in the innovation
      management system   53
   The scope of a manager's actions   55

Sequencing a change effort and involving other people   57
Categorizing the tools   63

4   A Framework for Thinking about Innovation   70

Overview of the innovation process   72
   Phases of the innovation process   72
   Goals: what does it mean to improve
      innovation performance?   74
   Components of innovation performance   75
   Goals for each phase of the process   76
Idea generation systems   79
   Old theories of how to get ideas   79
   Who generates new ideas?   81
   Children, newcomers, and other outsiders   82
   Why it can be difficult to accept new ideas, particularly
      from outsiders   83
   Idea diffusion in other species   85
   Managing the difference between old and young
      (or insiders and outsiders)   87
   Why experience and education limit idea generation   91
   Joining an organization   92
   New theories of how to encourage idea generation   95
   Objections to implementing the new theories   96
   Implementing the new theories   99
   Complementary theories of idea generation   102
Project funding systems   102
   Dimensions of a funding system   103
   Outcomes of a funding system   114
   Managing risk and evaluating outcomes   118
Development systems   119
   What development systems have in common   119
   How development systems vary: overall characteristics   121
   Speed in development   124
   Reducing cost of development   125
   Improving fit with customer need   126
Diagnosing problems in an innovation system   127
   A systematic method of diagnosing problems   129
   Executing solutions and evaluating the results   130
Identifying opportunities for improvement   132

**Part II   How to Plan and Implement a Program to
Improve Innovation Performance   135**

5   Planning and Sequencing Change   137

Organizing a change program   137
  Determining what to change   137
  Early change efforts: when a company is just beginning
    to worry about innovation performance   142
  Mid-range changes: fixing ongoing performance or
    alignment problems   146
  Advanced changes: fine-tuning the system   151
  Sequencing the changes, planning the change process   160
Why change programs differ   165
  Industry and strategic context   165
  Company history   168
  Power and control issues   168
What an individual can do to improve an innovation system 170

6   Different Managers' Roles in Implementing Change   171

A framework for understanding managers' roles   172
  The different levels of manager   172
  What managers do during a transformation   173
How managers performed the roles   176
  Industrial Chemicals   176
  Lawn & Garden   179
  Northern Pharmaceuticals   180
  Advanced Materials   182
Managers' roles in a diversified company   183
  Corporate management's role   183
  Division/group management's role   185
  Business unit management's role   186
  Project manager and team member roles   187
  Summary of management roles in a diversified company 188
Management roles in a focused company   188

7   Two Common Paths of Innovation System Evolution   191

Why innovation systems follow different
  evolutionary paths   191
Innovation system types   194
  Differences in organization structure, project structure,
    and communications   194
  The Traditional system   196

Reasons for moving away from the Traditional system   198
Methods of moving away from the Traditional system   200
The Focused system   202
The Multi-focused system   202
The Flexible system   204
The Advanced Flexible system   207
Company configurations

**8 The Evolution of Idea Generation, Funding, and
Development Systems**   **212**

Managing idea generation   213
Generating ideas in companies with Focused or Flexible
    innovation systems   213
Having the right competences   214
Assuring that new links are made   217
Managing project funding   218
A summary model: four types of funding system   218
Tools used to improve funding systems   221
Managing development   223
Distinguishing between different project types   223
Managing low-uncertainty projects   224
Managing high-uncertainty projects   226
Summary of system evolution   231

**9 The Impact of Industry and Strategy on Innovation
System Design**   **233**

Industry differences   234
How ideas and opportunities differ   235
How companies' environments differ   244
The stability and predictability of companies' environments 249
Other impacts on innovation system configuration   253
Competence   253
Management's level of interest in innovation   255
Management's level of interest in diversification   256
Product-market strategy   256
Company history   257

10 Conclusion   **258**

Summary   258
Conclusions   258
The message to managers   260
Next steps   262

Appendix: Notes for the Academic Community   **264**

The initial data collection framework   265
  Different levels of general manager   265
  Different types of general management activity
    (use of different tools)   265
  Impacts on the innovation process: phases of the
    innovation process   267
  The overall framework   268
Method of data collection and analysis   270
  The data   270
  Data collected outside the formal research project 272
  Method of data collection   272
  Method of data analysis   274

Bibliography   278
Index   283

List of Figures

1.1	Companies (primary sites) by innovation reputation and sector	8
1.2	Companies (all sites) by innovation reputation and sector	9
1.3	Outline of the main body of the book	11
2.1	Chemical Residues time line	23
2.2	Chemical Residues time line	25
2.3	Chemical Residues time line	28
2.4	Chemical Residues time line	31
2.5	Chemical Residues time line	41
2.6	Chemical Residues time line	47
2.7	Chemical Residues time line	52
3.1	Chemical Residues project history	54
3.2	Chemical Residues project history: the tools classified	56
3.3	Intervention types classified by scope	58
3.4a	Scope of senior management actions at Industrial Chemicals	59
3.4b	Scope of senior management actions at Northern Pharmaceuticals	60
3.4c	Scope of senior management actions at Lawn & Garden	61
3.4d	Scope of senior management actions at Advanced Materials	62
3.5	Intervention types classified by scope	65
3.6	Impact of tools/interventions over time	66
4.1	Key activities during the project life cycle	72
4.2	Goals by phase	77

4.3	Managers' goals as they intervened in the innovation system	78
4.4	The old theory of idea generation: separation	80
4.5	The new theory of idea generation: developing and mixing competences	97
4.6	Distance between ideas and funding sources: example from Bower (1970)	107
4.7	The funding system and diversification	112
4.8	How to find and analyze problems in an innovation system	128
4.9	How to find opportunities for improvement in an innovation system	131
5.1	Impact, ease of change, and riskiness of various tools	140
5.2	General sequence of change efforts	141
5.3	Knowledge, complexity and the change process	161
6.1	Framework of management levels and roles	175
6.2	Managers' roles in a diversified company	184
6.3	Managers' roles in a focused company	190
7.1	Evolution of innovation systems: general sequence	197
7.2	Evolution of workflows and organization in Focused systems	203
7.3	Evolution of workflows and organization in Flexible systems	206
7.4	Evolution of eight companies: 1984–95	208
7.5	Focused innovation system and Flexible innovation system compared	210
8.1	Types of idea generation system	215
8.2	Methods of improving idea generation	216
8.3	Types of funding systems	219
8.4	Improving funding systems	222
8.5	A low-uncertainty project	225
8.6	Methods of improving the management of low-uncertainty projects	227

8.7   A high-uncertainty project   229
8.8   Methods of improving the management of
       high-uncertainty projects   230

9.1   Industry differences listed   234
9.2   Scarcity of ideas and cost of investigating them   237
9.3   Summary of industry differences   254

A.1   General categories of methods for improving innovation
       performance identified in the literature (prior to 1994)   266
A.2   The preliminary view of general managers' methods of
       improving innovation performance   269

List of Tables

4.1 Tools that impact idea generation: 3M example   100
4.2 Dimensions of a funding system   103
4.3 Outcomes of a funding system   115
4.4 What development systems have in common   121
4.5 How development systems vary   122

5.1 Reasons why change programs differ   166

9.1 How ideas and opportunities vary   235
9.2 How industry environments vary   244
9.3 How industry stability and predictability vary   250
9.4 Other impacts on innovation system configuration   255

Preface

The ability to innovate is a source of sustainable competitive advantage, whether your business is the manufacture of heavy industrial equipment or the provision of virtual financial services via the Internet. But how do you breed innovation into the very bones of your organization, so that it becomes a repeatable, managed phenomenon? That is the question that Jim Christiansen addresses in this book.

There can be no doubt about the business value of innovation. Most of us running successful companies can point to some innovative, highly differentiated product that has become the most profitable in our portfolio, or to some process innovation that has enabled us to drive costs far below those of our competitors.

Innovation pays dividends for shareholders too. Today, the highest returns for investors are produced by the health care industry and the electronics and communication industries. These two sectors, driven by a continuous stream of innovative products and ideas (Viagra and the Netscape search engine, to name but two) have generated returns thirteen to twenty points higher than the stock market average. Innovation opens new markets, drives growth and differentiation, motivates employees and captures customers' attention using much lower advertising budgets.

Innovation, or lack of it, explains many of our most famous corporate sagas. I can find no other explanation for the birth, decline and recent re-birth of Apple Computers, which started with the development of the first user-friendly personal computer, then lost ground to more aggressive competitors, and is now rejuvenating the micro-computer business with new design and technology at a time when most industry observers had declared the company dead. Why is Renault, the French regional automotive manufacturer, in a position to acquire a significant share in Nissan, a global player? The explanation is that it has aggressively pursued product innovation and differentiation with its monospace vehicle strategy, including the large Espace, the medium Scenic and the small Twingo. These products now account for a fair share of Renault's profitability and hence its ability to acquire its larger competitor. The same applies to Cisco Systems, which started a little more than ten years ago in the field of communication routers for computers, and is now challenging Lucent, Alcatel, Ericsson, and Siemens in supplying the largest telecom operators.

Once senior managers have recognized the importance of innovation, however, they face another challenge: that of being innovative, in the sense of providing new and valuable products or services to the company's customers. New is nice; the French supersonic Concorde was in many ways new. Useful in its own right is not bad either, but the world is full of me-too ideas that never captured the price level or market share necessary to break-even. It takes the two together to hit the jackpot.

This kind of value-creating innovation is the result of a complex system that Jim Christiansen analyzes in detail, using real life examples. His approach combines a scholarly attention to detail with clear-eyed insights into the factors that really enable and drive innovation in the corporate environment.

The book is about creating a culture of innovation. Jim Christiansen's approach to the issue will strike a chord with experienced executives. It is practical, actionable and designed to help us to make effective improvements to our innovation system. His references are eclectic and instructive. Do you know, for example, how ideas are spread rapidly through a community of monkeys? The answer is here, and it might change at a stroke the way in which you disseminate new ideas in your company.

There are many ways to talk about innovation, but Jim Christiansen has made it simple. He structures his analysis in three stages. First, he deals with how ideas are generated in a company. How could 3M come up with the *Post-It*™ idea and manage the right mix of market and technology analysis, of hard work and serendipity to bring it to fruition? Second, how does an executive team recognize the value of an idea and decide to fund it? We all know that the first personal computer was developed in the Xerox Park Research Center, but less well known is the fact that the first Cisco router was developed by a skunk team from another electronics company, a company that decided to let the team leave with the results of their work.

Finally, how does the development process provide the rigour and flexibility to reduce new product development time, ensure product cost and performance objectives, and keep R&D within the agreed budget? Why is it that the faster developers in a given industry are often two to three times quicker than their slowest competitor?

The challenge is to accomplish all of this in an R&D environment that is evolving quickly. In the past ten years, most companies have globalized and distributed their R&D locations, as seen with Hewlett Packard which has expanded from a few United States sites fifteen years ago to more than thirty development sites today scattered across three regions of the world. Decentralization has also been driven by the need for business unit managers to master their own R&D budgets and teams; at companies such as Lucent, Texas Instruments and Danone, 90 percent of R&D budgets are today decentralized to the business unit level.

Developing an innovative culture and deploying the best R&D management practices requires great expertise and persistence. Faced with this increasing complexity and burgeoning of new ideas, a number of companies, for example Cisco, Pfizer, and Merck, have started to acquire technology companies and outsource R&D work. Taking advantage of these opportunities will require the provision of an environment that preserves the innovativeness of the acquired companies.

The message in Jim Christiansen's book is ultimately one of hope. He demonstrates that every executive, every company, can develop an innovation culture that is state-of-the-art. Occasionally this may require a little external help. This book is clearly part of that help. It is practical, precise, and extremely clear. Jim Christiansen's gift is his ability to combine step-by-step business practicality with the excitement and drama of a novel.

Does the book say it all? Certainly not, and there is more that some readers will want to know. But if you are deeply concerned about innovation, I believe that this is one of the best places to start. Read this book carefully, identify those areas in which you feel your company can improve most, implement change and experience the satisfaction of an even more efficient innovative system. The insights and sound practical advice in this book will prove enormously helpful and I feel sure that there is yet more to come from Jim Christiansen.

XAVIER MOSQUET
Senior Vice President
The Boston Consulting Group

Acknowledgements

Many people and institutions helped me to write this book. It will not be possible to list all of them, but I will mention as many of the key people as possible. I apologize to those who I have inadvertently missed.

First, I owe a large debt of gratitude to Arnoud De Meyer, Claude Michaud, Yves Doz, Dan Muzyka and Philippe Haspeslagh, all of the Institut Européen d'Administration des Affaires (INSEAD). They provided key help in getting access to twelve of my twenty research sites. I particularly thank Claude Michaud of the Centre Européen d'Education Permanente (CEDEP) in this respect. He single-handedly organized my access to four sites, and helped with access to four others. John Clarkeson, Rene Abate, Xavier Mosquet, and Jacques Garaialde of the Boston Consulting Group helped to arrange access to two additional sites. Without the help of all these people, it would have been much more difficult to obtain good access to such a large number of sites.

Second, I owe an even larger debt of gratitude to the more than 300 managers who agreed to speak with me about their companies' innovation systems. They were all quite open about both the successes and the problems their companies had faced in their innovation programs. Without their help this book would have been impossible.

Third, I owe an additional debt to INSEAD, CEDEP, the Boston Consulting Group, and the pseudonymous company MGE, all of which provided financial support for the research.

Many scholars contributed to the content of the research in one way or another. The first, chronologically, were a number of people at the University of Chicago, where I had my initial graduate-level training. I owe particular thanks to the late Morris Janowitz of the Department of Sociology, to Paul Peterson, Ira Katznelson and Lloyd Rudolph, then in the Department of Political Science, and to Akira Iriye, William McNeill, and Barry Karl, then in the Department of History. They and a number of additional staff members in the Department of Political Science and the National Opinion Research Center gave me my initial training in social science research methodology. It is from them that I learned how to conduct interviews, how to verify information obtained from interviews, how to collect and analyze historical data, and many other essential techniques of social science fieldwork. John Van Maanen of Massachusetts Institute of Technology (MIT) added additional insights on field research methods during his two visits to INSEAD.

Philippe Haspeslagh and Sumantra Ghoshal provided useful inspiration as I was designing the research. It was they who encouraged me to turn what was to be a study of the impact of communication on innovation into a larger study of the role of general managers in managing innovation.

Reinhard Angelmar, Arnoud De Meyer, Yves Doz, Christoph Loch, and Ludo Van der Heyden of INSEAD all participated in one or more of my initial interviews at the MGE sites. They all read the case studies I produced on the four MGE sites and commented on them extensively. Nine MGE managers and one researcher in an outside laboratory linked with MGE read and commented on the cases as well.

Yves Doz, Philippe Haspeslagh, and Dan Muzyka each read multiple drafts of my INSEAD dissertation, which became the core of this book. They and a number of other people at INSEAD, including Arnoud De Meyer, Chan Kim, Christoph Loch, Claude Michaud, Mark Lehrer, Kazuhiro Asakawa, Dana Hyde, Alice de Koning, Peter Moran, James Henderson, Bjorn Lovas, and Simon Rodan, made highly useful comments on presentations of the material. John Van Maanen of MIT also read and made many useful comments on an early draft of the dissertation. Finally, a number of people read and commented on the manuscript of this book. These included Arnoud De Meyer of INSEAD, Xavier Mosquet and George Stalk Jr of the Boston Consulting Group, Gary McGraw of Eastman Chemical, and Manley Johnston of 3M.

Various faculty members at the Institute of Management Development (IMD) in Lausanne, the Institute of International Studies in Stockholm, the Norwegian School of Management in Sandvika, the Copenhagen Business School, and Erasmus University Rotterdam made useful comments on the material during my visits to their schools. Several people at Renaissance Worldwide, including Roger Lewis and Steve Mecklenburg, commented extensively on presentations of the material. Several dozen other managers and academics from a variety of institutions participated in seminars where I presented the material as I was writing the book. Their comments were much appreciated.

Several other people saw presentations of parts of the material, or read papers derived from the material, and encouraged me to continue during that difficult stage when there was much work still to be done and the final product was still several years away. The most important of these were Deborah Dougherty of McGill University, Robert DeFillippi of Suffolk University, Raymond Calori of the Ecole Supérieure de Commerce de Lyon, Charles Baden-Fuller of City University London, Kathleen Eisenhardt of Stanford, and Rebecca Henderson of MIT. Gary Hamel, C.K. Prahalad, Howard Thomas, and Don O'Neal were kind enough to include a paper summarizing several of this book's main themes in their work, *Strategic Flexibility: Managing in a Turbulent Environment*.

On a more personal note, Norman, Linda and especially Christina offered help of incalculable value. Chan Kim, in a phrase I will remember for the rest of my life, encouraged me to, 'Never, never, never, never, never give up.' My family was highly supportive throughout. Countless others offered friendship and good company as I was carrying out the fieldwork, the analysis, and the final writing of the book. I especially thank Marie-Jo, who made life much more pleasant as I wrote the book. I also owe thanks to Sandra, who has shown herself many times over to be a true friend. Finally, I owe special thanks to my daughter, Gwen, who demonstrated incredible optimism, hope, and good cheer throughout the very difficult adventure that led to this book. It is to her that I dedicate this book. I also thank Gwen's cat, Moustache, for reminding me what it is like to be a hunter. Thank you Gwen, thank you Marie-Jo, thank you Moustache, and thanks to you all.

1 Introduction

Two companies

More than ten years ago, I was a member of a consulting team working for an American consumer products company, which I will call USF (for US Food Products, a pseudonym). USF was far from the largest company in its field. But it showed a record of steady growth and profits going back more than three decades. It was a solid player in its core markets, and had diversified into a few related businesses. USF management hired us to help them to find new growth opportunities, either in the businesses they had, or in related businesses.

What I learned by working with them was how easily companies could kill innovation. We looked at a number of their businesses and came up with many ideas on how to grow them. They killed virtually all of them. Some of them they disposed of right away, without even trying them seriously. It seemed that very few ideas could run the gauntlet of the objections that USF's management team was capable of raising. The few that did run the gauntlet died slow deaths as USF's sluggish operating practices gradually bled the life out of them.

The company's history showed that USF had, almost in spite of itself, come up with some breakthrough innovations. Just three years earlier, it had invented a successful new category in the food business. But it had not been able to turn its first-mover advantage into a successful long-term position. Within months, it had fallen into last place, and within a couple of years, it was out of the new market altogether.

The more we looked at USF, the more depressing the story became. It turned out that the company's record of steady growth was based on an illusion. When we analyzed the company's financial records, we discovered that sales and profits in ongoing businesses had been declining for many years. Management had covered up the decline by buying one or two smaller companies each year. But the ongoing business was dying.

Management blamed the decline in the core businesses on the 'inevitable demographic decline of its core markets.' In other words, its customers, the people who had grown to love its products decades ago, were dying off. However, other companies with similar products and the same original customer base were still growing. Somehow our client had missed opportunities that others had seen. Or had it failed to exploit its opportunities effectively? Why was USF failing so miserably at innovation while others in the same field were doing well?

A few years later, I worked with a very different consumer products company. This one I will call ConsumerCo (also a pseudonym). In its century-long history, ConsumerCo has created several consumer products categories, and unlike USF, it still dominates the categories it created. Better yet, it is still innovating continuously in nearly all of its operations. Unlike USF, it is growing strongly in its core businesses, and has been for many years.

When I first encountered ConsumerCo, I interviewed several dozen of its managers. I asked them how their company managed innovation, and was impressed, sometimes astonished, by their answers. The company had many methods for stimulating idea generation. Some of the methods were original; methods I had never seen used in any other company. ConsumerCo also had original and effective methods of funding projects and developing products. In some ways, ConsumerCo had turned the textbook rules of 'good business management' on their heads. The company did not follow the rules taught in business schools. They had invented their own rules and their own ways of managing innovation, and they were doing very well. In fact, they were doing so well that I began to wonder whether the 'business school rules' were such good rules after all. Managing innovation effectively seemed to demand something different.

The topic of this book

As I learned how ConsumerCo worked, I began wondering whether other companies could become more like ConsumerCo. I knew 3M; they were a lot like ConsumerCo. Although the two companies operated in very different markets, their ways of managing innovation were strikingly similar. Could other companies become more like them? Could USF and other less innovative companies become more innovative by copying the practices of innovation leaders such as 3M and ConsumerCo? How could they do that? What practices would they have to copy? And how would they go about changing some of the basic management systems and practices that were preventing them innovating?

After encountering ConsumerCo, I became obsessed with these questions, thinking about little else for the next five years. I read hundreds of books and articles on the subject of innovation management. I interviewed more than 300 managers on the subject of innovation, and carefully tracked how more than a dozen companies managed their innovation processes. I analyzed how eight companies had tried to improve their innovation processes over a period of ten years. I tried to understand both how the good innovators did it and how the not-so-good innovators could become more like the good ones. After gathering all this evidence, I analyzed the results and wrote the findings up. The results will be reported in two volumes, of which this is the first.

In this text, I will deal with four topics. First, I will show that *a wide range of everyday management structures, systems and practices (collectively referred to as 'management tools') have a significant impact on innovation performance*. The way in which you set up an organization, the way you manage resource allocation, the way you manage your people, and many other things all have an impact on innovation performance. In Chapters 2 and 3, I will develop an overall list of the management structures, systems and practices, at the corporate, business unit, and project level, that impact innovation performance.

Second, since I am looking at how the whole organization acts as an innovation system, it is useful to have a *base of definitions and concepts* to help to organize the discussion. Thus, in Chapter 4, I will lay out a method of thinking about innovation that will help us to look in detail at two things. The first is how the different phases of the innovation process work in large companies, and second, how the different management structures, systems and practices affect innovation performance during each phase.

Third, it is not easy to change a large company. Transforming a USF into a 3M would take a huge management effort spanning several decades. Yet transformations nearly this large have occurred, General Electric probably being the best-known example. How do companies do it? If you want your company to be more innovative, what do you do? First you need to know what it is you want to change. What do you want the company to look like at the end of the change process? Then you also need to know how to manage the change process itself. In Chapters 5 and 6, I will talk about *how to manage the process of improving innovation performance*: what to do first, what to do next, and who should be doing what.

Finally, in Chapters 7, 8 and 9, I will talk about *differences between innovation systems across industries*. Most books and articles on innovation do not make any distinction between different industries. They either focus on one industry (for example, pharmaceuticals or motor vehicles), or provide a general discussion of how innovation can be managed across a large number of industries. Such generic discussions can provide useful insights, but they can be misleading. Innovation in a diversified industrial products company is not the same thing as innovation in a pharmaceutical company or in an automobile company. The innovation problem is different across industries. The management structures, systems, and practices needed to manage innovation effectively are not the same in all industries. I will document this point and explore the reasons for the differences in Chapters 7, 8 and 9.

The purpose of this book

With this book, I hope to accomplish a number of different things. Primarily, I want to *help managers to improve the innovation performance of their companies*. On the way to doing that, however, I hope to *improve everyone's understanding of how innovation systems work and how they can be improved*. Understanding how innovation systems work is, in fact, key to improving them: the better we understand them, the more we can improve them. Virtually all of the discussion in this book will focus on these two topics.

One corollary of the first topic is that I want to *help companies innovate in their core businesses*. It is easy, although perhaps in the long term harmful, to separate innovation activities out from the rest of the business, to put them in a laboratory or a 'skunk works' that has limited interaction with the core business. But this avoids the issue of how to make the core business more innovative. In most companies, it is the core business that absorbs the most and often the best resources. In the most innovative companies, much innovation occurs in the core businesses. Why should that not be true in all companies?

While the book will focus primarily on accomplishing the above goals, there is another theme in the background: that I want to *help companies to create environments that are more hospitable to people's creativity*. People, particularly intelligent people, are often motivated by a desire to contribute, to create something that is useful for themselves and for other people. But companies often block this impulse. Creating something new involves a departure from routine. But companies need routines and they resist departures from them. We are good at managing routine. We are less good at managing creativity, diversity, experimentation, and difference. Hopefully, this book will increase our ability to manage creative, nonroutine processes.

A corollary to this is that I want to *give individuals who work in business enough information to be able to tell the difference between management practices that support innovation and those that suppress it*. People deserve to spend their work time within companies that use and encourage their creativity. This book will give individuals enough information to identify an innovation-supportive company when they see one. It will also tell them what kind of changes to lobby for if they find themselves in a company that does not support innovation.

This book will build on many previous books. Books such as *The Individualized Corporation* by Ghoshal and Bartlett (1998) and *Relentless Growth* by Meyer (1998) have demonstrated that we are at a stage in business history at which we are developing new and more effective ways of managing companies. In particular, we are learning how large companies can innovate more effectively. This book will demonstrate the principles and practice of how larger companies can do this.

Methodology

Most of the material presented in this book comes from a comparative study of innovation management practices in twenty companies. Since I studied eight of these companies in more detail than the others, I sometimes refer to these eight companies as the eight primary sites. Most of the conclusions presented in this book were developed from the study of these eight companies.

Four of these eight companies were independently managed divisions of a diversified European manufacturing group, the other four being fully independent. The eight companies competed in five different industries. Three of them were rated as excellent innovators, and four as average innovators. The last was somewhat below average. I interviewed more than 140 managers from these companies while working as a researcher at INSEAD, the leading European business school. I charted how these companies managed innovation at the time of the interviews, but also how their innovation systems had evolved over the ten years prior to the interviews.

Part of the material presented in this book, particularly in the section on industry variation (Chapter 9), draws on interviews I conducted with managers from twelve additional companies competing in eight additional industries. Two of them were rated as excellent innovators, seven of them as average innovators, and three as less than average. I interviewed managers from ten of these companies while working at INSEAD, and managers from the other two while working as a consultant.

The academic reader will be interested in knowing how the interviews were set up and conducted, what questions were asked, and how the analyses were done. Brief summaries of these issues are included in an Appendix at the end of this book. The more general reader will be more interested in knowing who the companies are. Most of them insisted on anonymity as a condition for participating in my research, but I can nevertheless describe them in general terms here.

Introduction to the companies

Four of the eight primary sites were independently managed divisions of a diversified European corporation called Manufacturing Group Europe, or MGE (a pseudonym). MGE is a diversified manufacturer with interests in a variety of chemical and materials science specialties, as well as in pharmaceutical and consumer products. Each of its divisions was rated (from polls in business magazines) as an average innovator. The four MGE divisions discussed in the text are Industrial Chemicals, Advanced Materials, Lawn & Garden, and Northern Pharmaceuticals.

Each division's management team had virtually complete independence in constructing its division's management systems. While each management team was supervised by a member of the Corporate Executive Committee, in practice the Corporate Executive Committee gave the division managers complete freedom to manage their divisions as they saw fit. As a result, the management systems and methods used in the four divisions varied considerably. Brief descriptions of the divisions follow.

Industrial Chemicals. In the 1980s, Industrial Chemicals produced and sold basic chemicals, but in the 1990s its management began putting more emphasis on developing and selling applied chemicals, that is, specialized chemical products designed to address specific customer needs. Industrial Chemicals was headquartered in the same city as corporate management, the links between corporate and division management being close.

Advanced Materials. More than Industrial Chemicals, Advanced Materials invested heavily in applied chemical products. Its products were mainly new and specialized materials used in the production of a wide range of industrial and consumer goods.

Lawn & Garden. The Lawn & Garden division produced and distributed a variety of agrochemical products, many designed for the home gardening market. One member of the corporate management team, Paul Thomas, had previously led the Lawn & Garden division.

Northern Pharmaceuticals. A mid-sized pharmaceuticals company, Northern Pharmaceuticals was run more independently than the other divisions. The pharmaceutical business was considered 'different' from MGE's other businesses. It was also consistently profitable. As a result, corporate supervision of Northern Pharmaceuticals had little visible impact. At times, Northern's management team acted in advance of the rest of the corporation. For example, Northern Pharmaceuticals began an innovation improvement program two years before corporate began its effort to improve innovation performance in the other divisions.

As noted above, the four MGE divisions were rated as average innovators. All were involved in chemicals, agrochemicals, or pharmaceuticals.

Of the four other primary sites, three were companies with reputations as excellent innovators. In two cases, the reputation was verified via poll results (large panels of managers placing these two companies' innovation performance in the top 10 percent of all companies in their respective home countries). The third was not rated in any available poll, but it had recently won a national award in its home country, an award that cited the high quality of its innovation processes.

One of these three excellent innovators was Eastman Chemical. As a chemical company, it provided a useful comparison for the three MGE divisions involved in chemicals and materials science. The other two were diversified manufacturers. One, ConsumerCo, focused mainly on consumer products. The other, 3M, produced a variety of both consumer and industrial products. These diversified manufacturers provided some variation with respect to industry.

The last of the eight companies was EurAuto, a motor vehicle assembler. I chose it to give industry variation, and, in particular, to obtain a comparison site within the automobile industry. Much research has been carried out on the management of innovation projects in the automobile industry (for example, Womack *et al.*, 1990; Clark and Fujimoto, 1991; Wheelwright and Clark, 1992), and the presence of EurAuto in the sample helped me to relate my results to that research.

Brief descriptions of these four companies follow (see Figure 1.1 for a summary of the companies' industries and innovation reputations).

Industry	**Innovation reputation**				
	Low	**Med–Low**	**Medium**	**Med–High**	**High**
Chemicals			*Industrial Chemicals* *Advanced Materials*	*Eastman* *Chemical*	
Agrichemicals			*Lawn & Garden*		
Pharmaceuticals			*Northern* *Pharmaceuticals*		
Industrial products					*3M*
Consumer products					*ConsumerCo*
Motor vehicles		*EurAuto*			

Figure 1.1   Companies (primary sites) by innovation reputation and sector

Eastman Chemical. This was a diversified manufacturer with interests in a variety of chemical specialties. It was an excellent innovator, although not as highly rated as 3M or ConsumerCo. Management had, since the mid-1980s, been very active in trying to improve innovation performance.

ConsumerCo. ConsumerCo was a diversified manufacturer focused on consumer products, having been rated as an excellent innovator for many years. Management had been concerned with innovation performance for as long as anyone could remember.

3M. A diversified manufacturer focusing on a variety of industrial and consumer products specialties, most of them related to materials and coatings, 3M had rated as an excellent innovator for many years. Management had been concerned with innovation performance for as long as anyone could remember.

EurAuto. The motor vehicle assembler EurAuto had an average innovation reputation, not being rated quite as well as MGE. Management had been very active in trying to improve innovation performance since the mid-1980s.

Periodically, I will cite examples of innovation management practices from twelve other companies, in all cases using their pseudonyms. Figure 1.2 shows these names, their industry focus, and their innovation reputations. Brief descriptions of these companies follow.

Innovation reputation					
Industry	**Low**	**Med–Low**	**Medium**	**Med–High**	**High**
Chemicals		EuroChem	*Industrial Chemicals* *Advanced Materials*	Eastman Chemical	
Agrichemicals			Lawn & Garden		
Pharmaceuticals			Northern Pharmaceuticals		
Industrial products					3M
Consumer products and food	USF		AmPro		ConsumerCo
Motor vehicles		*EurAuto*	USAuto		
Electronics and computing		ConElec	USComputers		
Telecoms			EurTel		
Industrial machinery				MachineCo	
Other manufacturing			CementCo	OptiCo	
Services			FinCo Admin		

Note: Primary sites in italics

Figure 1.2 Companies (all sites) by innovation reputation and sector

- *USAuto*. A US motor vehicle manufacturer. An average innovator.
- *CementCo*. A European cement manufacturer. One of the leaders in its field, but rated as an average innovator.
- *USComputers*. One of the world's leading computer companies. Rated as an average innovator.
- *EuroChem*. A diversified manufacturer with interests in chemicals, pharmaceuticals, and consumer products. Rated as an average innovator. Similar to MGE in terms of the nature and breadth of its businesses.
- *MachineCo*. An industrial machinery manufacturer. A leader in its niche, with several recent breakthrough innovations.
- *ConElec*. A consumer electronics manufacturer. Rated as an average innovator.
- *OptiCo*. A manufacturer of optical equipment. A leader in its niche, and an excellent innovator.
- *FinCo*. A diversified financial services company. One of several leading players in its industry, but an average innovator.
- *Admin*. A public bureaucracy focusing on defense. A mid-range innovator compared with other defense ministries.
- *AmPro*. A large American consumer products company. Rated as an average innovator.
- *USF*. A mid-sized American food processor. Rated as a below-average innovator.
- *EurTel*. A European telecommunications equipment manufacturer. Rated as an average innovator.

Outline of the book

The first point of this book will be that a wide range of management structures, systems and practices affect innovation performance. A manager should not think that he is finished once he has improved his company's project funding system and speeded up development: many other corporate structures, systems, and practices impact innovation performance as well. (See Figure 1.3 for an outline of the book.)

Since we will often refer to 'corporate structures, systems and practices,' let us provide a shorthand way of referring to these different management tools. At times, the word 'tool,' or 'management tool,' will be used to refer to 'anything that a manager can change that will have an impact on the functioning of the company's innovation system'. This is a very broad definition that includes corporate strategy, organization structure, incentives, project management systems, communications systems, and many other things influencing innovation performance. For the sake of convenience, however, a common word is needed to refer to all of the variables that a manager can manipulate. I have chosen the word 'tool,' since tool refers to an object that can be used to manipulate another object. In this case, the manager is using the communication system (the tool) to manipulate the way in which the company's innovation system (the object being worked on) works.

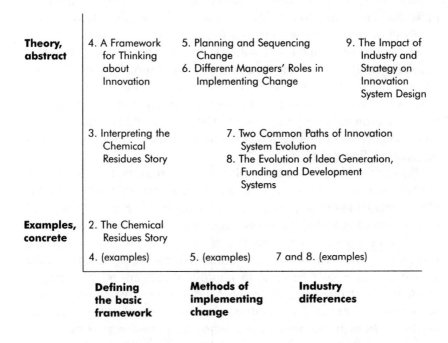

Figure 1.3   Outline of the main body of the book

In order to show that a wide range of tools can be used to impact innovation performance, I will take the reader through the story of an innovation project in Chapter 2. The project is called the Chemical Residues (CR) project. It occurred within MGE's Industrial Chemicals division. At the request of MGE management, the story is disguised. The industry, the technical details of the project, and the names of all individuals and locations have been changed, but all of the events recounted in the story actually happened. The management events and issues presented in the story are 100 percent fact. As I recount the story, I will show that a wide variety of management structures, systems, and practices affected the progress and performance of the project. Chapter 3 will list the tools involved, classify them, and briefly discuss how they influenced innovation.

In Chapter 4, I will draw back to take a more theoretical look at the innovation process. This chapter will introduce concepts that will facilitate a discussion and analysis of the innovation process and of managers' attempts to improve innovation performance. Some of these concepts relate to the different phases of the innovation process, others to how innovation works during the different phases.

At the end of Chapter 4, I will talk briefly about how to diagnose problems in an innovation system. I will then turn, in Part II, to the process of 'improving innovation performance' itself. Chapters 5–9 will look at how companies can most effectively structure a program to improve innovation performance. The work in this section is based on a comparison of innovation performance improvement programs at the eight primary sites.

Chapter 5 will look at how to plan a program to improve innovation performance, and Chapter 6 will consider the roles that different types of manager can play in such a program. Chapters 7, 8 and 9 will investigate how the problem of improving innovation performance differs between industries. For managers who have worked in several industries, it may be obvious that innovation systems are different, and that different things must be done to improve them, but most managers, and many academics who write about innovation, have worked in only one or two industries. The discussion here of how industries differ, and of how these differences affect innovation systems, should help managers to find ways of improving innovation performance that are adapted to their companies and to their industries.

In looking at cross-industry differences, two avenues will be explored. First, there will be a discussion of how the management teams of eight companies improved their innovation systems over a ten-year period (Chapters 7 and 8). The companies can be classified into two groups. The management teams in both groups were going to great efforts to improve innovation performance, but they were not doing the same things. I will show how the situations in which these two groups of managers found themselves, and the ways in which they changed their companies, differed.

After describing the differences among these eight companies, we will consider industry differences more generally (Chapter 9). Using other examples, I will illustrate a variety of ways in which industries differ, and will talk about how these differences affect the way in which a company's innovation system should be set up.

Chapter 10 provides the conclusion and is followed by a brief Appendix. This discusses methodology, sources, and other issues of interest to academic readers.

I wish the reader well in what I hope will be a useful journey through this discussion of innovation management.

Part I

A Wide Range of Management Systems and Practices Impact Innovation Performance

In Part I, I will develop a number of core concepts and frameworks that are useful for analyzing companies' innovation systems and the management systems that affect them. I will begin in Chapter 2 by recounting the history of an innovation project called the Chemical Residues (CR) project. The CR project ran into many difficulties during its ten-year history. Most of these difficulties stemmed from problems created by the management structures, systems and practices of the company that housed the project. This story will illustrate how everyday management tools can impact, for better or for worse, the progress of an innovation project.

In Chapter 3, I will use data drawn from the CR story to develop a list of management tools that can influence any company's innovation system. I will then briefly analyze and classify the list, describing briefly how and when these tools typically have their effect.

In Chapter 4, I will step back to take a more theoretical look at how companies' innovation systems work and at what managers can do to improve them. The theoretical concepts and definitions developed in Chapter 4 will be used throughout the remainder of the book.

2 The Chemical Residues Story

The aim of this chapter is to show that a wide range of corporate structures, systems, and practices (that is, management tools) impact innovation performance. This will be achieved by taking the reader through the story of the Chemical Residues (CR) project. By demonstrating, narratively, that a wide range of tools affected this project, I will make the more general point that a wide range of tools can, in principle, affect any project. I will then classify and analyze the tools in Chapter 3.

The story of the CR project begins in the mid-1980s. I visited Industrial Chemicals, the division of MGE that housed it, in 1994 and 1995. At that time, I traced nearly ten years of the project's and the company's history. The story was fascinating. Many delays had occurred during the early stages of the project, most of which had occurred as the result of problems created by Industrial Chemical's own management systems. After four years marked by serious delays, however, the project's fortunes changed. MGE's Executive Committee decided to put far more emphasis on product innovation. At that point, the roadblocks began to disappear. Many management systems and practices were changed as management made a serious effort to improve the division's innovation performance.

I documented the project's and the division's history during both phases, identifying what caused the roadblocks that the project encountered during its first four years, and documenting what was done to remove the obstacles during the next five years. Both parts of the story will be presented here.

The mother company: MGE

MGE was founded in the late 19th century. The core of the company lay in basic chemicals, but in the early 20th century, the company moved into pharmaceuticals. MGE continued to diversify into related businesses through the late 1960s. By then, it had significant positions in agrochemicals, applied chemicals, and chemical-based consumer products. In the 1970s and 80s, the company made significant international acquisitions so that, by the late 1980s, the company was a significant international player in its core businesses.

At no time during this long history had the company worried much about product innovation. Now and then it launched new products of course, but this was not the focus of its strategy. Although it took advantage of obvious opportunities for new products when they came up, no special effort was made to expand through new product development. What the company did focus on was process innovation. Here it was very successful. It brought the cost of its commodity chemical products down so low that its share of the world market kept expanding.

In the 1980s, the company was concerned with growth, but not with growth through new products. Rather, it grew through acquisitions, which absorbed all the company's free cash and left even fewer resources available for new product development. It was in this environment that the CR project was born. As will be seen below, the project team struggled for nearly five years to find sufficient resources to fund the project.

MGE's strategy began changing in the late 1980s, but the change did not happen entirely by choice. Both the 'growth through acquisition' strategy and the 'low-cost' strategy were coming under increasing pressure. By the late 1980s, MGE had acquired significant positions in all major world markets, and there was little left of interest to buy. At any rate, MGE had stretched its financial resources to the limit, so financing another major acquisition was not possible.

At the same time, the low-cost strategy was no longer working in some business units. There were several reasons for this. First, the chemical industry was changing. The basic chemical products that MGE produced were increasingly commodities, available in quantity from a number of producers, including producers in low-wage countries. MGE's excellent process technology was not always enough to overcome high wage differentials.

To make matters worse, in some business areas the low-wage producers had monopoly access to high-grade sources of raw material. MGE could not compete with producers who used raw materials of substantially higher quality than its own.

In other areas, customers were no longer interested in buying commodity chemicals. They wanted chemicals that would perform a specific function, but they did not want to have to design the chemical themselves, so they looked to chemical companies to do it for them. In short, basic chemicals were out. Custom-designed, high-value-added chemicals were in. But these were not the kinds of chemical with which MGE had much experience.

Facing all these changes, MGE's executive board decided to put far more emphasis on product innovation in the 1990s. Applied chemicals would be 'in' at MGE as well. Once this change in strategy was decided upon, things became much easier for the CR project. Funding and other much-needed support came easily, almost too easily, for the next few years. MGE's managers, all having grown up under the low-cost strategy, did not really know how to run the company in a way that encouraged product innovation. But they did know that if they starved innovation projects like CR, no innovation would occur. As a result, the CR budget went up dramatically.

At this point, I will stop my history of MGE to recount in detail the CR project's history. In the rest of this chapter, the project's story will appear in normal type. My comments on the story will be displayed in a different typeface. These comments will focus on how various management structures, systems, and practices impacted on the project.

The reader should note that all names in the story have been changed. The industry in which the story takes place has also been disguised. All of the events really happened, but not in the industry or in the places indicated.

The Chemical Residues project and the Industrial Chemicals division

The cast of characters:
- George Marsh. The chemist who identified the CR opportunity and headed the project for six years
- Ken Peters. Hired from a European regulatory agency to replace Marsh as head of the CR project

- Sam Johansen. Hired by Ken Peters to manage the CR project's activities in North America
- Jerry Roth. Head of the business unit producing the CR chemical. Funded the project during the third year of its existence
- Mark Quinn. Head of a second business unit that was interested in the CR opportunity. He funded the project for a year after Roth's business unit ran out of money
- John McCoy. Industrial Chemicals division director of research
- Ken Smith. A senior Industrial Chemicals division manager responsible for overseeing several business units and the CR project during the project's third, fourth, and fifth years
- Mark Green. Part of MGE's pharmaceutical group until he joined Industrial Chemicals in the CR project's sixth year. Supervisor of the CR project and head of the division from the project's sixth year on
- Paul Thomas. Member of corporate executive committee responsible for pushing innovation within the company. Also had supervisory responsibility for Industrial Chemicals.

A chemist discovers an idea

In the mid-1980s, Jerry Roth was the head of a business unit at Industrial Chemicals. Roth had a problem. The head of the division had asked him to find a job for George Marsh, a chemist who had worked in several different divisions of MGE as well as in a joint venture that MGE had created with another company. Most recently, Marsh had worked in another business unit within Industrial Chemicals. This unit had just been sold, and Marsh had exercised his option to stay with the company. Now the division faced the problem of finding something for him to do.

Finding Marsh a job was not easy, since, by MGE's standards, Marsh's career had been very unusual. Not only had he worked in four different units, but worse, he had also worked both in technical positions and in marketing. This was virtually unheard of at MGE. The 'proper' career path at MGE was to stay in one function, usually within one unit, and move up – people did not move across business unit and functional boundaries. But Marsh had. He had broken all the normal rules, and now Roth had to find him a job.

Roth did not mind much as he liked Marsh, a competent, although not outstanding, performer. The problem was that Marsh was not a specialist in anything in particular. Virtually all the jobs at MGE were designed for specialists, people who had spent their entire career in one function and in one business unit. There was no obvious fit for Marsh anywhere.

Then Roth thought of his co-products problem. It is a fact of life in the chemical business that many chemical processes produce co-products. A company might want to make a large quantity of chemical A since there is a high demand for it, but the process for producing it might also produce a co-product, chemical B. Given the way in which chemical processes work, it might not be possible to produce chemical A without simultaneously producing chemical B. (For example, if you produce hydrogen by splitting water molecules, you will also produce oxygen; there will be no hydrogen without oxygen as well.) The problem with co-products is that there is sometimes no market for them. So the company may have to bury them or unload them at ridiculously low prices just to get rid of them.

Roth's business unit was profitable, but it produced a large number of co-products. Two years before, Roth had asked two of his engineers to spend one-quarter of their time looking for new, profitable uses for his co-products. They had produced many reports, but no revenue. Why not add Marsh to the team? He was senior enough to lead the team, and maybe if Marsh were on the team full time, he would come up with something. Roth thought it was worth a try, so he called Marsh into his office and offered him the position. Marsh accepted on the spot.

Roth was not following any corporate strategy in trying to sell his co-products: there was no strategy in place to build revenue through internal product development. However, the goals Roth's boss gave him included building revenue and profits, and Roth would be rewarded for this. In effect, Roth decided that part of his business unit strategy would be to build revenues through new product development. He did not want to invest a lot of money in this, since the outcome was so uncertain. But he did not know what else to do with Marsh. Thus he put Marsh on the project and told him to find something to do with the co-products.

Several aspects of MGE's corporate management practices affected Roth's decision to find new markets for his co-products. The *goals* the corporation set for him included building more revenues and profits. There were *incentives* for meeting the goals, incentives such as pay rises and further promotion opportunities. These incentives made it very much in Roth's interest to achieve the goals. Finally, while corporate *strategy* did not focus on new product development, it did push him to grow his business unit. Thus, Roth set his own business unit *strategy* to include growth through finding new uses for his co-products.

After taking over the project team, Marsh spent a few weeks catching up on what the two part-time engineers had done. In two years, they had investigated over 100 ideas. There was a filing cabinet full of reports, and Marsh decided to read them. He could not believe that the team had investigated so many opportunities without finding any that would work.

After several weeks of reading, Marsh found one idea that he thought deserved another look: using one of the co-products as a catalyst in water depollution systems. The co-product would react with some hard-to-treat chemical wastes and cause them to precipitate out as a harmless solid.

Marsh thought that the idea made sense chemically, but it had been rejected and he wondered why. Reading the file, he found that only one study of the idea had been made. A test at an outside laboratory had 'demonstrated' that the idea could not work on a commercial scale, but Marsh was not convinced as he did not believe the assumptions behind the test.

Marsh had sold water treatment chemicals in one of his previous jobs at MGE so was familiar with how treatment plants operated. He was also a chemist, so he understood the chemistry of water treatment. In addition, he knew the chemistry of the co-products produced by Roth's unit. The way in which the outside laboratory had carried out the test did not make sense, but his engineers would not have recognized that: they did not know water treatment plants well enough, and they were not chemists.

No one else at MGE would have seen the opportunity either. There was no one else with the exact skills needed (water treatment chemistry, water treatment operations, and co-products chemistry) to see this particular opportunity.

So why did Marsh see this opportunity when no one else had? He saw it because of his particular mix of skills and experience. MGE normally hired people who were trained in only one function, but Marsh was trained in two: chemistry and marketing. MGE normally developed people by moving them up the ladder in the same function and business unit, but Marsh had somehow managed to get around MGE's normal personnel management systems, moving across function and business unit boundaries. Had he not done so, he would not have had the background to see the value of the CR opportunity.

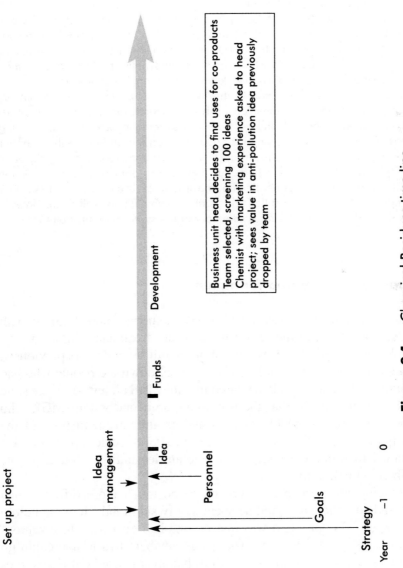

Figure 2.1 Chemical Residues time line

Set up project

Idea management

Development

Funds

Idea

Personnel

Goals

Strategy

Year   −1   0

Business unit head decides to find uses for co-products
Team selected, screening 100 ideas
Chemist with marketing experience asked to head
project; sees value in anti-pollution idea previously
dropped by team

What would have happened if MGE's personnel management systems had encouraged hiring people with more diverse backgrounds, and then moved them across function and business unit boundaries? What if MGE had hundreds of George Marshes instead of just one? Would the company have seen this opportunity, and others like it, earlier? Probably, yes.

I will infer from this that MGE's *personnel management systems*, particularly its career management practices, were preventing the company from recognizing innovation opportunities as quickly as it could have. Had MGE routinely rotated people through functions and business units, perhaps one of their people would have seen this opportunity, and others like it, faster.

Another feature of this story is the fact that Marsh and his two engineers were given no particular direction for how to search for uses of the co-products. Industrial Chemicals did not have any systematic *methods of generating ideas*. The engineers were simply turned loose on the problem without further direction. In the right circumstances, this can result in creative solutions, but it appears that the engineers here had neither the right background nor the right environment to generate the maximum of useful ideas. How other companies might have handled this situation is something I will discuss later in this book. (See Figure 2.1 for a summary of the story up to this point.)

Hunting for help and for money

Marsh wanted to discuss the idea with someone more familiar with water pollution and the chemistry of water treatment. Unfortunately, the company had sold its water pollution unit several years previously. Marsh spent several months trying to track down the people who had worked in this unit, but it appeared that they had all left MGE. Despite this, Marsh thought that there must be someone within MGE who would be knowledgeable about water treatment chemistry and the equipment needed to put his idea into large-scale operation. He decided to scour the company's laboratories until he found people who could help him.

Finding the right people proved to be much more difficult than Marsh had anticipated, and he spent nearly six months looking before giving up. One problem was that no one had ever tried to inventory what people at MGE knew. There was nowhere that Marsh could go to find out whether someone at MGE had ever carried out research or published a paper on this subject. The personnel department did not know, and neither did corporate R&D management, so Marsh ended up calling all the laboratory managers one by one.

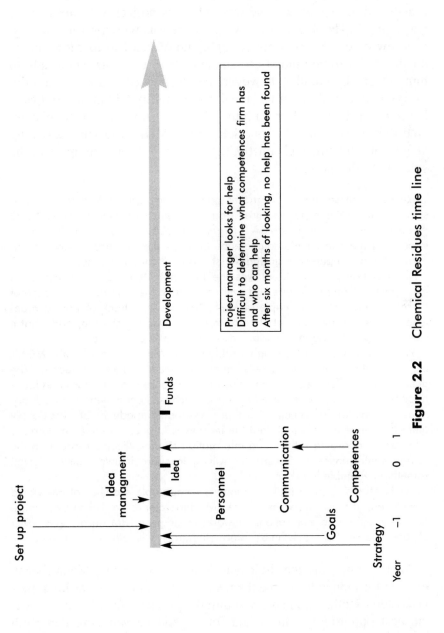

Figure 2.2 Chemical Residues time line

Set up project

Idea managment

Development

Funds

Idea

Personnel

Communication

Competences

Goals

Strategy

Year   −1   0   1

Project manager looks for help
Difficult to determine what competences firm has
and who can help
After six months of looking, no help has been found

Making these calls was quite laborious. In those days, MGE's people did not like to share information with strangers, even when those strangers carried MGE business cards. Each time he called, Marsh had to explain who he was, what his project was, and why he was doing it. He also had to say whom he was working for and why. In a few cases, that was not enough, and Marsh had to get an introduction from some mutual acquaintance before people would talk to him. Over six months, however, he managed to talk to virtually everyone in a position of technical responsibility within the company, but none of them could help him. After all that effort, Marsh discovered that he was the only one left within MGE who knew anything about water treatment chemistry. (See Figure 2.2 for a summary of the story up to this point.)

The story in these three paragraphs covers many corporate structures and systems. First, MGE separated itself from some key competences when it sold its water pollution unit. This M&A (mergers and acquisitions) activity had a key impact on the company's *competence* base as the absence of water-treatment-related competences slowed Marsh's project for some time.

Compounding the problem was the fact that MGE had no *competence management system*. No one had ever catalogued the skills and knowledge of the numerous technical people at MGE. No one kept track of what competences the company had, what competences it was investing in, and what it was gaining or losing in its various acquisitions and divestitures.

As if these were not enough problems for Marsh to deal with, MGE's communications and incentive systems hindered him in his search. The absence of an effective *communications system* between MGE's far-flung laboratories made the process of searching for technical competences quite laborious, and the lack of *incentives* to share information made the process doubly difficult. It appeared, in fact, that the incentives in place at MGE encouraged information hoarding rather than information sharing. People recognized the value of information and were not willing to share it unless they received something valuable in return.

While Marsh's search took six months, comparable searches at 3M would have taken, at most, two weeks, since 3M's laboratories are linked by a dense and very active communications network. In addition, 3M encourages, even obliges, people to share technical information freely with others in the company.

At the same time that he began looking for people, Marsh began looking for money to pursue the research. His first stop was his supervisor, Jerry Roth, who had given him the project. Water treatment was the best opportunity Marsh had found, and he was sure that Roth would fund it, but to his surprise, Roth would not. Roth knew nothing about water treatment and was in no position to evaluate what Marsh was saying about it. He could see that he might have to invest for three or four years before Marsh's idea would pay off. In the meantime, he would have to build a whole new set of customer contacts to sell it. This was not the sort of challenge he was interested in. He would move to another post within three years, and had no need for long-term investments. What Roth wanted Marsh to find were simple uses for the co-products that would pay off quickly and require little investment, so he said no to Marsh's idea. And that was that. Or so he thought. (See Figure 2.3 for a summary of the story up to this point.)

The reasons behind Roth's decision are worth exploring in detail even though this is in many ways a familiar story.

First of all, the *project funding system* at Industrial Chemicals gave business unit managers 'monopoly rights' over funding innovation projects within their business units. The business unit manager had sole discretion over whether or not to fund project ideas that came up within his unit. Officially, people within a business unit had no right to go anywhere else for funding. As we will see below, Marsh bent the rules a bit after Roth said no, but according to the rules, Marsh should have stopped right there.

So why did Roth say no? There was nothing in corporate *strategy*, in his business unit *strategy*, or in the *goals* he was given by senior management that would encourage long-term investment. If a project was likely to take more than two years to pay off, there was no reason, according to the official strategy and goals, to do it. The *incentives* that Roth faced put him in a position in which a long-term investment could reduce his compensation or harm his prospects for promotion. As if that was not enough, the company's *culture* discouraged people from taking risks. Thus it was logical for Roth to say no. The fact that no one besides Marsh had any *competence* in water treatment did not help, since that made it harder to for Marsh to build any credibility for the idea.

One other aspect of this decision must be mentioned. The *decision-making methods* in use at MGE at this time gave sole responsibility for each decision to one person, in this case the business unit manager. Since the water treatment idea did not fit well within Roth's business unit, it is not surprising that Roth said no. Had MGE practiced consensual decision making, however, other people, some of them probably from other business units, would have looked at Marsh's proposal. They might have seen in the proposal features of interest that Roth missed and given it a more favorable review.

Another aspect of MGE's *decision system* was that appealing against a decision was unheard of. People rarely 'went around their bosses' to appeal to a higher authority as doing so would have been seen as disloyal and embarrassing to the boss.

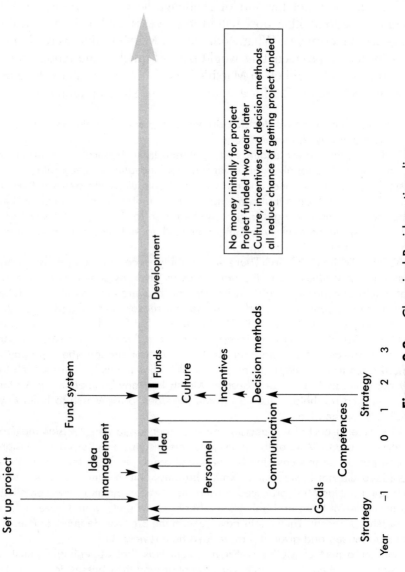

Figure 2.3   Chemical Residues time line

By MGE's rules, Roth's 'No' should have stuck, and Marsh should have quit his work on water treatment. Officially, there was nowhere else Marsh could go for funds. Nonetheless, he continued looking into the water treatment opportunity with whatever spare time and funds he could muster. Since he did not have enough money to do any new research himself, Marsh decided to call people he knew who worked in water treatment to see what they could tell him.

What Marsh found out was interesting. Other companies had seen the idea and were putting money into it, but none of the other companies had access to cheap supplies of the chemical needed, as MGE did. Thus, it looked like there was still room for MGE to develop Marsh's idea into a viable business.

Marsh decided to do a more general market survey, asking an acquaintance, an engineering consultant specializing in water pollution issues, to carry out the survey for him. Marsh wanted to find out whether the regulatory agencies would be interested in his idea. He knew that it would never fly as a business unless regulations were tightened to force industries and municipalities to reduce emissions of the residues that his system was targeting, but since Marsh did not have any money to pay for a survey, the consultant could only work on it on an informal basis. When he had other business with the regulatory agencies, he would take fifteen minutes out to ask them what they thought of Marsh's idea. After six months, he had visited most of the major water regulation agencies in the world, and he came back to Marsh with the results: the idea could work; the agencies were interested.

With this evidence, Marsh went back to Roth to ask for funding to undertake further research. This time he got it, but more than two years had passed since he first discovered the idea.

It is interesting that Marsh's extremely informal 'market survey' counted as evidence in the funding decision. There was no attempt to quantify the opportunity at this point, nor did he document possible competition. Even after Marsh received funding, there was no follow-up, no attempt to develop a more detailed or systematic view of the market, until many years later.

This shows, first, that there were no particular rules about what information should be used for *project funding* decisions. In fact, the system was so informal that each business unit manager could set whatever standards he wished in determining whether or not to fund a project.

The fact that there was no follow-up on this survey, even after the project was funded, is an indication of weakness in Industrial Chemicals' *project management systems*. No standards existed by which Marsh's performance as a project manager could be measured. No one was there to *mentor* him or to counsel him on what needed to be done to get the project off the ground.

The fact that Roth now said yes must be looked at. His incentives had not changed, nor had the project funding system been changed. What had changed, however, was that there was more evidence, an endorsement from a well-known expert in the industry. In addition, Roth might have been convinced by Marsh's sheer persistence. For nearly two years, Marsh had been badgering him about this idea. In the absence of any better ideas, Roth might simply have decided to give in to shut Marsh up. At any rate, the budget he gave was not particularly generous, and the money spent would not greatly damage the results of Roth's business unit.

With the money came formal project status and a name for the project. The name was Chemical Residues, since the idea was to develop a way to remove chemical residues from waste water. Marsh was named project manager, and used his limited budget to fund feasibility studies. As it happened, no one inside MGE could carry out the kind of tests he needed, so Marsh contracted with outside laboratories to test the feasibility of the chemical reaction. Unfortunately, he did not insist that the laboratories provide the type of documentation that would later be needed by the regulators, which cost the project team time later on. (See Figure 2.4 for a summary of the story up to this point.)

When Roth gave Marsh's work official project status (*project set-up*), he gave the work more legitimacy than it had had before. With official status, the project could have a budget and a project manager. Roth's decision to make Marsh the project manager (the selection of initial personnel, part of *project set-up*), while seemingly logical, would create problems later. We saw above that Marsh was not undertaking adequate market studies. We see here that he was also failing to develop adequate technical documentation (*project management methods*). This would cost the project team additional time at a later stage.

The results of the first tests were positive, but then disaster struck. Roth's business unit started losing money. Since Marsh's project was still years away from profitability, Roth decided to cut its funding; once again, Marsh was left out in the cold.

But Marsh did not give up. He decided to shop for funding elsewhere. Six months later, he met Mark Quinn, who headed a business unit in a neighboring division. Quinn's business unit was able do the processing that was needed to turn Roth's co-product into a salable product. Quinn offered Marsh a small budget and administrative support to continue his work and Marsh accepted.

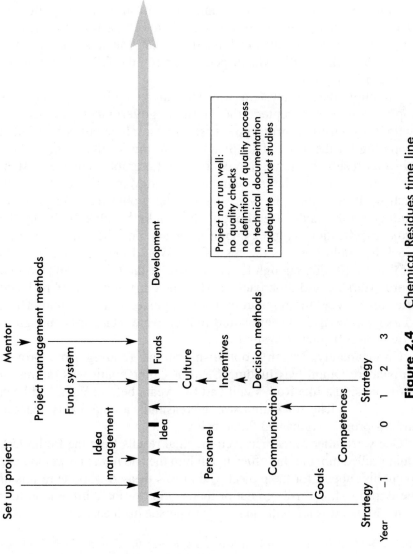

Figure 2.4 Chemical Residues time line

With the new money, Marsh ran more tests, although he still had to rely on outside laboratories for most of the work. With laboratory feasibility of the chemical reaction proven, he began looking for ways to generate more interest among potential clients and regulatory agencies.

Marsh soon learned that the German federal government was planning a series of tests on means of controlling water pollution. One, to be conducted in Berlin, would involve a full-scale test of ways to reduce the chemical residues that Marsh's catalyst was designed to deal with. Marsh petitioned for the CR solution to be included in the tests.

Although the CR system was still in an embryonic state, his application was accepted, the German government providing a budget to build a prototype system. Marsh spent six months preparing for the test and another year waiting for the results. When the final results came in, they were very favorable. The CR system was superior to all other systems tested, and Marsh was elated. With such positive results, he was sure that he would have no problem finding more funds. He thought he would be able to bring the project to fruition within a couple of years, and the only stumbling block he could see was the regulators. Would they tighten controls on water pollution enough to require use of the CR system? On that score, Marsh could look back at what his consultant friend had said after his survey: the regulators were interested in the system. Thus, Marsh was confident they would tighten water standards enough to require use of the CR system.

Unfortunately, Marsh's optimism on the funding front proved unfounded. Quinn was funding CR, but Quinn's unit was falling on hard times, just like Roth's unit had two years before. What had been a profitable niche for Quinn was increasingly a commodity market, and his profit margins had fallen below zero.

One week after Marsh received the final results from the Berlin test, Quinn called him into his office to tell him the bad news: he would have to cut his support for the project. Quinn was pleased with the results of the Berlin test, but had run out of money. So, for the third time in four years, Marsh was left with no money to pursue his idea.

Thus, after looking for money for two years, Marsh first found it in Roth's business unit. Then, after a year, Roth cut his funding. A few months later, Marsh found new funds, only to have them taken away again a few days after the Berlin test had demonstrated the feasibility of the idea.

Like Roth's early refusal to fund the project, the two decisions to cut funds were influenced by a variety of management systems and practices. The company's *strategy* (low cost) and *goals* (short-term profits) discouraged long-term investments in new product development. The structure of the *project funding system* and *decision-making methods* gave business unit managers sole responsibility to fund innovation projects. The *incentives* in place discouraged business unit managers from making long-term investments. Finally, as if this were not enough, the company's *culture* discouraged risk-taking.

Marsh was discouraged when Quinn cut his funding, but once again he did not give up. First, he took a long weekend in the country to think things over. Then, the day he came back, he called John McCoy, Industrial Chemicals' director of research. He told McCoy the story and asked him for help.

McCoy was quite impressed with what Marsh had gone through, as well as with the results of the Berlin test. While it was not his role to fund development projects, he did have some funds that he normally used to support fundamental research. There was enough to support Marsh until the end of the year, and McCoy promised to help Marsh to look for more permanent funding.

With a little breathing space, Marsh began planning how he would capitalize on the success of the Berlin test. More technological development would be needed, and he would have to go back and speak to the regulators. Most of all, however, he would have to keep working within MGE to find permanent funding.

When Marsh told me this story, he said that during the first four years of the project, he had spent more time looking for funds and other forms of help than he had spent working on the project. Had MGE's *project funding system*, *incentives*, and *culture* helped him, rather than working against him, he could have saved two and a half years.

Corporate begins supporting innovation

At this point, fate intervened again, but for once fate was on Marsh's side. Unbeknown to Marsh, MGE's executive committee was worried. In the previous two years, four business units had begun losing money. Seeing this, the executive committee investigated, and what they found was not reassuring.

In each of the four businesses, MGE had been one of a handful of Western companies dominating a market. Competition had revolved mainly around price reductions driven by improvements in process technology. MGE's process technology was good, and the company had been able to maintain high margins.

This situation, however, changed when new competitors, based in emerging Asian economies, entered the arena. These new competitors had lower labor costs than MGE. Several of them owned mineral deposits that were much richer than those to which MGE had access. Until the mid-1980s, these advantages had been offset by trade barriers and, more importantly, by high transportation costs. But trade barriers were coming down, and transportation costs had fallen significantly. There was no longer any way to keep the Asian competitors out of Western markets, and prices had fallen enough to make the businesses unprofitable for MGE.

Other trends were also worrying. Customers were becoming more demanding. In the past, MGE's chemical businesses had dealt mostly with other chemists, selling products to other chemical companies, or to companies that employed large numbers of chemists. MGE had never been obligated to understand what its customers did with its products as the customers had their own chemists on staff who did that. The business worked on the basis of specifications: the customers specified exactly what chemical they needed, and all MGE had to do was produce it at the desired level of purity. As long as MGE's products met specifications, things were fine.

But now the chemical business was getting more complex because of two factors. First, scientific progress in chemistry had greatly expanded the variety and complexity of molecules that could be produced. Whole new families of chemicals (including biochemicals) were being invented and no one could keep track of all developments in the field. Even customers with large numbers of chemists on their staff were unable to keep up with all relevant developments. Increasingly, they looked to MGE to help them understand what the new chemicals could do for them.

Second, the use of chemical products outside traditional chemical industries had increased dramatically. From agriculture to paper to plastics, one industry after another was finding that chemical products could help to improve product performance, lengthen product life, or otherwise increase product value. These downstream industries could not hope to understand the full range of chemical products that might be useful to them, so they had to rely on suppliers to help them understand what was available.

If it wished to serve these customers, MGE had little choice but to learn these new industries and sell products on the basis of what they could do for the customer. It could no longer sell products to established specifications with purity and cost being the only considerations. Thus, with new Asian competitors overrunning the commodity end of the business, and with customers demanding increasing value added at the other end, MGE could no longer compete with a simple, low-cost strategy.

One member of the executive committee, Paul Thomas, argued that the way out was to innovate more. MGE could move downstream from commodity chemicals to provide more complex and profitable products. This diversification could provide growth, growth that would never come from its current mix of commodity businesses.

After several debates, the Executive Committee made a decision. MGE would put a much higher emphasis on innovation, particularly on the development of new applied chemicals businesses. The only thing that remained was to figure out how.

Here the executive committee makes a change in corporate *strategy*. As we will see, this change in strategy had a far-reaching impact on the CR project and on the prospects for other innovations at Industrial Chemicals.

The question of *how* to increase innovation was an important one. All the members of the Executive Committee had spent their entire careers at MGE. While they had heard about more innovative companies, such as 3M, they knew little about how they worked. This did not stop them from saying that they wanted to make MGE look more like 3M, but they did not know how 3M worked. In fact, 3M's structures, systems and culture were very different from those of MGE, but no one at MGE had any clear idea about what the real differences were.

In addition, the Executive Committee members did not really run the company. The units were run by business unit managers, with the help of division-level management. Executive Committee members were responsible for overall supervision, but were far removed from operating decisions. Everyone liked it that way. The business unit managers knew their businesses far better than the Executive Committee did; everyone acknowledged that. What is more, most of them had been running their businesses quite well and producing steady profits. The successful ones would view any interference from above as an unwanted and unneeded intrusion, resenting and resisting it.

As a result, the Executive Committee didn't have a precise blueprint on how to proceed, having no idea of what kinds of new system and structure were needed. They knew if that if they tried to change divisional management systems, their efforts would be viewed as an unwelcome intrusion by division management, but they could not sit still and do nothing.

Competence is an issue here, but it is *management* competence, rather than technical or marketing competence that is the issue. The Executive Committee did not know how to set up or manage a company for product innovation: they had been managing a low-cost strategy for decades, and they had no experience with product innovation.

Another issue is the *organization structure*. MGE was, in effect, divided into independent fiefdoms. Control from the top was loose and based on personal influence. Top-down orders to change fundamental systems would have been completely counter to the culture. The Executive Committee could say that it wanted management systems to change, but, by tradition, its members would have to leave many of the details of the change process to their subordinates.

Paul Thomas was designated to spearhead the new innovation thrust. Thomas was a man of action. He had grown up in MGE's Lawn & Garden business and had later moved to Industrial Chemicals, before being promoted to corporate level. As an operating manager, he had always performed well. He had a reputation of making decisions and acting quickly, being more likely to do something and see what happened than to sit for six months thinking about what to do.

Thomas' only previous involvement with innovation had been as a business unit manager supervising projects. It was easy for him to equate innovation with projects, so for him, more innovation meant more projects. Thus, he decided to find and/or create more projects.

Thomas' solution may seem simplistic, but it was completely consistent with management practice at MGE. As an Executive Committee member, he could use corporate funds to create a project or increase a project's budget. He could establish a personal relationship, in effect a reporting relationship, with a project manager, or with anyone else he wanted. However, what he could not do so easily was to order division and business unit heads to reform their management practices to encourage innovation. He would not anyway have known what kinds of change to recommend. Focusing on projects may thus have been the best thing to do under the circumstances.

At that point, Thomas had never heard of the CR project. Although he supervised the Industrial Chemicals division, innovation projects had never had a high priority in the division, so no one ever discussed them with senior management. As luck would have it, Thomas soon heard about CR. However, he did not hear about it through normal channels, since no 'normal' channel existed. In fact, he did not hear about it through MGE channels at all. One day, several weeks after the decision to change strategy, he read about CR in his evening newspaper.

The newspaper article, on page three of the business section, reported the results of the Berlin test. It said that CR was the most promising solution to an important pollution problem. It quoted Marsh as saying that the project offered considerable promise for MGE's Industrial Chemicals division. Thomas was surprised: he had never heard about Marsh, CR or the Berlin test, yet here was an article in his local daily which said that the CR project was one of the keys to his company's future. He decided to look into it.

The nature of MGE's *communication system* in the 1980s is revealed here: vertical communication about product development did not exist. Thomas and his colleagues soon changed that.

The next day, not knowing whom else to call, Thomas called Marsh, and then it was Marsh's turn to be surprised. Marsh had heard of Thomas, to say the least, but he had never spoken to Thomas, or to any other member of the Executive Committee. In fact, he had rarely spoken to anyone within two levels of Thomas, other than the division's director of research. He did not know what to say. Of course he would come and see Thomas. But what was it about?

Thomas explained that he was interested in the CR project and wanted to learn more about it. Marsh put together a short, technical presentation and showed it to Thomas the next week. Thomas asked many questions in return. Then he told Marsh to revise the presentation to show it to MGE's Chief Executive Officer and to Industrial Chemicals management. After these presentations, Thomas told Marsh that he would get division-level funding, as well as corporate funding if he needed it. If he needed anything, all he had to do was ask. The CR project was going to be a high-level corporate priority, and he, Thomas, would assure that it got whatever resources it needed.

In effect, Thomas and the Chief Executive Officer began *supervising* the CR project themselves. They demanded monthly reports from Marsh and made sure that he got whatever resources he asked for. In effect, they made *funding* decisions about the project themselves, rather than leaving such decisions to be worked out through the normal project funding system.

Marsh was amazed. Within weeks, the project's budget increased to five times its previous peak. After four years of scrounging for resources, Marsh could hire anyone he needed and spend whatever money he needed to spend. He had never had so much support in his entire life. He immediately hired two technical experts to help him develop the system. He contracted other work out to internal and external laboratories. He also hired several part-time workers to develop contacts with the regulators. Some of these part-timers were MGE people who had other responsibilities, others being consultants or lobbyists. While Marsh continued to focus his attention on Europe, he hired a skeleton team, all part-timers, to manage development in the North American market.

Industrial Chemicals management, seeing corporate management's sudden interest in innovation, began paying more attention to the subject themselves. In effect, Thomas's decision to give so much support to an innovation project was a signal of how serious corporate management was about improving MGE's innovation performance. Division managers began looking at the situation. They saw the same problems that corporate management had seen – that in many businesses, the low-cost strategy was no longer working. Consequently, they decided to support innovation more fully.

Business unit managers did not react the same way. They figured that corporate management would still expect them to produce steady profits in the short term. In their annual performance reviews, they discovered that they were right: corporate management's evaluation of their work still focused on short-term profit. Thus, they remained reluctant to support long-term investments in product innovation.

The business unit managers' continued reluctance to support innovation was based on the fact that their *incentives*, particularly their promotion prospects, were still tightly linked to short-term profits. Corporate management began talking about the need for more risk-taking and long-term investment, but business unit managers did not believe this, since there was little action behind the words.

Their skepticism was reinforced by senior managers' behavior during their annual performance reviews. Senior managers still focused on and rewarded short-term profit performance. As a result, it was several years before business unit-level managers began placing any priority at all on product innovation.

Division-level managers got on board with senior management much more quickly, partly because they were much closer to the Executive Committee members. They saw each other regularly and felt that they were all part of the same team. In addition, division managers' promotion prospects were much less dependent on short-term profits.

Division managers, like the Executive Committee, first focused their attention on individual projects. Ken Smith was a member of the division's management committee. Since 1988, he had supervised three business units, which between them supported six innovation projects, one of which was CR. Smith had, however, never devoted more than 2 percent of his time (his estimate) to the project. But now that the project was a corporate priority, Smith began spending much more time with Marsh and his team.

One result of Smith's increased involvement was that a serious technical problem was solved. Scaling up the system for the Berlin test had proved difficult. As Marsh told Smith, the technical system that the team had used at Berlin cost so much that it made the whole project commercially unfeasible. Smith was a chemical engineer by training, and he saw a solution that Marsh and his team had not envisaged. Smith's idea worked, and the project got back on track.

Newly interested in the project, Smith, in effect, began *participating* in the project and contributing ideas, much as a project team member would. One of the ideas he contributed solved a significant technical problem.

Reforming project funding and management systems

A few months after becoming involved with CR, Smith decided to review the project's history. He talked with McCoy, the division's director of research, and the two of them undertook a careful review. They were concerned with how long Marsh had been forced to run around the company looking for resources before finding stable funding. They realized that if a similar idea arose again, it could easily go through the same endless search for funds since the division's project funding system had not changed.

After studying the problem for several months, Smith and McCoy proposed two reforms, both of which were implemented by division management. Projects were made a division-level responsibility, and business unit heads no longer had monopoly control of them. Business units could still support projects, if they wished, but they would have to report on what they were doing, and not doing, to a division-level committee.

Second, division-level funds were provided to support projects that did not fit within the charters of existing business units. It was hoped that the next CR-like project would quickly be reported to the division funding board and find stable funding there. In that way, the new project's manager would not have to do what Marsh had done, spending the majority of his time looking for money rather than working on the project. (See Figure 2.5 for a summary of the story to this point.)

The division's *project funding system* was changed radically as a result of Smith and McCoy's review.

In addition, Smith and McCoy looked in detail at what Marsh had done with the project. They decided that Marsh needed to put more emphasis on marketing and regulation. Despite his marketing experience, Marsh had focused on the project's technical development. He had made little progress in developing contacts with potential clients, industry partners, and regulators. So Smith urged Marsh to concentrate more on these neglected aspects of the project.

This was division management's first attempt to look at *project management methods, but* it was not its last. Up to that point, project managers had received little guidance or training in how to manage projects. They, like Marsh, had been left entirely on their own to figure out how to manage their projects.

With higher project budgets and other reforms underway, corporate management decided that it was time to publicize the company's new focus on innovation. The company was under pressure from its share-holders to produce more growth and profits, and as a result, corporate management decided to tell shareholders about MGE's most promising innovation projects, CR being on the list.

Marsh and others protested that it was far too soon to reveal the project to the public as they were still several years away from having a viable product. Corporate management, however, over-ruled Marsh and publicized the project anyway. They presented CR as a water treatment solution that was 'nearly ready'. The entire water treatment industry soon heard about the project, and the project team had to deal with numerous requests for information. Potential customers were disappointed to learn that CR was a long

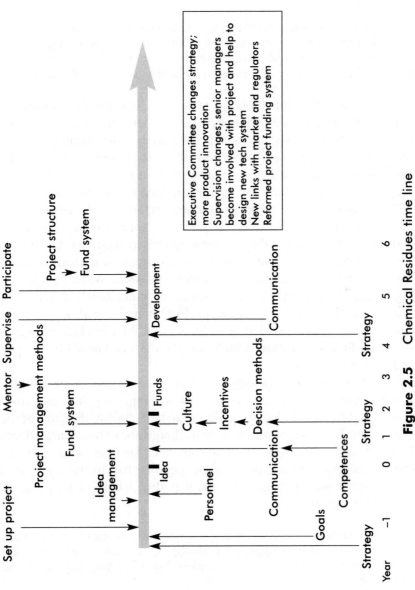

Figure 2.5 Chemical Residues time line

way from being 'nearly ready'. The team's credibility suffered, and it was harder to get cooperation from potential partners for several years thereafter.

Here corporate management made decisions about publicizing the project. In effect, they took over the management of the project with respect to the issue of publicity (taking *operational control* of a project). By doing this, they disempowered the project team and reduced the project's chances of success.

Two years after the huge increase in CR's budget, Smith and Thomas became concerned with Marsh's performance as a project manager as he did not seem to be getting much done. Although he was spending a lot of money, there was little visible output. Their initial analysis was that Marsh was 'not aggressive enough in pushing the project', and they began looking for someone to replace him.

About this time, the project got a new supervisor, the new division head, Mark Green. Green had more experience with formal project management than any other senior manager in Industrial Chemicals. He had spent the first twenty years of his career in a pharmaceutical company, where he had supervised many projects. When he saw how Marsh had been managing the project, he immediately agreed with Smith and Thomas that a new project manager was needed. For Green, however, the problem was deeper than Marsh's lack of aggressiveness. In Green's eyes, Marsh simply did not know how to plan and manage a project.

Marsh's technical knowledge was key to the project, so the problem was how to keep him on the team while replacing him as project manager. Smith decided to make Marsh technical director of the project, while putting someone else in charge above him. Surprisingly, Marsh was not unhappy with the change. He had always been a chemist at heart, and had never liked spending half his time preparing reports for senior management. He was thus happy to turn that job over to his new boss.

Here management began thinking about what was needed to run a project effectively (*project management methods*). Once senior managers saw Marsh's limitations, they decided to replace him (changing team personnel, part of *supervision*).

Green worked with Thomas to develop a profile of the ideal CR project manager. Green thought that the key issue facing the new project manager would be to get tough new regulations in place in Europe, regulations that required industries and municipalities to reduce chemical residues in waste water. He therefore decided to find someone who was experienced in working with European regulators. He also wanted someone who knew how to run a project and get things done.

With the help of a headhunter, Green and Thomas found their man, Ken Peters, working in a European regulatory agency. He had been promoted several times, and they took that as evidence that he could get things done, so they offered him the job. Peters accepted and took over the project more than six years after Marsh had started pushing the idea. More than two years had passed since the Executive Committee's decision to emphasize product innovation.

Some MGE managers did not like the fact that an outsider was hired to run CR, Peters not being part of the MGE network. He hardly knew anyone in the company. In most management jobs, his life would have been difficult for that reason as people would not have known who he was or whether to trust him. Peters, however, had plenty of resources, resources that came straight from the top of the company. He did not need to lobby his peers for support as his direct link with top management assured that he could get anything he needed.

The downside of Peters' connection with top management was that it generated talk of favoritism as business unit managers did not have such easy access to corporate resources. Some of them were jealous and complained, quietly, about the 'favoritism' being shown to this unproven manager and his unproven product.

The irony of the situation was that few MGE managers would have been willing to take a job as project leader. No one had ever moved up from a position like that, it was not on the career track. A job like that was too risky. If the project did not survive, its manager would be out of a job and, possibly, out of the company. Such things had happened before and no MGE career person would run that risk.

Top management had been talking about innovation for two years, but nothing had changed in the way in which they promoted and rewarded people. Would they do something different for an outsider? The skeptics, who were still in the majority, believed that they would not; they believed that top management would continue to reward steady profits rather than unpredictable ventures such as innovation success.

Here, despite their efforts to promote innovation, top management was running into a credibility problem. Their core management team, the business unit managers, did not believe that promotion criteria (*incentives*) had really changed. As far as they were concerned, the best way to move up in the company was still to produce steady profits and no surprises in an ongoing business. The career people did not know what to make of people who were willing to work on innovation projects. As far as they were concerned, it was obvious that they did not care very much about their long-term future with the company.

Once Peters took over the project, he was astonished at how little documentation existed. Marsh had been working on the project for six years, but there was no coherent record anywhere of what technical work had been done or of what progress the project had made on the various marketing and regulatory fronts. There was, in fact, little documentation of any kind, except for that which had been produced by outside laboratories. Peters could see that his first job would be to document what had been done and to determine what the next steps would be.

After losing 2–3 years because of delays in getting funding, the CR team lost another 1–2 years because of its failure to plan and document its work adequately. Peters was obligated to start from the beginning in terms of producing the kind of technical documentation required by regulators, customers, and potential industrial partners. With more effective *project management systems* and *project supervision*, Marsh's failure to document progress adequately would have been noticed far sooner.

Peters hired full-time people in North America and Asia to help him to run the project in those regions, but, unlike Marsh, Peters gave his lieutenants clear direction. Next, he hired an engineer to document all the technical aspects of the proposed system.

Sam Johansen was the man Peters hired to head the North American effort. Johansen had been working in antipollution for more than twenty years. As soon as he took over the North American operation, he took stock of what had been done. Like Peters, he was surprised and disappointed by the lack of documentation, so to remedy that, his first move was to conduct a thorough market study. What he found disappointed him still further.

Johansen was hired onto the project at the end of its seventh year. As he undertook his market study, he quickly learned that the regulations he needed, requiring reductions in water pollution, were already in place in the United States, having been passed three years before. The restrictions would tighten at the end of the project's ninth year (phase I), and again three years after that (phase II). Marsh's team had picked up this fact, but they had not appreciated its significance. Johansen did, and he knew he would have to work fast to get a system up and running to be tested in time for phase I. He wondered what other companies were working on the problem. Surely, with so much advance warning, there must be competitors, and indeed there were.

This incident points out the importance of maintaining effective contact with customer and regulatory groups during the early stages of a project (*communications* with customers and regulators; *project management systems*).

The industrial companies told Johansen that they were redesigning their processes to eliminate chemical residues in their effluents. Most of them had already advanced enough to meet the phase I regulations, and the rest were confident that they would be able to do so. None of them was interested in the catalytic process that MGE was proposing. Some said that they would have been interested had the process been ready two years before, when the regulations were passed. It would have looked cheap enough that they would have bought it to avoid an expensive process redesign, but by now they were well into the process redesign and saw no point in stopping. Most felt sure that they could meet the phase II regulations in the same way.

As a result, the industrial side of the North American market had evaporated from under the CR team. Had MGE funded the project more quickly, and had Marsh run the project well, CR could have been ready three years sooner and it could have captured the North American industrial market. But CR wasn't ready, and the market disappeared.

With such bad news from the industrial market, Johansen hoped that the municipal market would be more positive. It was, but it was far from a sure thing. While MGE's catalytic method had received favorable press, other methods also looked encouraging. Changes in filter technology looked particularly promising, being potentially cheaper and easier to manage than MGE's catalytic process. MGE still had a chance to capture this market, but it would be a race. Had they been ready three years earlier, they could again have discouraged competitors and preemptively captured the market.

For want of a good *funding system* and good *project management methods*, a large part of the potential market was lost.

Corporate and division management were located in Europe; they had never been very involved in the American market. The news that the market there would never be as big as expected was a disappointment, but they were too focused on what was happening in Europe to worry much about it. In Europe, the regulations still had to be written, and they wanted them to be written in the right way. They had good reason to be optimistic in Europe, since European industrial companies had not proceeded as far in developing controls for the chemical effluents the CR system was designed to control. They might still buy the CR solution rather than investing in process reengineering or other competing solutions.

The news that Marsh had missed some key information added fuel to Green's desire to reform project management. Working with Smith and others, he pushed for further changes. The reforms he implemented included the following. Standards for project managers were increased, and training programs were begun to train project leaders in the most effective project management methods. The newly trained project chiefs were given more power over their own budgets and more hierarchical control over the people who worked for them. The idea of the project team itself was strengthened, with cross-functional links becoming more common and more legitimate. (See Figure 2.6 for a summary of the story up to this point.)

At last, fundamental reforms in *project management systems* occurred. At the same time, *project organization structures* were changed. Project chiefs were strengthened, and cross-functional teams became the rule rather than the exception.

At the same time, Green made more reforms in the project funding system. He developed a new, detailed project evaluation form that was to be used to select projects for funding. The form included questions about the project's target market and the marketing efforts that had to be made before the project could reach fruition. Regulatory and technical issues were also covered. The revised funding system was designed to force project managers to think through all the issues relevant to the project early on, as well as to force them to plan how to deal with these issues.

This reform in the *project funding system* was designed to avoid situations in which project teams (like CR) missed fundamental issues.

In addition, Green required project chiefs to report to the division's head of R&D at least once every three months. The report was to

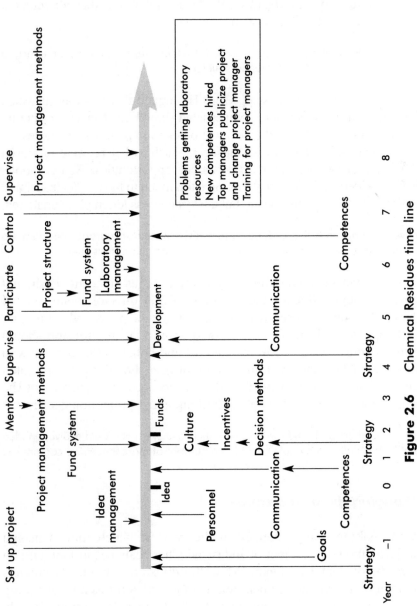

Figure 2.6 Chemical Residues time line

cover technical, marketing, regulatory, and any other relevant issues. This would allow the head of R&D to make sure that all relevant bases were being effectively covered.

This change in how projects reported to their superiors was, in effect, a change in the *project organization structure*.

At this point, Thomas stepped in. He argued that the way in which project team members were compensated should be changed, instituting a bonus system that would give small bonuses to members of successful project teams. Various project managers, such as Peters, were promised much larger bonuses and major career opportunities. Some people, including Peters, thought that this gave too much to the project leader and not enough to the project team, but the system was left in place unaltered.

It was thought that this change in *incentives* would encourage the teams to work harder, but it was not clear whether it actually had that effect.

Some managers, however, felt that the changes in incentives did not go far enough, McCoy, the division's R&D director, being one of them. He wanted to see real changes in career paths and promotion systems. He told anyone who would listen that the division should establish clear 'careers for innovation', and believed that anyone who had never taken part in an innovation project should not be promoted into division management. His ideas were not implemented, but (he hoped) they influenced people's thinking about promotion decisions.

Here was an idea about how long-term *incentive* systems should evolve, an idea that has actually been implemented in a number of more innovative companies.

Changing the organization

After making many changes in the way in which they managed projects, the management of Industrial Chemicals began looking at a more fundamental problem. While the division now ran its projects more effectively, management felt that the division was not generating enough new ideas. They wondered why thousands of bright people were producing only a handful of useful project ideas each year.

Division management were unsure of how to tackle this problem, so they brought in a group of organizational consultants. There were other reasons for bringing in the consultants too; for example, the division did not respond very quickly to customer requests for solutions to new problems. Perhaps if it learned to respond more quickly to customer requests, it would be able to generate more new products.

After talking over the issue with the consultants, management decided to reorganize the whole division. The twelve business units had traditionally been organized around four core technologies. New product development, when it occurred, had been driven by technological advances. There were no contacts between customers and the laboratories. According to the consultants, this was a problem. They said that if the division wanted to increase idea generation, it should put its technical people into direct contact with customers. At the same time, the consultants suggested, it would be a good idea for business units that served the same customers to work together. Up until this point, for example, there had been no contact between the four business units that served the paper industry. If there were, perhaps they would find ways to combine their technologies to create new, synergistic products.

As a result of these discussions, new sales teams, combining technical and sales people, were set up within each business unit. In addition, they put technical people from each business unit into direct contact with their customers. Management hoped that this would lead to more new product ideas and to a much quicker response to customer requests.

At the same time, management decided to reorganize the division's business units around customer groups. The business units were left intact, but they were linked into groups focused around major customer groups. In cases (and there were many) where several business units served the same customers, combined sales teams were set up that included technical people from each business unit. By putting technical people from different business units into direct contact, it was hoped that synergies between business units would be brought to light, paving the way for additional specialized products.

Here management implemented a major reform in *organization structure*, hoping that this would lead to more ideas and a quicker implementation of the ideas that arose. The organizational changes were designed to cause substantial changes in the division's *communications system*.

Management designed other reforms to remove other roadblocks that innovation projects had run into. Marsh had told many people the story of his six-month-long search for people with the competences he needed to pursue the CR idea. People remembered it, particularly when they heard other project leaders telling variations of the same story. As part of the organizational reform, division management decided to address this problem. They appointed a group of mid-level managers to conduct an inventory of the division's technical competences, an inventory that would be kept up to date on an ongoing basis. People would be informed of its existence, which would, it was hoped, allow them to find needed competences far more quickly than they had been able to in the past.

Thus, years after Marsh spent six months looking for people to help him advance the CR idea, management decided to implement a *competence management* system. Had it been in place years earlier, Marsh could have saved six months of his time.

As an additional move to speed up response to customers, many responsibilities were pushed down to lower levels of the organization. Decisions that had been the responsibility of division-level committees, such as product configurations and investments, were reallocated to the business unit level.

This was an additional reform in *organization structure*, this time focusing not on hierarchical links, but on decision territories.

Green continued to push for more training for innovation product managers, as well as for more routinization of project procedures. According to one of his subordinates, he still looked to his project management experience in pharmaceuticals as a model for what should happen in chemicals. But not everyone was convinced that projects such as CR could be planned and routinized to the same extent as pharmaceutical projects. CR, after all, faced an uncertain regulatory environment (in Europe), and had many sources of technical and market uncertainty that pharmaceutical projects rarely had to face. The division tried, nonetheless, to develop more effective methods of planning and managing projects.

Reforms in *project management methods* continued.

As all these reforms were being implemented, the CR project continued its technical and market development. The North American team was confident that it would gain some clients for the phase II tightening of regulatory requirements. It was also negotiating with potential partners who could build the equipment needed to implement the residue removal system.

The European team was focusing major efforts on the regulatory process. Much tighter regulations were under discussion, but were not yet written into law. In addition, the European team was beginning to develop close relationships with several potential industrial clients. Joint research activities were taking place on industrial scale methods of chemical residues control. The European team was optimistic that it could gain a significant market share once tighter regulations were implemented. (See Figure 2.7 for a summary of the project's history.)

Epilog

The CR project team continued to work on the project. While the market was difficult, there was still hope that CR would become a profitable niche product in the waste treatment business. This eventually happened, but the product has not been able to achieve the level of revenues and profits originally hoped for.

Meanwhile, the zeal division management had shown for improving innovation performance diminished after a few years. Several years after instituting his organizational reforms, Green moved on to another job. His replacement was not as committed to improving innovation performance.

The CR experience was disappointing for some in the division. So much effort expended for so many years, all for limited results, they said. Others argued that innovation is an uncertain game. The companies that win at this game take a lot of bets. They know that most of the bets will not succeed, but they also realise that the few that do succeed will more than pay for the rest. CR did not make it into the big leagues; it was not a blockbuster, but it was paying its way. Critics hoped that the company would take more such bets in the future, and this time, maybe, it would manage them better.

As you see, this is not the kind of 'I conquered the world' or 'My favorite CEO conquered the world' type of story that you sometimes find in business books. It is a story of real managers, not too different from those in most companies. It is the story of how they struggled with the problem of improving innovation performance in a company that had never before put much emphasis on product innovation. In the next chapter, I will analyze what they did and look at some more fundamental patterns behind their behavior.

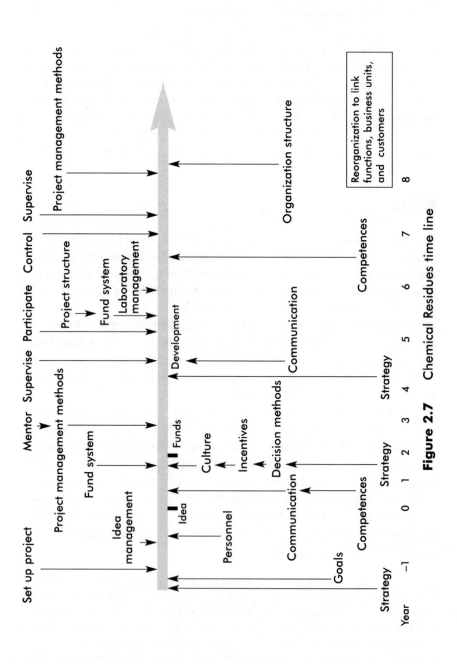

Figure 2.7   Chemical Residues time line

Interpreting the Chemical Residues Story

Roadblocks encountered and management tools used during the CR project

In the last chapter, it was noted that the CR project ran into many different kinds of roadblock during the first four years of its existence. Many different management structures, systems, and practices caused delays in the project. Later, division management changed many of these same systems and practices in an effort to improve innovation performance. It is useful to look more analytically at what they did.

Different types of intervention in the innovation management system

Figure 3.1 is a time line showing the history of the project over nine years. I have noted, with arrows, each time a management system, practice, or structure worked as a roadblock that slowed the project. Other arrows signal efforts to improve the management systems, practices, and structures around the project. Several interventions have been left out in cases of repetition. But the time line is a fair summary of which management tools affected the project and when. (Rather than repeatedly using the awkward phrase 'management systems, structures, and practices', I will frequently abbreviate it to 'management tools'. The logic behind this usage is that senior managers can, in theory, change all of a company's systems, structures, and practices. By changing systems, structures, and practices, they in effect use them as 'tools' to improve innovation performance.)

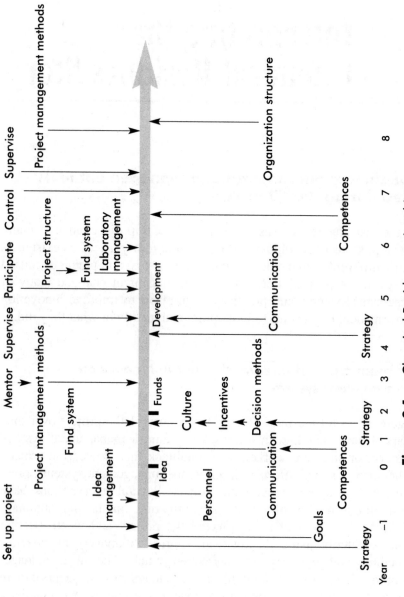

Figure 3.1 Chemical Residues project history

In Figure 3.2, I begin classifying these management tools. Anyone who wants to improve innovation performance can work on *one project at a time*. The top line of this chart reflects this type of activity. Once Industrial Chemicals senior managers discovered the CR project, they funded the project, supervised the team (skipping three intervening layers of managers), made operational decisions for the project (deciding to promote it, against the will of the project team), and changed the project manager.

Later, Industrial Chemicals senior managers worked on *the whole project management system*. This affects all projects, or, in some cases, all new projects. In the Industrial Chemicals case, senior managers worked on the project funding system, the organization structure of project teams, and project management methods. They could also have worked on methods of generating ideas within project teams, laboratories or other technical areas, as well as on other aspects of laboratory management.

Finally, Industrial Chemicals management worked on systems, structures, and processes that affected *the entire business*, operating units included. They did this by changing strategy, organization structure, incentives, goals, communications systems, and the methods of competence management. They could also have focused on other personnel management systems, culture, and methods of decision making.

The scope of a manager's actions

The difference between working on (a) one project at a time, (b) all projects, and (c) both operating units and projects is one of *scope*. Scope is measured in terms of what part of the company is affected by the action. A manager's action can have a narrow scope (one project) or a wide scope (the whole company). A general list of intervention types, classified by scope, is included in Figure 3.3.

Industrial Chemicals managers, like many others I observed, began to reform their company by experimenting with narrow-scope changes, altering the budgets and reporting structures of individual projects. These were very low-risk actions that had no likelihood of impacting negatively on the core business. After making alterations in a number of individual projects, managers then began changing project management systems. They modified funding systems, project

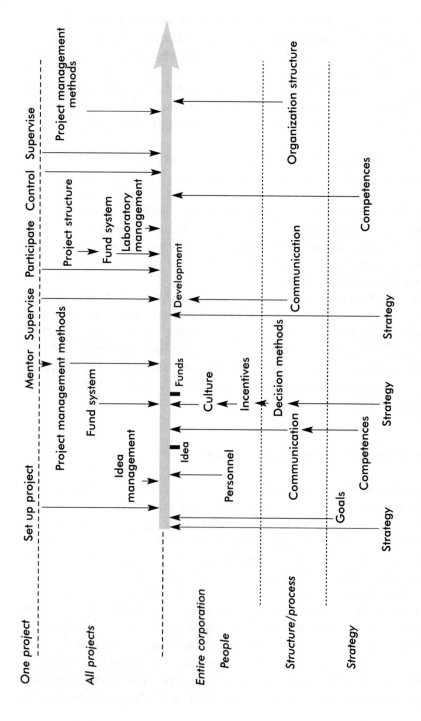

Figure 3.2 Chemical Residues project history: the tools classified

management methods, and project structures. They began reshaping company-wide systems and structures only after working with projects and project management systems for several years.

Scope is not the only dimension that we can use to classify managers' actions, but it is a key one. It is a quick way to judge the risk involved in an action, the complexity of a change, and thus the difficulty of implementing it. As a result, it helps to explain the sequence of actions that managers often take (see next section) as they try to improve their innovation systems.

Sequencing a change effort and involving other people

Figure 3.4a shows the scope of senior managers' actions at Industrial Chemicals over a five-year period. Beginning when the Executive Committee decided to change strategy, the chart shows, in chronological order, the scope of each action taken by division management in their efforts to improve innovation performance. Each diamond is an action. The bulk of activity in the first 18 months focused on individual projects. During the middle period, lasting about two years, the majority of activity involved the project management system. Finally, during the last 18 months, most activity was concerned with business-wide systems.

I charted the history of the reform efforts of three other organizations in the same detail as for Industrial Chemicals (Figures 3.4b, 3.4c and 3.4d). Brief histories of these cases are included in Chapter 6, and a more complete version of each story can be found in Christiansen (1997). In each case, managers focused first on individual projects, and then began changing project management systems. Finally, only after the reform effort had been under way for several years did they begin changing company-wide systems.

In several of these histories, the alert reader will have noticed that there is a category of intervention not mentioned above, that of 'reflection' interventions. These interventions do not fit easily into the dimension of scope. In three of the four cases studied, senior managers either brought in consultants to look at how the company was managing its innovation system, or asked an internal team to look at the same issue. This action – asking people to analyze a company's innovation system and find ways to improve it – I call 'stimulating reflection'.

| Changing the way in which business systems are managed | | | Changing the way in which projects are managed | Intervening in single projects |
Strategy/goals	Structure/process	People		
Strategy	Organization structure	Incentives	Management of idea generation	Set up
Competences and M&A	Communication and information management	Other personnel management systems	Management of laboratories	Supervision
Goals	Decision-making methods	Culture	Funding system	Participation
			Project structure	Mentoring, consulting
			Project management methods	Operational control

Figure 3.3   Intervention types classified by scope

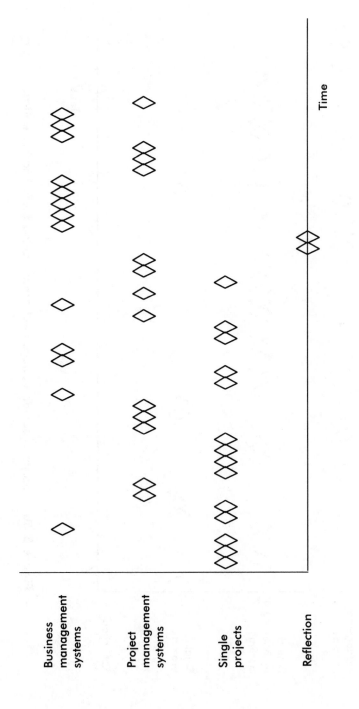

Figure 3.4a Scope of senior management actions at Industrial Chemicals

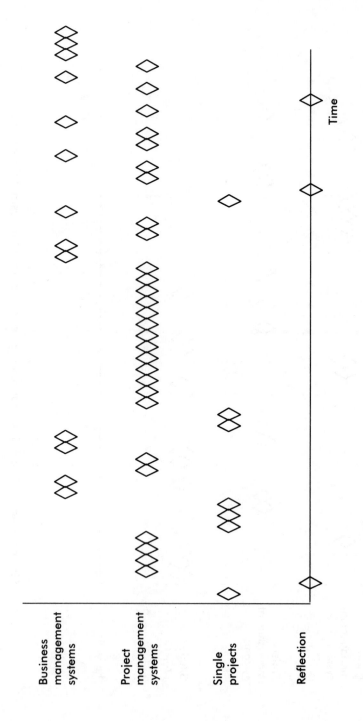

Figure 3.4b Scope of senior management actions at Northern Pharmaceuticals

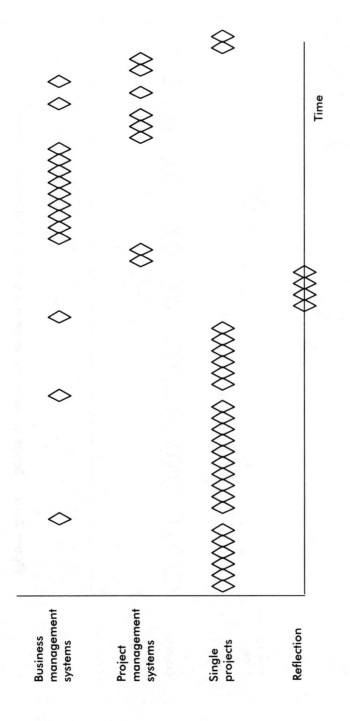

Figure 3.4c   Scope of senior management actions at Lawn & Garden

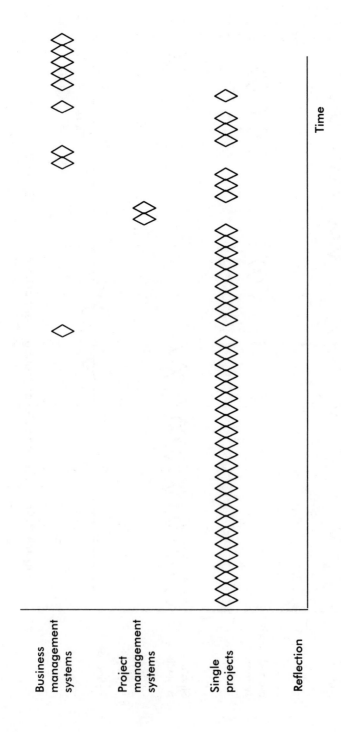

Figure 3.4d   Scope of senior management actions at Advanced Materials

While asking people to 'think about innovation' did not directly change anything, these reflection periods often led to substantial reforms in business management systems. For example, managers who were considering changing organization structure often brought in consultants as a way of reducing risk. They could draw on the expertise of consultants or other outsiders (new hires or academics) who had observed or participated in other organizational reforms. This reduced the risk of making an obvious mistake. Alternatively, they could bring several layers of their own management team into the planning process. This was seen as killing two birds with one stone: bringing lower-level managers into the process encouraged their mobilization as well as helping to improve the design of the new system.

Industrial Chemicals management brought in consultants to help them to design the division's new organization. Alan Grage of Lawn & Garden, another MGE division, was one leader who took a quite different path. (A brief summary of the Lawn & Garden story appears in Chapter 6. The full case study is reported in Christiansen, 1997.) When Grage decided that his division needed reform, he spoke to an academic consultant about what he wanted to do. Then he announced his plan to his people. Subsequently, he asked his managers, down to a very junior level, to think about the plan and determine what parts of it they would like to implement and how.

When I talked to Grage, he said that there was no way he could have designed the new system entirely by himself. Even bringing in his direct reports would not have been enough. The only people who knew how Lawn & Garden was run in detail were the people who ran it, and the people who ran it were his managers down to a very junior level. While he could give them broad outlines, Grage said that it was up to them to fill in the detail needed to make the plan work. It would then be up to them to implement it. He argued that they would be much more likely to implement a plan that they had developed themselves rather than one that had been imposed on them from above.

Categorizing the tools

Figure 3.5 lists the types of intervention found at Industrial Chemicals, classified by scope. There are additional dimensions, besides scope, behind the ordering of the lists. The items under project management follow a rough chronological order. The items listed under business management systems are not classified chronologically since they tend to have an impact throughout a project's life. Instead, they are classified according to whether they impact most closely on the company's strategy, structure, or people management systems.

Some readers may prefer the more recent formulation of purpose–process–people (Bartlett and Ghoshal, 1994, 1995; Ghoshal and Bartlett, 1995) rather than the older categorization of strategy–structure–systems. Purpose–process–people is a more lively, action-oriented formulation, capturing what companies 'do,' particularly with reference to process, better than the strategy–structure–systems approach. Purpose–process–people will therefore be included along with the more traditional dimension.

Figure 3.6 shows graphically when each management tool has its most important impact on the life of an individual innovation project. Starting from the top, managers can be involved with individual ideas or projects at virtually any time during the course of a project, but at no time is their involvement necessarily crucial. Good *project management methods* are key at the early stages of the project when the most crucial decisions are made. Later on in the project, when most of the key decisions related to the project have already been made, good management methods are somewhat less important.

Project organization structures are key, for different reasons, at both the beginning and the end of the project's life. The strength of the project manager and the project's formal links with the organization can be crucial in giving the project an effective start. However, the links, and the project manager's weight, can continue to be crucial if the project team needs the cooperation of other units in the organization during the development process. Finally, at the end, the project's links into the organization can make a crucial difference as the project is launched and integrated into ongoing operations.

The *funding system* is, obviously, crucial during the initial funding stage. It continues to be important later on because most projects are not given all the funds they need at the beginning. Milestones or hurdles are set up, and the project must be refunded when it passes these.

Laboratory management is vital at the beginning because laboratories and other technical areas are usually involved in the generation of ideas. Specific *methods of idea generation* are also key at this stage. Neither is very important as the project searches for funds, but both become somewhat more important during the development process,

Changing the way business systems are managed			Changing the way projects are managed	Intervening in single projects
Strategy/goals	Structure/process	People		
Strategy	Organization structure	Incentives	Management of idea generation	Set up
Competences and M&A	Communication and information management	Other personnel management systems	Management of laboratories	Supervision
Goals	Decision-making methods	Culture	Funding system	Participation
			Project structure	Mentoring, consulting
			Project management methods	Operational control
Other: Stimulating reflection				

Figure 3.5   Intervention types classified by scope

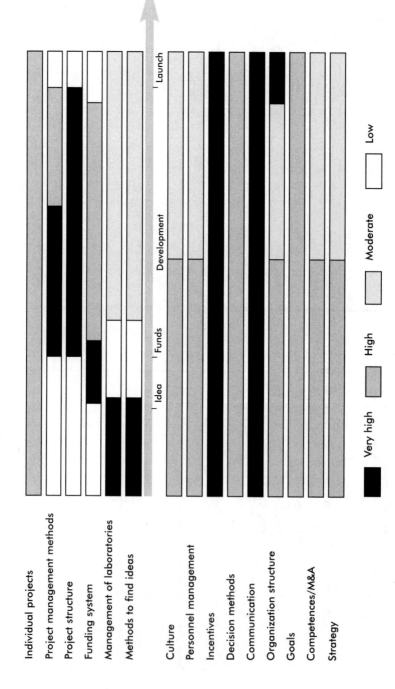

Figure 3.6   Impact of tools/interventions over time

since ideas for improving the product may arise during the project itself. Ideas for spin-offs (new projects) may also become evident at this time as well.

Of the business-wide systems, *incentives* and *communication* have a substantial impact on ideas and projects from beginning to end. Academics (for example, Allen, 1977) have been looking at the impact of communications systems on innovation since the mid-1970s. They have found a link between the amount of communication between units and the likelihood that those units will produce interesting innovation ideas. A connection also exists between the extent and types of communication link that a project team has and the team's success during development. Communication between people with diverse viewpoints stimulates idea generation. Communication between technical areas (or other areas where ideas may be generated) and funding sources affects the speed with which projects are funded. Communication between the project team and the rest of the organization, as well as outsiders, during development influences the ability of the project team to draw on outside resources.

Incentives impact on people throughout the process. They may motivate people to suggest and pursue ideas or to ignore them. They may encourage funding sources to be generous or ungenerous. They may cause project team members to work single-mindedly towards the completion of a project, or they may discourage full commitment to a risky project by discouraging risk-taking of any kind.

Methods of making decisions (by consensus among a large group versus by a single decision maker, appeal process, and so on) similarly have an impact throughout the innovation process. However, while I found cases where decision-making methods had a visible impact on outcomes, such cases were rarer than for communications or incentive systems.

Strategy sets the direction for the company. It guides people when they make decisions about where to look for ideas, what competences to invest in, and which projects to fund. It has a considerable impact on the early life of an idea or project, but less influence later on. Corporate or business unit strategy, however, may still guide a project team's decisions, or influence the amount of money invested in the project.

A company's competence base and its *competence management systems* have a role in idea generation and in the company's ability to exploit ideas in the early stages. Chemist Marsh would not have pursued the CR idea had he not himself had a peculiar mix of competences. The project team was slowed by the fact that MGE had no way to help Marsh find the additional competences he needed to pursue the idea.

Such competence deficits, the ability easily to find and track competences, and the ability to transfer competences can all have a large impact on a project in its early stages. Later on, competence management is still important. But a project team, once set up and going, usually knows what it needs and where it can get it. This makes it less dependent on the company's competence management system.

Goals, whether for business units, project teams, work teams, or individuals, can influence the innovation process. In companies where goals are cascaded down to the individual level, the impact is obvious. Individuals may or may not have goals that encourage them to innovate, or to help others who innovate. Even when goals are not cascaded down to the individual level, however, business unit and team goals can affect individual behavior, either encouraging people to innovate and support those who do, or discouraging them from doing so.

Organization structure has an important effect on communication patterns in a company. As a result, it has an impact throughout the innovation process. However, organization structure as it is defined here also involves distributing power. Organizational position determines who is responsible for specific units within the company, as well as who is responsible for specific activities. As a result, it determines who is in charge of controlling access to the resources that an innovation system needs.

Organization structure provides a hierarchical context around individuals and teams. Its effect on innovation, in the early stages, is indirect, as it probably has less impact than communications and incentive systems. Later, during development, the project team becomes an independent unit, often separated from the rest of the organization. Here, the impact of the organization structure around the project is limited. But later, when the project is launched, the team is integrated into the overall organization. Then, the dynamic aspect of the organization structure is key. How easily does the organization accept and integrate new products and business units?

Personnel management systems (other than incentives) involve such things as hiring, career development, and rotation systems. These can have an important impact on idea generation. Marsh acquired the competences that helped him to see the CR idea by moving around the company. Highly innovative companies, such as ConsumerCo, encourage people to move around.

Personnel management systems also have an impact on a project's ability to bring on new people. A company where people stay within the same business unit and move straight up a functional silo will find it difficult to set up cross-functional project teams. People will simply not have enough familiarity with the vocabularies and work practices of other functions to be able to effectively work with them. In addition, it will be difficult to create project teams outside an established business area (CR being an example of this), since this will involve leaving the traditional, safe career track. A project that is unable to assemble an effective team will find it difficult to make progress.

Organizational *culture* is defined here as 'rules, written or unwritten, that guide people's behavior in ambiguous situations (that is, situations where the best course of action is not clear)'. The dimensions of culture that are most important for innovation include 'willingness to take risks,' 'willingness to innovate or change', and 'willingness to support risk-taking or innovation undertaken by others'.

More innovative companies often have explicit rules about risk-taking. People are supposed to take calculated risks, innovation and experimentation being viewed as good. Less innovative companies, however, often have unwritten rules that discourage risk-taking. Risk-taking is, at best, not rewarded, and at worst, actively discouraged. Such cultural norms can have a vast impact on people's willingness to take risks and on their willingness to support others who take risks.

As a result, I have coded culture as having a large effect during idea generation, initial funding, and the early stages of development. By the time a project is well into development, it will be clearer to fence-sitters whether or not the project is a winner, and the cultural rules will have less impact.

This analysis gives the reader an idea of which management tools are important at different times over the life of a project. In the next chapter, I will present some general theory explaining how the various tools can be used to improve innovation performance. Chapter 5, as well as other sections throughout the book, will provide examples of how to use the tools. Limitations of space make it impossible to present a complete discussion of how the various management tools impact innovation performance. That will be tackled in another book.

A Framework for Thinking about Innovation

As I said in the introduction, innovation can be a very complex process. Many steps can be involved in generating an idea and bringing it to fruition. To be able to think clearly about this process, it is useful to be able to break it into phases, and then to develop a clear theoretical understanding of each phase. That is what I will do in this chapter.

In some ways, innovation can be compared to a complex manufacturing process. The manufacture of a computer memory chip involves several thousand steps, each of which must be performed correctly if the chip is to function. A mistake at any point can ruin the whole chip. Understanding this process involves knowing the tasks that need to be performed and how they are linked to each other (for example, what has to be performed first, and so on). Improving the process can involve improving the performance of each of the individual steps, changing the order of the steps, and/or identifying and eliminating unnecessary steps.

Developing a new product can involve many more steps than the several thousand it takes to manufacture a computer chip. To make matters more complicated, innovation projects are not repeated as often as manufacturing processes. Chip lines run for many months and may manufacture millions of identical chips. The process can be optimized over time. Experiments can be run and improvements put into place because the same process is repeated over and over again.

Innovation systems do not repeat things this often. While a pharmaceutical company may run dozens of compounds through similar regulatory tests, the differences between the compounds and their intended uses will require customization of much of the process. The process of setting up clinical tests may be the same from one compound to the next, but the investigation sites used and the exact data collected, for example, may vary.

In some industries, each project may be unique. A diversified manufacturing company may have hundreds of projects running at once in dozens of different business units, each targeted at a slightly different product–market niche. Nonetheless, there will be certain regularities in the innovation process, regardless of how different the projects are. Some of these regularities may, once they have been identified, seem simple and obvious. But once identified, they will allow us to think about the process more systematically. For example, identifying the key phases in the process will allow us to ask questions about the key management problems during each phase.

So, what are the key phases of the innovation process? To answer that question, it is useful to identify events that occur in every project. Each project originates in an *idea,* which will have arisen at a specific time and in a specific place. The idea for a product innovation will include some kind of *technical solution* to a current or possible future *market need.* The people proposing the idea will have looked for and found *funding* to pursue the idea. Exploring the idea might involve a few days of work in the case of a very simple idea, or many years in the case of a very complex and difficult one. This process of pursuing the idea to fruition is called *development.* When development is finished, a decision is made to *launch* the product. After launch, additional *post-launch development* may occur (Figure 4.1).

Development is largely an extended exercise in problem solving. Can the vision implied in the idea be made reality? If so, how? What technical problems are involved? What are the solutions to these problems? What kinds of marketing and regulatory problem are involved? How can the company solve these? The process of identifying and solving these problems is usually the longest and most expensive part of the innovation process. But the earlier parts – generating the idea and finding funding – should not be ignored. Improving these processes can radically shorten the cycle time between the appearance of an opportunity and a product launch. It can also result in products that meet market needs more effectively.

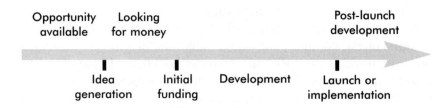

Figure 4.1   Key activities during the project life cycle

In the next part of this chapter, I will give an overview of the innovation process, discussing in more detail why it is useful to look at the process as a series of phases. I will explore how managers try to improve innovation performance during three key phases of the process. I will then discuss in a general way how each phase works, starting with idea generation, and moving on to the process of finding funding, and finally, development.

Overview of the innovation process

In this section, I will set up an analytic framework that will give the reader a background for understanding how managers can improve an innovation process. I will first identify and discuss three key phases of the process. Then I will consider the goals of the process, particularly the question, 'What does it mean to improve innovation performance?' In answering this question, several components of innovation performance will be identified. I will then discuss how these components apply to each phase.

Phases of the innovation process

Chapter 2 described the story of the CR project. This story showed how the actions, past and present, of Industrial Chemicals management had impacted the project. Chapter 3 provided a more structured analysis of certain key management systems, processes, and practices that had impacted the project. From this data, I constructed a table that listed a wide variety of ways in which managers could influence the innovation systems of their companies.

In that discussion, the concept of *scope* was introduced. I defined the scope of a manager's action as being the breadth of its impact across the company. The most narrow-scope interventions impacted only one innovation project. The most wide-scope interventions affected the entire company. In between lay mid-scope interventions that affected only the project management system.

In the discussion of CR, I implicitly used another set of concepts in the form of a phase model, describing the CR project as going through several steps. First came a *pre-idea period* in which an opportunity existed, but no one had identified it as a potentially viable economic proposition. The starting point of this pre-idea phase is undefined, but we do know that the CR idea could have been pursued many months, perhaps even years, earlier. When Marsh discovered it, ideas like it had already been under discussion for several years.

The pre-idea period ends when the idea is discovered and recognized by someone as being a potentially viable economic proposition. In the CR case, this happened when George Marsh discovered the idea and decided that it was viable and worth pursuing. Ideas can, however, be discovered and forgotten. Had Marsh not pursued the idea, it might have been overlooked, perhaps to be rediscovered by someone else later. It had already been forgotten once: one of Marsh's engineers had discovered the idea, but then discarded it when early test results were negative.

In the pre-idea period, the likelihood of generating an idea is particularly affected by the company's competence base, by its strategy, goals and incentives, by other personnel management systems, and by its communications systems. How these systems affect idea generation will be discussed at several points later in the book.

Through the rest of this book, I will use the term 'idea generation' to refer to what happens when someone has an idea (or discovers a forgotten idea) and recognizes it as a potentially viable economic proposition. Idea generation occurs at a specific point in time. It is followed, sometimes with a delay, by a period of searching for support. (An early description and analysis of idea generation can be found in Morison, 1966.)

Most business ideas of any significance are beyond the power of one person to pursue. So the idea generator will have to seek help. He may have resources already available to him that he can use to pursue the idea. This will allow him to delay the point at which he will have to ask for corporate support. At some point, however, he will almost certainly have to go beyond his immediate resources to seek help elsewhere. I call this period of looking for support the *funding search*. Systems like the funding system, the communications system, and strategy, goals and incentives all affect whether potential projects can obtain funds. They also affect how long it will take potential projects to find funds.

The funds search ends when *initial funding* is obtained. Once funding has been obtained, the project enters the company's *development* system. Development is a period that can last indefinitely. During this period, all of the company's project management systems affect the project. Senior managers may intervene personally as well. Business management systems will have an effect, since project personnel will continue to be part of the company. In addition, business management systems will have an influence when the team needs help from business units. They will also impact the project when the time comes to move the project into a business unit.

Goals: what does it mean to improve innovation performance?

I have noted that many different management systems and practices influence the innovation system. Managers at all the companies I have worked with have gone to considerable effort to change practices and systems to improve innovation performance. But what does that mean, to 'improve innovation performance'? The phrase can be taken to mean the production of more new products, and thus new revenues. It can also mean the implementation of more process improvements, and thus more cost reductions.

New products and process improvements are the final result of an innovation process, but we miss a lot if we simply try to link each management intervention with the final outcome without looking at what happens in between. Managers may change the communications system in a laboratory in the hope that, six years later, they will have more new products on the market. But what happens in between? And why do they think that changing the communications system will help laboratory personnel to develop more or better ideas than they have developed in the past?

To answer these questions, it is useful to break the goal of 'improving innovation performance' into components. Generally speaking, managers in the companies under study were not just focusing on final outcomes when they tried to improve their innovation systems: they had much more specific and short-term goals in mind. To understand what they were trying to do, we need to look at the short-term goals they tried to achieve across the phases of the process.

Components of innovation performance

In analyzing managers' efforts to improve innovation performance at eight companies, I was able to identify four key components of innovation performance. The first two are related to *fit with customer need*. To have any chance of being successful, new products under development have to fit with either *current customer needs* or *future customer needs*. Managers sometimes try to improve their companies' ability to react effectively to current customer needs (that is, to find ways of fulfilling the needs that customers are expressing right now). At other times, they try to build a capability to anticipate future consumer needs. The two are conceptually and operationally different, so we will treat them as two separate components of innovation performance.

The third and fourth components of innovation performance are *speed* and *cost*. Speed refers to time to market or time to implementation. How quickly can a company get a new product to market? How quickly can it implement a new process? Cost refers to the cost of the innovation system itself. Is money wasted? Could new products and processes be developed at a lower cost?

As an illustration, I will give examples of the methods that managers used to achieve each of these goals. When the managers reorganized Industrial Chemicals, they established new industry sales teams that would do a better job of identifying and reacting to customer needs. In part, the sales teams were to transmit information about current customer needs back to technical people much more quickly. But they were also designed to identify needs, either current or future, that the company had not been recognizing in the past.

3M set up multiple links with its customers partly to do a better job of picking up current needs. They began interviewing customers' customers on the theory that this would help them to identify their customers' future needs before the customers began to express them.

3M also sited laboratory resources in some of its overseas business units in order to be able to react more quickly to customer needs, and thus speed up its innovation system.

ConsumerCo insists that its managers talk with customers at least weekly. This helps them to pick up current customer needs. It was also thought that this high level of contact would develop their intuition and enable them to better sense unexpressed needs (that is, possible future needs).

EurAuto put great effort into reducing the time needed to develop a new car. Northern Pharmaceuticals successfully reduced the time needed to move a new compound through clinical trials. Both were concerned with speed. EurAuto was also concerned with cost. EurAuto management viewed cost reduction as being just as important as time reduction. They believed that by reducing the time needed to develop a car, they would reduce the cost as well.

Eastman Chemical's managers were also concerned with cost. When they discovered that terminated innovation projects cost just as much as those which produced viable products, they decided that something was wrong. They changed project teams' incentives so that less viable projects would be terminated more quickly, thus saving the company money.

Goals for each phase of the process

While managers would at times say that they wanted to 'reduce innovation cycle time' or 'achieve a better fit with customer needs,' most of their interventions were in fact even more focused than that, being designed to impact not on the whole innovation process, but on one part of the process.

When they worked on speed, for example, managers did not try to speed up idea generation, funding decisions, and development all at once. Instead, they conducted separate interventions for each phase. Some interventions were designed to speed up development, others to speed up funding decisions. A few were designed to speed up idea generation (that is, to help the company to recognize opportunities more quickly).

By analyzing managers' interventions, I identified eight phase-specific goals that they worked on. During the idea generation phase, they tried (1) to generate more ideas in relation to current customer needs (following the market). They also tried (2) to generate more ideas in relation to future customer needs (leading the market), as well as (3) to speed up the idea generation process overall. This latter goal contributed to the goal of hastening the overall process, but the interventions needed to speed up idea generation were quite different from those needed to quicken development.

When they worked on the funding phase, managers tried to assure that the company (4) made better funding decisions. They thought that they could accomplish several goals at once by improving their funding processes. The first goal was (4a) to fund more ideas fitting either current or future customer needs, which would assure that more good ideas would get through the system. The second was the converse of this: (4b) to fund fewer ideas that did not fit current and future customer needs. This would help to reduce the overall cost of the system. In addition, managers tried (5) to reduce the amount of time it took to make funding decisions. This increased overall speed and decreased innovation cycle time.

During development, managers had three phase-related goals. They wanted project teams (6) to make better operational decisions while running the project so that the final outputs would better fit current and future customer needs. In addition, they wanted teams (7) to work more quickly, part of the program of decreasing overall cycle time. Finally, they aimed (8) to reduce the cost of development.

The relationships between these phase-related goals and the overall goals is depicted in Figure 4.2 in the form of a three-by-four matrix. Figure 4.3 shows the causal links.

	Idea generation	Funding	Development
Fit with current customer need	More ideas: current customer needs	Better funding decisions: a. Fund ideas that fit	Better operational decisions
Fit with future customer need	More ideas: future customer needs	b. Don't fund ideas that don't fit	
Speed	Quicker idea generation	Quicker funding decisions	Quicker development
Cost		Less money wasted (result of better funding decisions)	Reduced development cost

Figure 4.2   Goals by phase

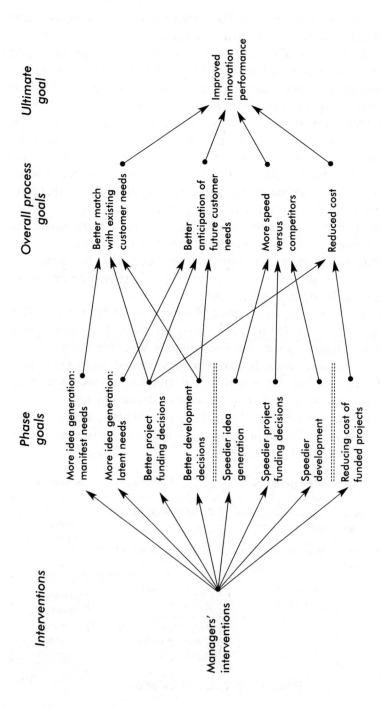

Figure 4.3 Managers' goals as they intervened in the innovation system

On the left-hand side of Figure 4.3, I have put 'managers' interventions'. In effect, managers intervened in individual projects, or changed project and business management systems, in an effort to improve innovation performance. They often worked on only one phase or one goal at a time, but a few interventions, such as those related to culture or incentives, had an impact across all the phases.

I identified and listed the general categories of intervention in my earlier discussion and analysis of the CR case. But there is not enough space in this book to explore each of the categories in detail. The remainder of this chapter will therefore provide a more general discussion of how companies' idea generation, funding, and development systems work, as well as of how they vary. I will also talk in general terms about what kinds of management tools can be used to improve these systems.

Idea generation systems

Where do ideas come from? The man on the street may believe that they come out of the blue, or maybe out of a research organization that functions as a black box, the inner workings of which are opaque to those on the outside. Some managers may share these views, not really understanding where ideas come from or how to generate them. Increasingly, however, better theories of idea generation have been developed, which managers can use to improve idea generation.

Old theories of how to get ideas

Before we investigate contemporary management theories of idea generation, let us first go back a few decades. At one time, ideas were the province of *lone inventors*, or at best of *a research organization separated, geographically, and organizationally*, from the business it supported. The theory that ideas came from somewhere 'out there,' from somewhere outside normal business activity, was a theory that lasted well into the 1980s in many organizations.

For example, Bell Laboratories was organizationally separate from AT&T for many decades. Indeed, it produced many good ideas, some of them ultimately used by AT&T. However, the model of a laboratory wholly divorced from operating units has fallen into disfavor. The story of Xerox's invention of the personal computer (PC) shows some of the reasons why. Figure 4.4 illustrates how this theory imagined idea generation to work.

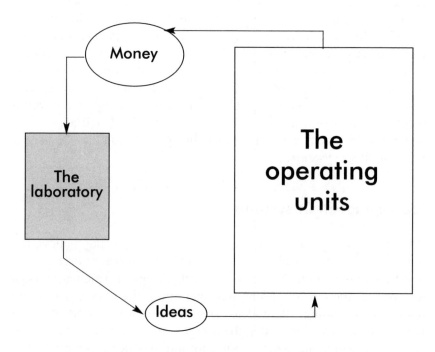

Figure 4.4   The old theory of idea generation: separation

It has become well known that the first PCs in the United States were built by Xerox's Palo Alto Research Center (PARC). PARC built the first PC, the Alto, in 1973 (Smith and Alexander, 1988), but PARC was unable to commercialize the product since the rest of the Xerox organization rejected it. Why did this happen? – because the organization had not had anything to do with the idea, did not understand it, and saw it as useless. Apple went on to develop the first commercial PC by adopting much of PARC's technology (Smith and Alexander, 1988). Within ten years of Xerox 'fumbling the ball', the PC became a major new industry.

Complete separation of laboratories from operating units often leads to this kind of situation, as ideas and projects do not transfer back and forth between the two areas. The laboratory may ignore ideas that arise in the operating units (for example, ideas from customers), or may be unresponsive to the short-term needs of the customer. Meanwhile, the operating units may ignore good ideas developed in the laboratory.

Who generates new ideas?

So if separation and the black box theory of idea generation do not work, what does? To address this issue, it is useful to consider the problem from several different perspectives. One approach is to look at individuals: Who is creative?, Who comes up with lots of new ideas? Another approach is to look at environments: What types of company, with what types of management system and practice, encourage the most idea generation? Let us look at each perspective in turn.

When faced with the question of what part of the population is most creative, problem-solving experts often come up with a surprising answer. Some say that small children are more creative than adults. According to some experts, children aged between five and seven are particularly creative. They are much more likely than adults to come up with original ways of interpreting phenomena and original ways of solving problems (see, for example Ackoff, 1978).

Some researchers on creativity, however, disagree with this stance. They say that children are not creative because they are not in a position to bring their ideas to fruition (see, for example, Czikszentmihalyi, 1996). Similarly, children do not know what has been tried before, so they sometimes propose unworkable solutions to a problem, solutions that an adult would not propose because of knowing from experience that they are ineffective.

The two groups of researchers disagree because they define creativity differently. For the first group, creativity is the ability to look at things in an original way. Whether these original ways of looking at things are fruitful or not is of secondary importance to these researchers. What they are concerned with is the process of idea generation itself, rather than the ultimate outcome of the process.

For the second group, in contrast, it is the outcome that counts. What matters is the ability to bring something entirely new into the world and have other people accept it. Both groups admit that young children are quite good at coming up with new ways of looking at things and new ways of approaching problems. What they disagree on is whether that constitutes creativity.

For our purposes, generating ideas and having effective outcomes both matter. There are no innovative outcomes without creative ideas. Many companies are either short of ideas, or miss good opportunities that their competitors see first. At the same time, however, companies need filters to sort the good ideas from the bad. I will focus on the problem of *generating* more and better ideas in this section, and on the problem of *filtering* the ideas in the next section, on funding systems.

Children, newcomers, and other outsiders

We do not normally take the ideas of young children seriously when we are looking at adult problems. Similarly, children do not have the kind of training or experience needed to understand most problems that adults face, much less solve them. Nonetheless, when problems are stated in terms they understand, young children have an ability to look at them in an original way. In most children, however, this capability diminishes as they grow up (Ackoff, 1978). It is interesting to look at both why they have this ability when they are young, and why it diminishes as they grow up.

Part of the reason that young children come up with original ways of looking at things is that no one has so far told them the right answers. They have no trouble thinking 'out of the box' because they have not yet learned where the box is. They can be original: indeed they have little choice but to be original, because they do not know the common wisdom. This is, in part, a handicap as they do not know how to make good judgements about their ideas. But it is also an advantage: they are far less inhibited about coming up with new ideas and sharing them.

There is evidence to suggest that something similar happens in the business world. On the larger scale, young, upstart companies often lead technological revolutions. The leaders in a business are rarely the first to develop or market truly new technical solutions (Tushman and Anderson, 1986; Anderson and Tushman, 1990; Christensen, 1997). At the micro level, work groups go stale if new members are not added to them regularly. These new members not only bring new ideas and new interpretations, but also prevent the group from becoming closed to ideas from the outside (Katz and Allen, 1982).

A willingness to entertain new interpretations of data may be particularly important in larger, older organizations. Dierickx and Cool (1989) have made the point that companies that have succeeded do not always know why they have done so. Complex companies in complex industries cannot keep track of everything that impacts on their performance; they may develop theories of why they have succeeded that are simply wrong. New people may see the real reasons for success, reasons that are quite different from the company's common wisdom. They may also see the early signs of change in the market, or the failure of an old strategy, long before anyone else.

In general, there is something about youth or newness in a situation that helps to facilitate idea generation. New people in a work group contribute more ideas, also serving as a conduit for new ideas from the outside. New companies pioneer new technologies and new approaches to markets. There is something about bringing in new people who are able to take a fresh look at a situation that leads to the generation of more ideas, children being an extreme example. But new people in a work group or new companies in an industry are not extreme examples: they are an everyday occurrence. Why is it, then, that existing work groups have difficulty bringing in new ideas? Why do existing companies have difficulty pioneering new industries? Companies that are able to solve these problems are much better equipped to innovate.

Why it can be difficult to accept new ideas, particularly from outsiders

Reasons for resistance to new ideas. So, why are older companies and stable work groups less able to generate new ideas? One issue is organizational. Older companies may be organized in ways that prevent them from effectively seeing or analyzing new ways of configuring their product (Henderson and Clark, 1990). They may not have the right skills in house. Another issue is political: key skills or key information may be held in functions that are not favored or taken very seriously (Leonard-Barton, 1992). Alternatively, key insights may be proposed by people who are new to a situation. The bearers of the insight/idea may not be in a favored position in the power structure, and may thus find it difficult to get their ideas seriously considered. It is this latter, more political, problem that I will explore in this section.

In many companies, the power of older managers is, in part, based on their 'superior knowledge and skill'. The senior managers of the company have supposedly reached their positions because they are the best managers. Their aura of competence may extend beyond people management and organization to technical and marketing skill. In such a company, saying that young people in the company are more skilled at anything can be disturbing. For if young people are more skilled than the old, why are the old on top? Why, indeed?

Silicon Valley has turned the old power structure on its head. There, young people with ideas manage their own companies, and an entire infrastructure has been set up to support them. Skills in electronics, computers and telecommunications, Silicon Valley's stock in trade, are freely available throughout the valley. Capital, too, is freely available to people with good ideas. As a result, young people do not have to put up with navigating the power structure of older companies to get what they need. They can simply go off and form their own companies. This has long been recognized as one of the reasons for Silicon Valley's success.

Reasons why older companies stay in business. 'Why do so many large companies stay in business?', the reader may ask. There are two reasons. One is that many large companies recognize that the young have lots of ideas. They welcome them and exploit them. They are blessed with management teams who are not embarrassed to admit that junior people have valuable ideas, and that older people are there to help to develop these ideas, rather than just oppose them.

The other reason why older companies survive is because they have assets they built years, even decades, ago. They have strong positions in mature industries. Often no one is able effectively to challenge them. Strong consumer brand names, if well taken care of, live for decades. Some companies, automobile companies for example, organize such complex and expensive tasks that their assets can simply not be duplicated by a young, innovative start-up. In addition, many older companies compete in industries where all their competitors are as old and conservative as they are. Companies in such industries do not have worry that much about innovation, since no new company is in a position to threaten them, and their existing competitors have little interest in doing so.

Sources of difficult to accept ideas. I have focused here on the issue of young people and young companies versus older people and older companies, but there are other dimensions of difference that are also important. Ideas can come from functions that are not favored in the company (Leonard-Barton, 1992). These ideas may be ignored because the functions they arise from are not seen as key to the company's competitiveness. Here, the dynamic is similar to that between young and old. The more powerful group, the favored function, gets more management attention for its ideas and activities. It will fear the diminution of its power if the less powerful group gets attention for its ideas.

Ideas can also come from outside the company and be rejected because of the 'Not Invented Here' (NIH) syndrome (Katz and Allen, 1982). Ideas can relate to a new technology, one not currently used by the company, and thus not understood by management (Christensen, 1997). Alternatively, ideas can come in a form (a new product architecture, for example) that is difficult for the current organization to assimilate, or even recognize (Henderson and Clark, 1990). In any of these cases, the dynamic is the same: the new idea is seen as illegitimate because it comes from some person or group that is near the bottom of the current power structure, or from some group outside the organization that is not listened to.

Many illustrations of this phenomenon of the rejection of ideas by those in positions of power are possible. Most published examples are drawn from business organizations. But anthropologists have found that animals behave in the same way.

Idea diffusion in other species

In the 1950s, Japanese anthropologists observed several large groups of monkeys on different Pacific islands. One of the things they studied was what the monkeys ate. In some cases they provided new types of food to see whether and how the monkeys adopted it. Once a day, they gave sweet potatoes to members of a particular group of about 150 monkeys. When the monkeys came to get their sweet potatoes, the researchers were able to identify each individual, which allowed them to track what each monkey did.

On one occasion, one of the younger female members of the group began washing her sweet potato before eating it. She liked it better that way and continued doing this each day. Gradually, other members of the group noticed what she was doing and began to wash their sweet potatoes too. Within eighteen months, 51 percent of the 150 or so monkeys had begun washing their sweet potatoes. Interestingly, those holding out included all of the older, male monkeys who were recognized as the leaders of the group. They would have nothing to do with the new way of eating.

Curious, the anthropologists wondered whether this diffusion pattern would be repeated if a new type of food were introduced. They thought that eighteen months was a reasonably fast period of time for half of the group to try something new, but they wanted to see if the same thing would happen in response to a new food. Thus, they introduced caramels to the same group of monkeys. The same pattern ensued. The young monkeys tried the caramels first. They liked them, and the habit of eating caramels slowly spread, passing mostly among the young and among females. Older males never tried the caramels at all.

Intrigued and eager to bolster their findings further, the anthropologists decided to try the same experiment with a different group of monkeys. They introduced wheat seeds to a group of over 100 monkeys on a different island, with the aim of seeing how long it would take members of the second group to adopt wheat as part of their diet. They spread quantities of wheat seed on a riverbank where the monkeys frequently came to drink. They were utterly astonished by what happened next.

By chance, the first monkey to try the wheat seeds was an older male monkey, one of the leaders of the group. He came to drink, saw something new on the ground, sniffed it, tried it, and liked it. It was obvious to the monkeys around him that he liked the new food, so they tried it, too. Within four hours, every monkey in the group had tried the new seed. They continued eating it as long as the anthropologists made it available. (The story is recounted in Ardrey, 1970. The original sources are Itani, 1963, and Kawamura, 1963.)

So, that's *eighteen months* for a 51 percent diffusion in one group versus *four hours* for a 100 percent diffusion in second. Diffusion in the second group thus proceeded *two thousand times faster* than in the first group. Why? Was it a coincidence that in the first case the idea came from an individual at the bottom of the group's social ladder, while in the second case it came from a leader? Probably not. The lesson is that, among monkeys, the animals most closely related to man, innovations are accepted two thousand times more quickly when they are proposed by a leader, rather than by a junior member of the group. Are groups of people very different? The answer from my personal observation is that some are, and some are not. Less innovative companies can be much like the monkeys. The leaders ignore or kill every idea that comes along, unless, of course, they can claim it as their own. More innovative companies find ways of getting around these basic primate instincts, identifying and exploiting ideas from junior as well as senior employees. Status issues, such as power and seniority, somehow do not get in the way of innovation.

Managing the difference between old and young (or insiders and outsiders)

One way in which to interpret the monkey story is to say that the leaders of a social group can slow or speed up the adoption of an innovation simply through their willingness to ignore or embrace it. If they are not interested, other members of the group will not try the new idea as fast. If, on the other hand, they are interested, others will imitate them, and the new idea will spread more quickly. By implication, leaders of business organizations can encourage innovations within the organization by adopting or supporting them.

Marketers have long used this principle in advertising products to consumers. Endorsements from 'leaders' are known to have a positive affect on the adoption of a new product. Do people within organizations act any differently? Assuming that they do not, the leaders of business organizations can influence people to innovate simply by showing an interest in innovation. Or they can discourage innovation by ignoring it.

Obviously, supporting innovation in a large company is not as simple as product endorsement. Many everyday management systems and practices must be brought into line if the company is to support innovation effectively. Nonetheless, the social side of the relationship between old and young, between insiders and outsiders, must be looked at carefully if one is to understand the dynamics of idea generation within a company. Let me illustrate this with two examples.

Young and old at ConsumerCo. Many companies, ConsumerCo being one of them, recognize the fact that younger people (or outsiders, or 'fresh faces') have new ideas. A country manager at

ConsumerCo told me how he and his colleagues managed this issue. Each year, he made sure to hire one or two young people, fresh out of university, onto his management team. They always came with new ideas on how ConsumerCo's products could be improved and/or marketed more effectively. They were particularly good at thinking of ways in which ConsumerCo's products could be adapted for young people, he said. But that was not all they were good at. They also had useful ideas on ways to appeal to all age groups.

The country manager went into more detail on how he managed young people. He and his peers listened to their ideas and utilized many of them. Some they had to shape to be more practical, more executable, whereas others could be used much as they were. Experimentation and testing determined which would work. Sometimes the younger people proposed ideas that had been tried several years before. But evidence of past failure would not necessarily kill the idea. If a case could be made that the situation had changed, or that the previous failure was an unusual result, they would try the idea again.

As ConsumerCo's young people gained experience, they received more and more responsibility. It was not unusual to see a successful thirty-year-old in charge of a product line or even a small business. Those who wanted to move up, and who proved themselves in lower posts, could become heads of major business units by the age of forty, or even earlier.

As they moved up, their roles and responsibilities would change. Regular movement into new posts would keep their minds fresh. For as long as several decades, they would move into a new post every three or four years. This would ensure that they always had fresh perspectives, something to stimulate their minds, and new problems to solve. For it is not just the young that have new ideas, but also older people who are new to a situation.

Gradually, as they moved into positions of higher management, they would not be expected to have so many ideas themselves. Rather, they would be expected to facilitate the implementation of others' ideas. At the level of country manager, this would be their whole job. Only those who recognized that other people had ideas, and that their role was to help to implement these ideas, would be allowed to reach the level of country manager.

Young and old at AmPro. AmPro (short for American Consumer Products, a pseudonym) illustrates another, less healthy way of managing the relations between young and old. The head of a laboratory employing more than five hundred people recently shared with me his concerns about how AmPro was managed. In five years, the company had undergone three reengineering programs. Each time, the budget for his laboratory had been cut, while the workload stayed the same or was increased. More and more, he was forced to monitor and control what his people were doing on a day-to-day basis. Laboratory scientists' work was scheduled, virtually to the hour, to be sure that all the work that needed to be done got done. There was little room for flexibility in time allocation, since the job of maintaining and gradually expanding the product line took so much time.

So, were laboratory scientists able to spend any time working on their own projects? They would have been allowed 15 percent of their time to do their own projects at 3M, but they had no time at all at AmPro. Personal projects were ruthlessly hunted down and screened out, since top management dictated that laboratory time be spent working on 'corporate priority projects'. And who decided what these projects were? Did the laboratory scientists have any say? Of course not: it was corporate and business unit level boards who decided.

What kind of situation did this lead to in the laboratories? The laboratory manager described it in detail. He was involved in recruiting, and had long been impressed by the quality of the young people whom AmPro attracted. In interviews, they would talk about ideas they had for the company's products: how they could be improved, how product lines could be extended. Some had ideas for new products or new businesses. They were eager to join the company and get a chance to apply their ideas. The laboratory manager and other recruiters liked that attitude, and they hired people who wanted to contribute. The new hires, fresh with their PhDs and other degrees, and full of new ideas, eagerly joined the company. They were full of enthusiasm and eager to contribute.

But what happened next? The answer is depressingly obvious: reality hit quite hard. An entire generation of laboratory people were heavily constrained by the successive waves of reengineering. For five years, management told them, almost continuously, that they had to work more efficiently, that they had to focus on corporate priorities.

AmPro had never been particularly generous about giving time for personal projects, but any thought of pursuing such avenues went out the window in the 1990s. All those young people who had come into the company full of ideas and eager to contribute found themselves spending more than full-time working on 'corporate priorities'. 'Corporate priorities' should be translated here as 'old ideas', 'other people's ideas', or 'ideas that had nothing to do with the ideas the young people had brought with them when they joined the company'.

Finding themselves in a management straitjacket, unable to even spend 5 percent of their time working on their own ideas, an entire generation of laboratory scientists had become frustrated, cynical and depressed. The ideas that they had brought with them when they joined AmPro were still sitting on the table, unexplored. They had joined AmPro thinking that they would be able to contribute ideas, to create new products, in addition to working on old 'corporate priorities', but this had not happened. As the months went by, they became more and more discouraged by and disengaged from their work.

The laboratory manager, who had watched this happen, did not know what to do. He had not expected this kind of reaction when he implemented corporate reengineering programs, but he understood it. He knew the people well enough to know that they were good people, and had become disillusioned for good reason. The question was what to do next. Corporate management still expected him to keep costs down while completing a large number of corporate-inspired projects. He felt he had no flexibility left to loosen the straitjacket that was suffocating his people's creativity.

Ironically, I learned from a colleague a few weeks later that the top management of AmPro felt that the company did not have any inspiring directions for the future. They had set ambitious goals for financial growth, but were not coming up with any ideas on how to achieve them. They were worried that the company had gone stale as it was not producing the ideas that it needed to grow. Management invited in more than a dozen teams of consultants to see whether they had anything useful to say, but rejected all of their advice. What management did not realize, or were not willing to face, was the fact that they had killed their own company's idea generation engine by reengineering it out of existence.

AmPro is large and strong enough that it will survive for a few decades even if it never launches another new product line. This management team, or another one, may possibly find a way of reversing the damage done to the laboratories. But in the meantime, the company has gone stale, as its own senior managers privately admit. How AmPro's management might turn the company around and restart its idea generation engine will be discussed briefly in a later section of this chapter.

Why experience and education limit idea generation

Earlier in this chapter, I noted that young children were very good at finding original ways of interpreting data, and original solutions to problems. It is useful at this point to return to that story and to ask the question, 'Why does children's creativity decline?', or, more precisely, 'Why do children become less able to generate original interpretations of data or original ways of looking at problems as they grow up?'

Researchers who look at children's creativity believe that it declines as they go to school (Ackoff, 1978). What do children discover at school that reduces their creativity? They in fact find two things at school, two things that are very interesting to our argument.

First, children find that there are right answers, and in most cases only one right answer, to virtually every question asked in school. And it is the teacher who knows the answer, rather than them. Instead of looking for multiple explanations for a phenomenon, or multiple solutions to a problem (both keys to creativity), they will immediately try to home in on the single 'right answer'.

The second thing that they will realize is that there are a large number of mechanisms for keeping order and focusing their attention on the officially approved ways of interpreting things. They will learn that it is not safe to propose a solution that is not 'the right answer'. Other pupils will laugh at them; the teacher may criticize them. Potentially creative variation, the seed of new explanations and new understandings, is punished (Henry, 1963; Laing, 1967; Ackoff, 1978).

When I recount this argument to people, some people, especially school teachers, take issue with it at this stage. They say that schools *must* teach the right answers: there is a lot that adults know that kids do not and kids have a lot to learn.

Of course kids have a lot to learn; I agree with that. The point is that in the process of learning it, they lose the habits that allow them to take a fresh look at things. They lose the willingness to speculate about multiple possible explanations for events, the willingness to propose different and unusual solutions to problems. They lose, in short, their originality. Or at least many of them do. Some educators try to get around this problem by creating schools that focus more attention on developing the child's creative abilities, or on letting the child proceed at his or her own pace. But schools of this type, like Summerhill (Neill, 1960) or the Montessori schools, are still rare in most parts of the world.

To speak in very general terms, there are three different ways in which children can react to school. Some survive years of schooling with much of their creativity intact. For whatever reason, they maintain a willingness to look at things in their own way, not simply accepting given explanations and solutions, but looking at problems on their own and making their own judgements. If they come up with a judgement different from that of the teacher, they stick with their own opinion, rather than automatically deferring to the teacher. These children are willing to say, 'I'm right', even when every one else has a different opinion. I will call these the *Individualists*.

At the other extreme can be found children who give up on forming their own opinions, deciding that there is no point in risking confrontation by not conforming. They devote their energies to figuring out what the officially declared 'right answer' is and sticking to it. I will call this group the *Conformists*.

In the middle lies a group that includes many of us. Lots of children learn that there is a time and a place for bringing up ideas and a time and a place for conforming: different situations demand different behavior. These children might focus on learning the right answers in a math and history class, while being quite creative in a creative writing class, an art class, or extracurricular activities. This group I will call the *Adaptables*. This group is influenced by the environment. If people around them, particularly those in authority, listen to ideas and encourage them to share their ideas, they *will* share them. But if people around them ignore their ideas, or ask for conformity, they will clam up and conform.

Following this story line, children become less creative after they go to school for two reasons. First, a lot of them become Conformists and decide that it is just not worth sharing their ideas. Second, many Adaptables discover that there are a lot of places where new approaches are just not wanted, so they rarely share their ideas. They lose the habit of sharing them spontaneously. The only ones who remain creative are the Individualists and those Adaptables who find themselves in situations where those in authority encourage them to share ideas.

Joining an organization

Extending the story line still further, let us look at what happens when people join organizations. The situation is strikingly similar to what they find at school. First, there are 'right answers'. Most companies have a base of common knowledge and common wisdom that people who have been in the company for a long time know. This knowledge may be knowledge of technical concepts, of how markets behave, or of how to manage the company. The common wisdom may relate to ways of interpreting market phenomena, judgements about what technologies are likely to be key for the future, or understandings of how to motivate people.

These bits of knowledge and wisdom are accepted as 'right', by junior people as well as senior managers. Those who disagree with the common wisdom lose credibility and risk being ostracized from the company. So, new people learn the common wisdom and learn that it is best for their careers to endorse the common wisdom, even if they sense that it may be wrong. It may be incorrect because the market has changed, because a revolutionary new technology is just over the horizon, or because the company never understood in the first place why it had succeeded (Dierickx and Cool, 1989).

Admittedly, some companies are more open than others to new ideas. But all companies have some common wisdom that is difficult, if not impossible, to challenge. The more successful companies are those whose common wisdom is most in accord with reality.

Thus, when joining companies, as when going to school, people find that there are right answers. The second thing they find is that, as in school, there are many mechanisms for keeping order. There are training programs that advise them of the company's common knowledge and wisdom. There are supervisors who will monitor what they are doing and tell them when they are deviating from the company's common wisdom. The supervisors will 'gently or forcibly guide them' back to conformity with the company's said common wisdom.

How, then, do people react when they join the organization? We can speculate that there are three possible responses. A few will stick to what they think, whatever anyone in the organization tells them. One example is the IBM manager who, in 1979, was convinced that PCs would become a big market while everyone around him was saying that PCs were a fad and that mainframes would dominate for ever. Another example is the GM manager who, in 1972, said that his company should pay more attention to the small car market. We can call these the Individualists.

There is one form of Individualist who plays a key role in some innovations, that is, the *Lone Inventor*. Some people either do not know or ignore the common technical wisdom in their companies. They work in laboratories alone for long periods and invent things that others think are either impossible or unsalable. Sometimes they end up inventing things that are, obviously, possible, and also quite salable. A famous example of a Lone Inventor is Art Frye of 3M. Frye worked for many months to develop *Post-It*™ notes, even though many of the managers around him thought that they would never sell. Thus, Lone Inventors, like other Individualists, resist pressures for conformity and keep on looking at the world in their own way. They provide one valuable source of ideas for innovative companies.

But few people are Lone Inventors. How else might people react when they enter an organization? Obviously, many will conform. Conformism was synonymous with American management in the 1950s, or so we are told (Whyte, 1956). Indeed, the 1950s were not particularly rich in innovation. The Conformists are not a source of ideas for anyone, their whole goal being to figure out what the common wisdom is and to endorse it. Doing so is a way of playing it safe and establishing a secure (so they think) position within their organization.

The third way of reacting to the organization is to be adaptable. The Adaptables, like their counterparts in school, learn that there are times and places to propose new ideas, as well as times and places to conform. When they are in an environment that encourages people to propose ideas, they propose them. When they are in an environment that encourages conformity, they conform. Some companies are innovative in part because they have found ways of encouraging the Adaptables to generate and share their ideas.

So, if companies want to have lots of ideas, they are advised to do two things. The first is to hire more Lone Inventors. Since people do not come with such labels stamped on their foreheads, they would do well to look for the CVs of people who take individualistic paths through life, for people who show a creative or inventive flair. Both ConsumerCo and 3M, the two most innovative companies in my sample, told me that they look for these features in people they interview. No other company mentioned this as something they search for in new people.

The second thing companies should do if they want more ideas is to put normal people, the Adaptables, into situations where they are encouraged to generate more ideas. Once again, ConsumerCo and 3M have been doing this for years. Eastman Chemical has been moving its management practices in this direction for more than ten years, and other companies are also trying to do likewise. Part of this book will focus on the issue of how to manage people in a way that encourages them to generate and share ideas. I will discuss some of the principles behind management to generate ideas in this chapter. Unfortunately, a lack of space precludes a detailed discussion of all the management tools that impact idea generation.

New theories of how to encourage idea generation

At the beginning of this section on idea generation, I talked about an old theory of how to generate ideas. Under the old theory, ideas were generated by specialists in research laboratories. These laboratories were often separated, both geographically and organizationally, from the rest of the company. Management poured money into the research laboratories, and the more money that went in, the more ideas came out. Or so they thought.

The newer and more effective theory involves recognizing the fact that ideas often develop when people encounter either (a) new phenomena, (b) new problems, or (c) people who think differently from them (see, for example, Van de Ven, 1986; Dougherty, 1992). Thus, a manager who wants more ideas is well advised to do two things. He should regularly put his people in contact with new phenomena and new customer problems, and he should put them into regular contact with people who think differently. This might involve exposing them to phenomena and people outside the company. But it can also mean structuring communication and work practices within the company in such a way as to encourage more contact between people who think differently.

In more abstract terms, people have different skills and different knowledge bases. We often refer to skills and the knowledge that goes with them as competences. People often have competences that they share with others. All biologists have certain competences in common. But, when you look in detail at what people know, and know how to do, people are rarely alike. There are shades of difference even between people in the same specialty.

These shades of difference do not always matter. But the larger differences between people, and especially between different kinds of specialist, do. Contact with new information can give a person a new idea, as can learning a new skill or a new body of knowledge (in other words, a new competence). Discussions with others who have different bodies of knowledge can likewise lead to a new idea.

Following this logic, there are, from the manager's point of view, several things that can lead to new ideas. One is contact with new information. So why not encourage people to absorb and seek out new information freely? Another is learning a new skill or a new body of knowledge. So why not encourage learning, not just learning that is immediately relevant to the job, but even more broadly based learning? A third factor is discussions with others who do not have the same mix of competences. So why not encourage a large number of horizontal links? Why not encourage discussions between people from different functions, for example? Figure 4.5 illustrates the way in which the new theory conceives of idea generation.

Objections to implementing the new theories

The usual complaint about 'letting people talk and learn', which the complainers equate with 'letting people get distracted from their work', is that it will not work. 'People who work in business need to be disciplined', the complainers say. They need to get work done. If they spend all their time learning, 'like kids in school', they won't get their work done. Or so they say.

The problem is that companies that encourage their people to learn are still disciplined. They build much of the cross-functional communication and contact into the work, and much learning happens *while* people are getting work done. It is quite possible to encourage creativity *and* be disciplined. The problem in many companies is that management views creativity and experimentation as being in opposition to discipline and hard work. In fact, in the most innovative companies, they are quite compatible.

Several decades ago, most Western automobile companies thought that cost reduction and increasing quality were opposed. Cost reduction meant reducing quality; increasing quality meant higher cost. It was 'either/or': *either* cost reduction *or* higher quality. Then the Japanese began building cars in the West that were *both* less expen-

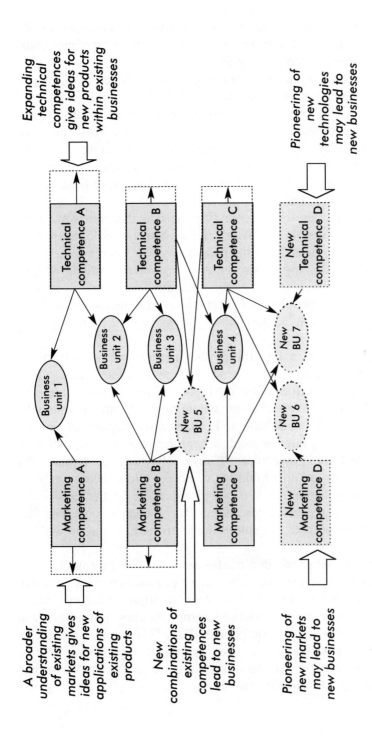

Figure 4.5   The new theory of idea generation: developing and mixing competences

sive *and* of higher quality than those which Western companies built. The Japanese showed that *either/or* was not correct. Companies could have *both* cost reduction *and* higher quality.

Something similar may be happening today in the realm of innovation. Many managers seem to think that they can have *either* hard work and a tight, efficient operation, *or* a lot of creativity and freedom to experiment. Doubtless, this is in part true. Cost reduction can go so far that there is simply no time left to think about any improvement or try anything new. But most companies are not that close to starvation. They can get more innovation out of their system at less cost than they believe.

The other objection to implementing the new theories is a variant of the Lone Inventor theory. Won't the inventive people, those who are going to have ideas, have their ideas anyway wherever they are? Does it really make any difference how you manage them, or how you manage the other people in the company? Of course it matters how you manage people. It matters how you manage the Lone Inventor types, and it matters how you manage the other people as well.

Here, in brief, are a few things that matter to Lone Inventors. They are attracted to certain kinds of environment, ones which provide them with information on topics related to their interests. They are attracted to environments where there are other people who are interested in the same things. Perhaps most importantly of all, they are attracted by environments where they can use much of their time to explore their own ideas. Conversely, they are repulsed by environments that are unstimulating or do not allow them to explore their ideas. If your company is not designed to fit the needs of a Lone Inventor, it will not attract them. If, by chance, one does join you, he will not be able to explore the ideas he has, and he will not stay long.

Other things matter to people who are not Lone Inventors, and a manager can do much to encourage them to innovate. New information and knowledge can stimulate them to think differently about things. Publicizing innovations and complementing innovators will encourage them to present and pursue ideas. This is only a sample of ways in which a company can encourage the average person (that is, someone who does not fit the Lone Inventor profile) to contribute ideas and to work to support innovations.

Implementing the new theories

Of course, it is not enough just to encourage Lone Inventors and other people to come up with good ideas. A company is well advised to support them in other ways if it wants to maximize idea generation. If you want quickly to diagnose how well a company is doing in this area, the following questions should be asked.

How often do the company's employees see new phenomena? How often are they exposed to new knowledge? How often can they pick up new skills? Are they encouraged to seek these things out? And do they have the right to seek them out?

How often do the company's people talk with other people who think differently from themselves? Is this kind of cross-boundary contact built into their jobs? That is, is work done by cross-functional teams, or by teams that include people from different product lines or regions? Are people encouraged to cross boundaries during their careers? That is, do they gain experience in different functions, product lines, and regions during the course of a career?

These preliminary questions will provide a good idea of how effectively the company is stimulating individuals and teams to generate new ideas. Other support is also necessary. During the discussion of the CR case, I showed that a broad range of management structures, systems, and practices could either inhibit or support innovation performance. Using the same general categories, I will show here that a company such as 3M uses a wide variety of different tools to encourage idea generation (Table 4.1).

Strategy and goals. 3M's strategy is to focus on areas where innovation can give a competitive advantage, and to be a leader in those areas. Everyone in the company knows this. So, innovation, and idea generation are known to be legitimate activities for everyone.

The company contains a range of technologies centered on the areas of materials and coatings. For anyone interested in these technologies, 3M is one of the world's best places to be. The necessary equipment, knowledge, and other resources are already available in the company. In addition, the company serves a wide variety of markets, and 3Mers are regularly made aware of new needs in all these markets. This rich mix of technologies and markets allows 3M's employees to combine things the company knows how to do in many new ways. This leads to a rich set of ideas and a diverse mix of new products.

Table 4.1   Tools that impact idea generation: 3M example

Type of tool	Tool	Impact
Strategy and goals	■ Focus on areas where innovation can give a competitive advantage ■ Range of linked technologies and markets in fertile areas ■ Business unit goals for innovation	■ High pay-off to innovation ■ High potential for new activities ■ Incentive for managers to innovation support
Structure and process	■ Horizontal interest group networks ■ Networks of laboratory managers and business unit managers ■ Processes for transferring technologies ■ Flexible organization structure	■ Technical progress and best practice spread quickly ■ Easy to find technical help when needed ■ Technology transfer possible when needed ■ Easy to form innovation teams, easy for teams to evolve into business units
Personnel management systems and culture	■ Financial, social, career and intrinsic rewards for innovators ■ Cultural norms support innovation	■ People know that they will be rewarded for innovating ■ Constant reminders of importance of innovation and need to support it
Project management systems	■ Many potential sources of funds ■ Many projects, much mentoring, coaching for project managers	■ Relatively easy to sell a new idea ■ Easy to learn project management techniques

As if this were not enough, the company also sets clear innovation goals for each business unit. Thirty percent of sales in each unit should come from products or processes introduced within the past four years. This encourages each manager to look for useful new ideas all the time.

Structure and process. 3M has numerous horizontal interest group networks. So if people want to find out what other people working on adhesives are doing, they need only to join the appropriate networks. There are also numerous networks among laboratory managers and business unit managers that help to communicate information about market needs and potential technical solutions. These stimulate idea generation by (a) keeping technologists informed of what the market needs, and (b) keeping market-facing people informed of what the company has to offer.

3M also has effective internal processes for transferring technologies and other best practices across the company. If a business unit in Asia needs a technology being developed in the United States, the company has methods of transferring the technology.

In addition, 3M has a very flexible organization structure. It is easy to form new innovation project teams, and it is easy for such teams to evolve into business units. People are also aware that it is easy to form new teams and business units. This doubtless encourages them to develop and share ideas, since there appear to be no downstream barriers to bringing their ideas to fruition.

Personnel management systems and culture. Innovators are rewarded at 3M. The rewards are not just financial. People can become heroes within 3M by contributing significantly to innovation. The personnel development and promotion system assures that people who are promoted to positions of responsibility have experience with innovation projects and are known to support innovation. In addition, all the cultural norms, the rules of behavior, in the system encourage people to support innovation.

Project management systems. Besides these company-wide features, 3M has a project funding system that provides many different potential sources of funds. A person with an idea has many alternatives if the closest source of funds says 'no'. This encourages a free flow of ideas, since even if the closest funding source refuses, there are many other places where one can ask.

In addition, 3M practices numerous methods of encouraging idea generation. The ideas, once funded, fit into 3M's well-developed project management system. The company has considerable experience in project management, experience that is imparted to new 3M people in several ways. People begin to learn effective project management techniques early in their careers as they participate in innovation projects. In addition, 3M senior managers will act as mentors to project managers, helping them to navigate their projects through difficult competitive environments, as well as the sometimes difficult internal environment.

Complementary theories of idea generation

Certain writers, notably Kim and Mauborgne, have developed some very interesting theories about idea generation in existing businesses that complement the theory discussed here. In a recent article, Kim and Mauborgne (1997a) recommend a method of generating ideas within an existing business that involves redesigning a product or service. They suggest that companies can often generate considerable value by identifying dimensions of the product where they can add considerable additional value to the customer, while, at the same time, identifying areas where they are offering more than the customer really wants or needs. By offering more in areas where the customer wants more, and by offering less in areas where the customer does not care, they can often construct a more valuable but less costly product for the customer. Kim and Mauborgne cite Formula One hotels in Europe and Cineplex Cinemas in Belgium as examples of products that have gained high market shares using this method.

In a second article, Kim and Mauborgne (1997b) discuss the impact of the level of fairness of a company's policies on the willingness of people within the company to share ideas. This article points to what could be a very rich vein of insight into the development of trust and willingness to share ideas within a company. Unfortunately, this discussion is beyond the scope of this book and will have to await a later one.

Project funding systems

When a person has an idea, she may be able to work on it alone for some time. But, if the idea is significant, it will at some point be necessary to ask for help. At this juncture, the company's resource allocation system comes into play. Where can the person go to for help? What does she have to do to get help? How likely is it that she will get help? The answers to these questions are all heavily influenced by the dimensions of the company's funding system.

In the first part of this section, I will discuss the dimensions of a funding system in detail. Afterwards, I will consider the outcomes of the funding system and how they are affected by the system's design. Finally, I will briefly outline the issue of managing the risk and evaluating the outcome of a portfolio of innovation projects.

Dimensions of a funding system

At its core, a funding system consists of people with ideas, people with resources, and communications links between them. There are several key dimensions of this constellation (Table 4.2).

Table 4.2   Dimensions of a funding system

Dimension	Impact
■ Distance between people with ideas and people with resources	■ Affects speed of communication, distortion of communication, and level of knowledge of those making decisions
■ Time to make decisions and obtain funding	■ Affects overall speed of innovation process and response time
■ Distortion of information communicated between people with ideas and people with resources	■ Affects appropriateness (correctness) of decisions taken
■ Level of knowledge of those making decisions	■ Affects appropriateness of decisions taken
■ Number of possible funding sources available	■ Likelihood of diversification; likelihood of an unusual idea getting funding
■ Type and quantity of information demanded by funding sources	■ Affects appropriateness of decisions taken; may force teams to think about things they would not otherwise consider; can also slow decision
■ Incentives of those making decisions	■ Affects their willingness to support innovation

One key dimension is the *distance between people with ideas and people with funds*. By 'distance', I mean the number of intervening people or intervening hierarchical layers between the person with the idea and the funding source. Can the person with the idea obtain resources from people he knows, perhaps from the people he works with every day? Or must he go to some other unit in the company to obtain resources? Is only one level of approval required? Alternatively, must he get approval first from a business unit board, then a division board, and finally a corporate board? Can he present the idea to the funding source himself, or does he have to through intermediaries who will do the presenting for him? For example if a corporate board has to approve a project, it will probably not be the laboratory scientist who presents the idea to them.

Distance has three key effects. First, long chains of communication or approval mean that decisions will be slow to be taken. If these chains are short, decisions may be made much more quickly (*speed of decision making*). Second, if the contents of a innovation project proposal must be communicated through a number of people, there is likely to be some *distortion of the information presented*. This will lead to a lower decision quality. Third, if the funding source is distant from the source of the idea, the people making the funding decision are likely to have little knowledge of the technology, the market, and other key issues involved. This also will lead to a decision of lower quality. On the other hand, if the funding source is close to the source of the idea, those making the decision are likely to be more knowledgeable and the decision quality is likely to be higher (*knowledge of decision makers*).

In addition to distance, the system has other dimensions, one being the *number of funding sources available*. One person or position may have a monopoly of innovation project funding, as business unit heads did in Industrial Chemicals in the 1980s. Or the idea generator may have many potential sources of funding, both in his own business unit and elsewhere, such as is the case at 3M.

Another dimension is the *type and quantity of information demanded* by funding sources before they give resources to a project. This can range from minimal information about the goals of the project to detailed information on the technology involved, key marketing issues, and other relevant aspects. In addition, there may be formal requirements for what information will be given. Alternatively the system may be informal, the funding source asking for whatever it wants. In this latter case, some project teams may be required to provide extensive and detailed information, while others are not required to provide anything more than a minimal amount of information.

Finally, the *incentives facing those who make funding decisions* are key. How those who control resources are rewarded, and what they see as the strategy and goals of the company, will have a great influence on how many resources they dedicate to innovation and what they decide to fund.

I will discuss each of these issues in more detail here, illustrating these key dimensions and how they work by giving examples. In a later section, I will show how these dimensions impact the outcomes of the funding system as a whole.

Distance between people with ideas and people with resources. Once people have an idea, they may be able to work on it for some time alone. They may already have resources that they can allocate to any project they wish. In this case, there is no distance between the person with the idea and the person with the funds, as they are the same person.

This is often the case at 3M. In effect, 3M pre-allocates time and resources to its technical people so that they can follow up immediately on any ideas they have. It does this through its 15 percent rule, and through a liberal policy on the use of company resources, such as machinery and supplies. If employees have an idea and want to pursue it, they are allowed to spend 15 percent of their time on it without question. They are also allowed to use any spare machinery and materials that are available within their laboratory. Many ideas, including the famous *Post-It*™ note, have benefited from this policy.

In some companies, however, there is no 15 percent rule. Working without authorization on a personal project would still be a serious breach of policy in most MGE divisions, and there is no time left over for such work at EurAuto. As a result, good ideas wait until they can get attention and funding from senior managers. The CR idea had to wait for four years before it found stable funding.

The first outcome of distance: the time needed to make decisions and obtain funding. A comparison of the 3M and MGE cases points to one of the key issues in funding: how long it takes to make funding decisions. When they look at funding decisions, most companies focus first on making sure that the decision is right. They do not want to spend money on useless projects, but they sometimes also worry about spending too little on promising projects. The issue of how long it takes to get funding more rarely gets attention, but it can have an important influence on the ultimate success of the project. Time lost at the funding stage is lost forever; it can not be regained. And, as the famous saying goes, time is money. Pharmaceutical companies estimate that one day of delay in a pharmaceutical development project means $1 million in lost revenues.

Both the time needed to obtain funding and the quality of funding decisions are affected by the number of 'intermediaries' who have to be involved in the funding decision. By 'intermediaries,' I mean people who have to transmit information between the idea generator and the funding source, or people who make a preliminary screening decision before the proposition is presented to the funding source.

An example will illustrate this (Figure 4.6). In the late 1960s, Bower documented how funding processes worked in several divisions of a large American chemical company (Bower, 1970). Most ideas came from functional specialists, some below the level of department head. Their ideas for new products, processes, and plants had to be approved by the department head (in some cases), the business unit head, the group funding board, and finally the corporate funding board before they could be worked on. Even quite small projects (a few tens of thousands of dollars) had to be approved at the corporate level.

In this cumbersome process, there were as many as three intermediaries between the source of the idea and the final funding authority. Waiting for approval from these three intermediaries, and from the final funding source, took months. Proposals were edited on the way up in order to be more 'palatable' to those making the final decision, and this editing could involve some distortion of the idea.

In practice, the corporate board acted largely as a rubber stamp. The last people to make any serious study of the proposition were usually members of the group-level board. But no one could officially work on the idea until corporate management had approved.

Compared to this cumbersome process, the process that Industrial Chemicals ran in 1985 looks streamlined. At Industrial Chemicals, business unit heads could approve innovation projects on their own account. Projects could thus, at least, be approved quickly. Nonetheless, many companies possessed such unwieldly processes until the 1980s and 90s, when the need for speed forced many companies to streamline their funding processes.

Companies with cumbersome funding processes do survive in some areas. I am aware of one company that requires at least seven different committees to approve any investment over $200,000. In some special cases, the approval of nine different committees being required. Also, while $200,000 is a relatively large investment for this company, it is

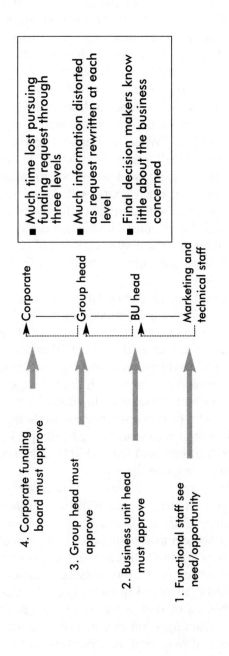

Figure 4.6 Distance between ideas and funding sources: example from Bower (1970)

not large relative to the company's revenues (being less than 1/20th of 1 percent of its annual revenue), and investments of this size regularly occur. At best, the process of getting all the necessary approvals takes five months. This is a serious handicap in a business where competitors make such investment decisions in, at most, two weeks.

The second outcome of distance: the distortion of information and decision quality. The time needed to get a proposal through seven (or even three) levels of approval is obvious, but less obvious is the distortion of information that occurs. When a proposal has to be approved by people at least three levels away from where it originated, it is almost certain that the proposal will be altered to make it more palatable to those 'on top' who must approve it. In addition, since the originators of the project will almost certainly not be presenting it themselves, it may be people who do not know the project who will do so. What they present may resemble the project, but it is unlikely that they will capture the key issues as well as those more closely involved.

In addition, there may be simple misunderstandings that occur as information about the project is passed through multiple people. Many people have played the children's game where a number of children all line up in a row and pass a message from the child at one end to the child at the other. Each child whispers the message to the one next to him, and all are greatly amused by how much the message has changed by the time it reaches the end of the row. Hopefully, information will not be distorted as much by grown-ups who are discussing an innovation project. But nonetheless, if information is passed up a hierarchy along a chain of three or four people, there is likely to be some misrepresentation of the information along the way.

The third outcome of distance: the level of knowledge of those allocating funds and decision quality. Another aspect of distance from the idea is the level of knowledge of those allocating funds. Let us consider, for example, a diversified company. Suppose, in a particular case, that a funding decision is being made three levels above that at which the idea originated. Will those making the decision know much about the technology or the market involved in the project? Unlikely, at best. The project may deal with a market or a technology that they once worked in, ten or fifteen years ago, but that market/technology will have changed. Alternatively, it may deal with markets and technologies with which the funding board members have never dealt. If they are unfamiliar with the market and technology, their decision quality will suffer. On the other hand, if they are quite close to them, the quality of the decision is likely to be higher.

In such a situation, the 'real decision' is often made one or two levels below the final authority, but the extra step(s) in decision making still lose time. In addition, any alteration in the decision made lower down is likely to diminish the quality of the decision.

The distance dilemma: speed and decision quality versus fiscal responsibility. If funding decisions are made closer to where ideas originate, the chances are that those making decisions will know more about the technologies and markets involved. In addition, there will be less distortion of information, and the decision will be finalized more quickly. This is part of the genius of the 3M system. People can allocate their own time to projects, or they can seek funds and support from the teams or business units with whom they work every day. Only if these immediate sources of support fail do they need to go further for funds.

Of course, the 3M system does not work for all companies. 3M works in an area where most ideas can be pursued inexpensively, the cost of most projects being small enough that they do not represent a significant corporate commitment. The financial health of the company is therefore not at risk.

The situation in a pharmaceutical company is quite different. The price tag for clinical trials of one molecule can reach several hundreds of millions of dollars. This is a significant corporate commitment, and the financial health of the company is at risk. Thus, such decisions cannot be made in the laboratories: they have to be made by high-level corporate officers. Most pharmaceutical companies, however, have recognized that it is still necessary to make quick decisions, to transmit information without distortion, and to assure that those making the decisions are knowledgeable about the products and markets on which they are deciding.

As a result, funding decisions in pharmaceutical companies are made by high-level boards, but there are few or no intervening levels of review. The connection between project teams and the funding board is quite direct, and every effort is made to keep the board in close touch with the relevant products and markets. Pharmaceutical companies get into trouble only when there are too many projects for one board to understand them all. Some pharmaceutical companies are finding their way around this problem (Sharpe and Keelin, 1998); this will be discussed in the next section.

Number of possible funding sources available. Three other aspects of the funding problem are worth mentioning. One is the importance of the number of funding sources available to the person who has generated an idea. This can vary from *none* in companies where certain departments are not viewed as potential sources of ideas, and are thus starved of innovation funds, to *many* in companies such as 3M, where anyone can go anywhere in his or her search for funds.

If no resources for innovation are available in a disfavored department, this will effectively quash innovation in this department (Leonard-Barton, 1992). It is, however, probably rare for a whole department to be completely starved of innovation funds. More commonly, there will only be one source of funds that is considered legitimate. This may be a department head or a business unit head to whom the department reports.

The effect of having only one source of funds is either positive or negative, depending on the company's strategy and situation. If the company is practicing a focus strategy, having only one source of funds will help to maintain this focus. As long as the funding board understands the technologies and markets involved, the system will work. If a large number of projects are involved, or if the technologies involved are more than one person, or one board, can learn, the task will be difficult. Some companies, such as SmithKline Beecham, have developed the means of managing such situations. Sharpe and Keelin (1998) told its story in a recent *Harvard Business Review* article.

SmithKline Beecham faced the problem of how to select among dozens of potential pharmaceutical projects. In the proposals, all the projects looked promising. Since the company was becoming very large and the number of projects was increasing, the funding board could not master all of the technical and market details of each project. As a result, it had to devise a number of ingenious methods of getting the project teams to reveal more information about their projects (Sharpe and Keelin, 1998).

The most ingenious, and perhaps most useful, method was to have them develop three scenarios in addition to their basic request for funds. To do this, the project teams had to answer three questions: What could they do with a significantly larger budget?, What could they do with a significantly smaller budget?, And how would they salvage what they had learned if the project were closed down? Their answers to these questions revealed much about the options available in pursuing the project, giving the funding board a much better base on which to make decisions than the simple take-it-or-leave-it propositions of the past (Sharpe and Keelin, 1998).

Another useful method for managing complex project selection problems is to compare the projects to seek synergies; pharmaceutical and chemical companies sometimes do this. They find that it simplifies the problem of selecting among projects. By identifying common themes, the company can eliminate duplication and assure that sufficient resources are devoted to problems that are key to several projects.

If a company is trying to maintain a focus, having several funding sources can be a problem because it may lead to a lack of direction. If two individuals or groups handle funding, they may not have the same vision of the company's future; they may simultaneously try to lead the company in two different directions. If senior management is not sure which direction is best, and has deliberately set up the two funding boards so that both paths will be explored, having two funding committees makes sense. But if the duplication is an accident of history, and senior management would really rather pursue only one path, possessing two funding boards is a waste of money and leads to an undesirable lack of focus.

If, on the other hand, the company wants to diversify, having multiple sources of funding will be very useful. As each funding source will develop its own ideas of how the company could expand. Each will very likely fund different types of project. This will allow the company to explore a number of possible avenues of expansion (Figure 4.7).

If a company wanting to diversify has only one source of funding for innovation projects, it may find it difficult to diversify effectively. With only one funding source, it will be much more likely that there will be only one vision of the company's future – the one held by the funding source. This will limit experimentation to areas consistent with that one vision. As a result, the company might miss a number of promising areas not covered by the 'official' vision.

Type and quantity of information demanded. Another dimension of funding systems involves the type of documentation required for a funding request. This dimension controls the amount and type of information that will be exchanged between the person(s) proposing the project and the person(s) deciding whether the project will be funded.

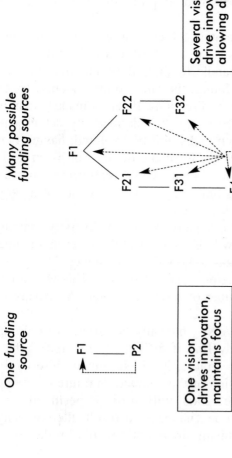

One funding
source

*One vision
drives innovation,
maintains focus*

Many possible
funding sources

*Several visions can
drive innovation,
allowing diversification*

Key:

F# = Funding source X
P# = Project idea X

Figure 4.7 The funding system and diversification

Normally, exchanging more information is better, assuming that the exchange does not unduly slow the decision-making process. Exchanging a greater amount of information normally allows a better decision to be made, since more potential problem areas will be explored. Potential problems of market acceptance, technological feasibility, the problem of finding suppliers, and so on should all be considered in judging a funding application. In addition, if the project team is forced to consider a broad range of issues and potential problems in its funding request, this ensures that the issues will be thought through. If the team is never required to do so, this thinking may never occur.

There are exceptional cases where forcing teams to think through marketing, technology, and other issues is not necessary. When an existing product development team at 3M begins work on a new project, they may not be required to produce any particular documentation.

In cases where the new project lies in an area on which the team has already been working (for example, a variation of an existing product), management may not see any need for documentation or a detailed review of the decision. They may have confidence that the team already knows the technology and the market in question, and that the team will make appropriate judgements about what to invest in. Adding a further burden of documentation would not increase the team's knowledge of the area, but only slow the team down.

Such a documentation-free system has obvious limits. Industrial Chemicals did not require any particular types of information in funding requests in the 1980s. Business unit heads were responsible for approving projects, and they could ask for any kind of information they wished, but they were not required to collect any information at all. This system was quick and simple, like that at 3M, but it did not work in all cases. Two problems occurred at Industrial Chemicals that would not have occurred at 3M.

The first problem was that the business unit head did not necessarily have the kind of knowledge needed to effectively evaluate all the projects with which he was presented. When George Marsh asked his business unit head to fund CR, the business unit head knew nothing about water treatment, which made it more difficult for him to evaluate the proposal. A team at 3M might run into a similar situation, in which case it would have referred the proposal to someone who did know the area. In most cases, however, department-level teams received propositions that they fully understood.

Second, the informal system at Industrial Chemicals allowed some project teams to make proposals without thinking through key issues. George Marsh received budgets for several years of work without ever carrying out a serious study of the product's market potential. This would probably not have happened at 3M, since teams there included marketing (and other) professionals trained to consider such issues.

The incentives for those making the decisions. The last key dimension I will discuss is the incentives facing those making funding decisions. Are they encouraged to support innovation or not? This will be affected by a number of aspects of the company's management systems.

Obviously, the explicit incentives, such as compensation and promotions, have an impact. If those supporting innovation receive large bonuses and promotions, this is a strong signal that managers should support innovation. However, if noninnovators, those who focus on the short term and invest nothing in the long term, are promoted, a strong signal is emitted that one should not invest in innovation.

More subtle aspects of the culture affect this too. Who are the company's heroes? Are they people who have innovated? Or are there other, better routes to hero status? What kinds of story do managers tell? Are there stories about heroic efforts to innovate? Are there stories that show the value of innovation? Or are there stories about how people hunkered down, cut costs and put short-term profits ahead of everything else? If the company's heroes are innovators and the stories that managers tell focus on the importance of innovation, there is a high chance that the people in a position to fund projects will support innovation.

Finally, the company's strategy and goals can have an important impact on managers' behavior. Does the strategy give any importance to innovation? If so, are people aware that innovation is key to the strategy? Are there explicit goals in relation to developing innovations? If the strategy and goals place an emphasis on innovation, it is much more likely that the people in a position to provide funds will support innovative projects.

Outcomes of a funding system

A number of outcomes are driven by the structure of the funding system (Table 4.3). Some of them, such as the *time needed to make decisions* and the *accuracy of decisons* will be familiar from the last

Table 4.3   Outcomes of a funding system

Outcome	Impacted by	Importance
Time needed to make funding decisions	■ Distance between idea source and funding source (for example, number of levels of decision needed) ■ Funding system procedures (for example, frequency of meetings)	■ Affects overall speed of innovation system
Accuracy/appropriateness of funding decisions	■ Amount and quality of information about project available to decision makers ■ Amount of knowledge decision makers have about technologies and markets involved	■ Inappropriate decisions may result in missed opportunities or wasted money
Number of projects funded	■ Funds available ■ Incentives of decision makers ■ Average project budget	■ Affects number of new products company will have downstream ■ But funding too many projects may slow them all
Breadth of projects funded: product markets	■ Company strategy ■ Number of different, independent funding sources	■ Affects range of potential diversification and expansion
Breadth of projects funded: competences	■ Company strategy ■ Number of different, independent funding sources ■ Existence of competence management program	■ Affects company's competitive position in the long run ■ Affects ability to develop new activities
Risk profile	■ Company strategy ■ Incentives of decision makers	■ Affects risk/payoff profile of project portfolio
Project outcomes	■ All of the above	■ Drive company's future competitive position and learning

section. Also familiar from the discussion of the number of funding sources will be the *number of projects* funded and the *breadth or variation of projects funded*. Breadth, in turn, has two key subdimensions, the *product markets worked on* and the *competences worked on*. More global outcomes include the *overall risk profile* and the *outcomes of the projects themselves*.

Time needed to make a funding decision. The time needed for funding decisions is an important competitive variable: the longer it takes to make decisions, the longer the time to market will be. The time required is most importantly affected by the number of levels of decision needed, and the distance between the source of the idea and the funding source. Simple procedural issues in decision making (for example, how often a funding committee meets) are not discussed here, but they too can have a significant impact on the time to make a decision.

Accuracy of decision making. Companies can spend too much or too little on a project. While they more often worry about spending too much, spending too little can be just as serious a mistake. By spending too little, they may sacrifice the chance to build an important competitive advantage for the company. Spending too much is at worst, only a loss of money; spending too little can mean the loss of a competitive position in a new market. Pharmaceutical companies quantify the loss by looking at the average revenue of a typical pharmaceutical product. For them, the loss equals 'one million dollars per day', each day of delay resulting in one million dollars of lost revenue. As a result, pharmaceutical companies are willing to spend more to speed up projects.

The accuracy of decisions is driven by two things, the first being the amount and quality of information about the project available to decision makers. This is determined by how distant they are from the project, and by the type and amount of information demanded as part of a funding request. The second aspect that drives the accuracy of any decision is the amount of knowledge that the decision makers possess concerning the technologies and markets involved in the project. If they are more knowledgeable about them, they will make better decisions.

The number of projects funded. All things being equal, the greater the number of projects funded, the more new products the company will have a few years down the road. The number of projects funded is influenced by the money available, the average project budget, and the incentives facing those who make funding decisions. If the latter have any discretion in the amount of resources they apply to innovation, their incentives may have a large impact on the amount of resources applied.

Breadth of projects funded. Companies that want to diversify are well advised to fund a broader mix of projects than companies focusing on just one or two markets. The breadth of the project mix is influenced by the number of different and independent funding sources available. In general, the more funding sources there are, the broader the project mix. The breadth of projects funded is also affected by the company's strategy. Companies may deliberately choose to develop new product markets and competences – or they may choose not to.

Breadth: product markets. One aspect of the breadth of a project mix is the range of product-market positions covered. Is the company developing new items in each of its current product markets? Or has it stopped development in some existing areas, potentially abandoning those territories to more aggressive competitors? Is it expanding into new product-market areas? Are the new areas judged by management to be desirable areas for future expansion? Are there enough new thrusts? Or are there more than the company can really manage?

The breadth of the product-market mix is affected by the company's strategy and goals, as well as by the location of funding sources. If some business units dedicate funds to innovation while others do not, the project mix will obviously favor the product markets served by the more generous business units.

Breadth: competences. The other aspect of breadth is, in effect, the mirror image of product markets: it is the range of competences being developed through innovation project funding. Product markets are the external side of the projects, competences the internal side. Process development projects work on process competences. Product development projects may work both on product and process competences. In addition, they may develop the company's understanding of specific markets (market competences).

As in the case of product markets, the company may want to look at the ensemble of its innovation projects to determine what competences are being worked on. Are key competences being advanced, or are they left to stagnate? Is enough being invested in the key competences? Are any desirable new competences being developed? If not, should some be developed? A good competence management program will ensure that these questions are answered.

Once again, the breadth in terms of competences is partly the result of the company's strategy and goals and partly the result of the location of funding sources. If one technical area receives the lion's share of innovation funding, the competences in that area will be well supported, while other competences will risk being short-changed.

Risk profile. Companies usually want a mix of low-risk and high-risk projects. The low-risk projects can be counted on to advance the company's technologies and improve its product mix. High-risk projects should also be high-payoff projects, offering the potential for a significant improvement in process technology and/or significant new market positions. A company wanting to expand will be well advised to take bets on a number of high-risk, high-payoff projects, while simultaneously advancing its existing positions through more predictable, lower-risk projects.

Project risk is importantly affected by company strategy and by the incentives of those who make funding decisions. If the incentives discourage risk taking, the company will very likely end up with few high-risk projects in its project mix. The issue of managing risk will be discussed in more detail in a later section.

Outcomes of the projects. Project outcomes are the indirect results of the funding system. Obvious outcomes include new products, new product features, new revenues, and process improvements resulting in time or cost reduction. Less obvious outcomes include learning about technologies and markets, and spin-off products or process improvements.

Spin-offs can be defined as new products or process improvements developed as a result of work carried out on a project, but not being the original target of the project. Such spin-offs can be quite valuable. Projects that officially have failed, since they did not reach their original goals, may still make very important contributions to company learning, thus paving the way for new products or processes developed by later projects (Leonard-Barton, 1995, Chapter 5).

Both project risk profiles and project outcomes are important and complex issues that are best discussed in the context of a company's whole portfolio of projects. This will be attempted in the next section.

Managing risk and evaluating outcomes

Projects have both obvious and less obvious outcomes. The obvious outcomes include new products, improved products, new revenues, and cost and time reductions. These are the outcomes most often evaluated by management when they ask whether a particular project has been a success.

Less obvious outcomes include learning and spin-offs. A project team may learn much about a set of technologies and markets, even though it does not reach its original goal of producing a viable new product. While a traditional evaluation may brand the project a failure, this is a mistake. The learning may turn out to be valuable elsewhere (Leonard-Barton, 1995, Chapter 5). In particular, it may allow another project to make a breakthrough in the area addressed by the first project. The learning may support a new, more successful thrust in the area, or result in spin-off products in an entirely different area.

These less obvious results should be taken into account when evaluating the success of a project. In addition to asking what revenues were won and what costs were reduced, the evaluation team should ask the following questions. What was learned? What new thrust in this area will the project's results support? What kinds of spin-off product and process may come out of this? These questions will point to valuable results that might be overlooked by a more traditional evaluation system.

The issues of learning and spin-offs should also be considered in evaluating risk. Will high-risk projects produce useful learning even if they do not meet their goals? If they will, the risk is not as high as the simple financial figures and probabilities indicate. Is there a potential for spin-offs, or for synergies with other projects? If there is, the risk in relation to immediate payoff may again be high. However, the potential for unforeseen payoffs downstream is also high. These unplanned benefits should be thought about as thoroughly as possible when funding decisions are made. Projects rich in learning and in spin-off possibilities should receive funds before projects with fewer potential beneficial side effects.

Development systems

What development systems have in common

All development systems have some things in common. At their core, they are charged with the job of *taking ideas that have been funded and bringing them to fruition.* The ideas may be good, but they are worth little to the company until they turn into new products, improved products, process improvements, and so on. The commonality, however, goes further. All companies appear to have common subgoals: to develop products that *fit customer need*, developing them *quickly*, and at *reasonable cost*.

The work done in a development system is normally organized as a set of *projects*. In most companies today, each project will have a designated project leader and a designated project team. In some cases, the same people, or the same team, may handle several projects. Innovative companies in industries where technology is moving quickly will often set up permanent innovation teams. These teams may handle long series of product improvement and new product projects in one area or in a set of closely related areas. Such permanent teams may be linked to operating units. It may in some cases be hard to draw the line between the operating part of a business unit and the innovation team, since members of the innovation team may also have operating roles.

Project organization has not always been the rule in development systems. Before the 1980s, many companies simply let the R&D department work on innovations in whatever manner it pleased. Projects were often passed from one laboratory function to the next, and then to operating functions, without any project structure being put into place. This type of organization led to very slow execution of innovations, so it has largely been replaced by project organization.

Each project can be seen as a *set of tasks* that need to be performed for the idea behind the project to come to fruition. The tasks that need to be accomplished in any particular project are determined by the nature of the product envisioned, the nature of the process needed to produce it, the newness of the product and process, the technologies behind them, and the nature of the market, including the regulatory environment.

Projects vary in size and complexity. Simple product adaptation projects may last as little as a few days, in some cases even a few hours. Such simple projects may involve only a few tasks. The first tasks may involve a discussion of how to solve the adaptation problem technically. Then preliminary batches will be produced and tested. If the first attempt does not work, further formulations and tests will be needed, and tests on customer sites may follow. Half a dozen tasks may be all that is needed to finish the project.

At the other extreme, the most difficult new product development projects may last for several decades. Thousands of separate tasks may be involved as a company repeatedly formulates and tests its answers to a complex set of technical problems. Market tests may not take place until years of internal testing have occurred. Given that development systems have much in common, it is not surprising that there are common approaches to improving their performance. I will discuss these common methods in the later sections on 'Speed in Development, 'Reducing Cost of Development', and 'Improving Fit with Customer Need'. (See Table 4.4 for a summary of what development systems have in common.)

Table 4.4 What development systems have in common

Area	Common feature	Importance
Goals	■ Common goal: take ideas that have been funded and bring them to fruition ■ Common subgoals – Fit customer need (present or anticipated) – Speed – Cost	■ At a general level, all companies have a similar overall goal and similar subgoals
Organization	■ Project organization	■ Similar organizational concerns, and similar organization structures across many companies
Structure of work	■ All projects can be subdivided into sets of tasks, work packages, work units, and so on	■ Certain methods of structuring tasks are useful across a wide range of projects and industries

How development systems vary: overall characteristics

Size and length of projects. Development systems vary in line with the types of project they are designed to execute. Companies manufacturing simple but rapidly changing products have a large number of short projects. Such systems are likely to have permanent innovation teams that handle large numbers of these small projects. Companies manufacturing complex assembled products are likely to have large teams dedicated to only one project. These teams may be organized much as business units are organized, each function being represented on the team. (See Table 4.5 for a summary of how development systems vary.)

Table 4.5 How development systems vary

Area	Varying feature	Importance
Size and length of projects	■ Number of tasks to be performed; number of people involved in a project	■ Long, complex projects are more difficult to manage than shorter, simpler projects
Project similarity	■ A company's projects may be similar to one another, or may vary considerably	■ If projects are similar, it is easier to rationalize innovation activity
Project tasks foreseeable or not	■ In some projects, it is possible to foresee all the tasks that will need to be done at the beginning; in other projects, there is much more uncertainty	■ Planning and rationalization is much easier when tasks can be foreseen; management of uncertainty is much more important when they cannot
Centralized versus decentralized control	■ Projects may be controlled by one R&D hierarchy, or by a number of different business units and other groups	■ If many projects are similar, centralized control allows rationalization and more consistent management; if projects are all different, dispersed control allows adaptation to their needs

Project similarity. Diversified companies may run projects that vary enormously from one to another. These projects may be dispersed widely throughout the organization. More focused companies may have projects that are much more similar from one to the next; their projects may all be located within the same R&D department. In diversified companies, the tasks to be performed may be very different from one project to the next, so each project team may have to follow a unique path in finding a way to bring its project to fruition.

By contrast, in focused companies, the tasks to be performed from one project to the next may be very similar. If they are similar, the development system may include people who are specialized in performing these repeated tasks efficiently.

Task similarity from one project to the next may be driven by several factors. One is the *regulatory environment*. If all products must pass through the same regulatory hurdles, each development project will include the same battery of regulatory tests. The second factor is *market requirements*. If customer profiles are consistent across several product areas, the same battery of market tests may be performed. Third, if *product technology* or *product architecture* is similar from one generation to the next, many of the same steps may have to be followed during the course of technical development. If none of these factors applies, tasks may vary considerably from one project to the next.

Project tasks being foreseeable or otherwise. When a project is being carried out in a relatively stable industry, and the technology used by the project is stable, it may be possible to foresee all the tasks that will need to be performed to get the new product out of the door. The necessary technical tests, market tests, and regulatory tests may all be foreseeable before the project starts, which allows the project to be planned well in advance.

By contrast, when a project exists in an unstable or new industry, or when it uses an unstable technology, it may be impossible to foresee what tasks will have to be undertaken before launching the product. Here, planning beyond a short horizon (perhaps three to six months) may be irrelevant. The real test of the project team's skill will lie in how well they react to the unexpected events that occur during the course of the project.

Centralized versus decentralized control of projects. All projects may be controlled in a centralized fashion by a single R&D hierarchy, or they may be attached to different laboratories and business units distributed throughout the organization. In this case, there may be no central control of innovation projects and the system can be described as decentralized.

As noted above, if all the projects have many tasks in common, it is likely that they will all be housed within the same R&D organization. Since the projects are similar, they can be resourced from the same departments and supervised by the same R&D management team. This is the logic of the centralized development system.

By contrast, if the projects are all quite different, it is probable that they will be attached to different units, for example the unit within which they originated. Alternatively, they may be attached to whichever unit is best equipped to help them get their tasks finished. For instance, if a project needs access to technical or marketing competences housed in a business unit, it may be attached to that business unit. In addition, the fact that the projects are different will make it difficult for a single management team to supervise all of them (Prahalad and Bettis, 1986) as no one management team will have all the necessary knowledge and perspectives. As a result, the projects will be distributed to different units, each project being supervised by a management team that understands the issues involved. This is the underlying logic of a decentralized development system.

Speed in development

One of the primary ways in which managers have tried to improve development systems in the past fifteen years has been to speed them up. Managers in many industries have figured out that if they are not quick to develop new ideas, their competitors will enter the market first (Clark and Fujimoto, 1991; Wheelwright and Clark, 1992; Meyer, 1993). In some cases, patent life plays a role in pressuring companies to speed up. This has been particularly the case in pharmaceuticals, where companies have become acutely aware that the patent clock starts ticking early in development. Each day spent in development is a day's revenue lost. At one million dollars per day in pharmaceuticals, this is a lot of money.

Managers have used two methods to speed up projects. One is to inject more resources: if more people are working on a project, it can, all things being equal, be finished more quickly. This method of speeding up works in companies that have been spreading their resources too thinly over too many projects, as well as in companies that have simply been starving their projects. In other situations, a more finely tuned approach is usually needed.

The second approach is more complicated. It involves carefully modeling the tasks that must be undertaken to complete the project, identifying the links between the tasks (that is, what must be done before what), identifying the critical path, and doing whatever is possible to ensure that tasks along the critical path are culminated as quickly as possible. This second approach assumes that it is possible to foresee what tasks will be required to finish the project.

The assumption behind the second approach does not, however, always hold. It is not always possible to foresee what will have to be done to finish a project. Changes in the market, unexpected problems with the technology, and alterations in the regulatory environment may all force the project team to add additional tasks to their work plan. Uncertainty is likely to be particularly high when a team is developing not just a new product, but a new business.

Since the second approach does not work well in situations of high uncertainty, a third approach is needed. This third approach involves training the project team to identify factors that might force changes in the project plan, to monitor these factors, and to react quickly to changes. In short, alertness and flexibility are needed more than planning and rationalization. Some companies, particularly in fast-moving industries such as electronics, apply this kind of solution in new business development projects (Muzyka, 1989; Eisenhardt and Tabrizi, 1995).

Reducing cost of development

The second goal that managers have pursued in trying to improve development systems has been to reduce the cost of development. Cost has taken a back seat to speed in many industries (for example, pharmaceuticals), but it is nonetheless important, particularly in industries where the cost of product development is a large part of the ultimate cost of the product.

The primary method of reducing cost is to inspect the project plan carefully to determine whether all the planned activities are really needed. Critical components of the project need to be identified. Then anything not identified as critical should be evaluated in terms of whether it needs to be done at all.

Costs are sometimes reduced as the result of an effort to speed up development. The careful task analysis employed during a reengineering project often identifies tasks that do not need to be done. Cutting these may reduce cost as well as time. In addition, speeding up the project reduces the interest charges involved in financing the project. If the project is finished more quickly, the capital costs of financing it do not have to be borne for as long.

Another method of reducing cost relates to the incentives of project teams. Project teams often feel that they have to produce a successful product in order to have a chance at promotion and other good opportunities later. As a result, they may be unwilling to face evidence that the project will be unsuccessful. They may continue working on the project even in the face of evidence that it will fail, just because they believe that they have to make it succeed. As long as they think they have a chance of success, even if that chance is very small, they may pursue it, because they believe that, for them, the alternative – a failed project – is worse.

In this situation, money can be saved by changing the goals and incentives of the project team. If the team's goal is to 'find out whether a particular idea will work', rather than to 'make it work', the team can successfully achieve its goal and be rewarded, even if it has to terminate the project. The difference is subtle, but important. If management makes it clear to teams that their goal is to 'find out whether something can work', terminating a project becomes easier, and much less money will be wasted investigating dead ends. Eastman Chemical has implemented such a system and estimates that it has saved considerable money by not pursuing lost causes.

Improving fit with customer need

The third area of improvement is fit with customer need. There is no point in developing a product if it does not fit with some current or future customer need, as if it does not match customer need, no one will buy it. Yet companies are aware that many of the products they develop miss their target. Either they do not fit the need for which they were originally targeted, or the need itself does not materialize.

The main method that managers have used to avoid failures of this type has been to improve the links between project teams and customers. This can be done by building ongoing communications links with customers at several levels, and by embedding a customer-facing perspective in project plans and project management methods.

Communication with customers can begin as soon as the idea is generated. In evaluating an innovation system, managers can ask the following questions. Are the ideas tested with customers before significant funding is given? Are customer tests performed throughout the project to verify fit? Does the project team have ongoing links with potential customers that help it maintain awareness of evolving customer need?

A customer-facing perspective can be established via several means. First, project managers and team members can be trained in marketing. They can also be frequently reminded to pay attention to customers. Second, standard project plans and project management methods can be developed that include regular contacts with customers. Teams can be encouraged to follow these plans through training and supervision. Repetition of the message that the team must listen to customers will eventually have an effect.

In some cases, a company may choose to develop a product to fit needs that customers are not yet expressing. This sort of speculative product development is known as 'leading the market', rather than 'following the market'. Here, the team will still benefit from listening to customers, but they will not be following what customers say to the letter. Instead, they will be trying to imagine how customer taste will evolve, and how the product they are developing should be configured to appeal to this evolving customer taste.

In such cases, the appropriate questions are the following. Is the project team knowledgeable about current customer needs? Is there any sign that the product would be accepted by current customers? Does the team have a plausible vision for how future customer needs might develop? Is there any way to verify or test that vision? Is there any flexibility in the vision? That is, if the team is partly right and partly wrong, will they be able to alter the product to fit the situation? Or are they making a 100 percent bet on one possible product configuration? Thought experiments and contingency planning can be built into the project plan to increase flexibility.

Diagnosing problems in an innovation system

The advantage of having a theoretical understanding of the innovation system is that it gives us tools that will help us (a) to diagnose problems in an innovation system and (b) to identify the means of fixing problems. Even if no difficulties are manifest, it will allow us (c) to identify opportunities for improvement and (d) the means of making that improvement.

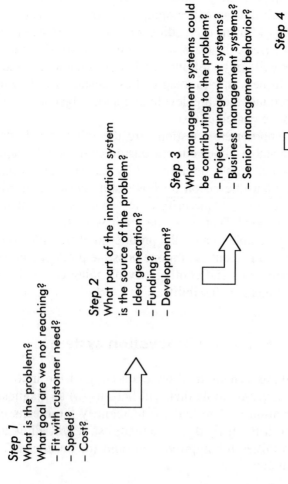

Step 1
What is the problem?
What goal are we not reaching?
– Fit with customer need?
– Speed?
– Cost?

Step 2
What part of the innovation system
is the source of the problem?
– Idea generation?
– Funding?
– Development?

Step 3
What management systems could
be contributing to the problem?
– Project management systems?
– Business management systems?
– Senior management behavior?

Step 4
How do we change the
management systems that are
contributing to the problem?

Figure 4.8   How to find and analyze problems in an innovation system

The best way to demonstrate this is to illustrate how the theoretical structure just presented can be used to find problems, diagnose their source, and design a solution.

A systematic method of diagnosing problems

If your innovation system is not performing up to your expectations, the best way to figure out what to do about it is to ask lots of questions. The general sequence of questions that is most likely to lead to a solution is the following (see Figure 4.8 for a summary):

1. What *is* the problem? On which performance dimension is the innovation system failing to meet management's expectations? In other words, which of the typical innovation system goals is the system not reaching? Is the innovation system (a) producing products that do not *fit customer needs*, (b) too *slow*, or (c) too *costly*?

2. What part of the innovation system is the source of the problem? During which phase does the problem arise? If the problem is *lack of fit with customer needs*, where in the system does this problem arise? Do our people (a) come up with *ideas* that do not have much relevance to customer needs, present or future? Do we (b) have some good, customer-relevant ideas that we fail to *fund*, while supporting others that are not so customer relevant? Or (c) do we fund customer-relevant ideas, but somehow lose the customer focus and customer relevance somewhere in the *development* process?

    If the problem is *speed*, where does this problem arise? Is it that we (a) do not recognize opportunities (that is, generate *ideas*) until long after competitors do, or that (b) our *funding* system takes a long time to allocate funds to new ideas, or underfunds good ideas? Or does it lie in the fact that (c) our *development* process is slower than that of our competitors?

    If the problem is *cost*, why does the overspending occur? Is it that we (a) *fund* too many projects that bring nothing to the company, or that we (b) spend more than necessary on projects during the *development* process?

Answering the questions under items 1 (what goal is not being reached) and 2 (what phase the problem arises in) will go a long way towards helping a management team to specify the problem and identify where it arises. Once the location of a problem has been identified, however, it is still necessary to determine its cause. To do this, it is useful to ask still more questions. Assuming that the management team has succeeded in defining the problem in more detail and in identifying what phases of the process it arises in, the following questions are relevant.

3. What aspects of the company's *project management systems* and its *business management systems* could be contributing to the problem? What aspects of *senior management behavior* could be involved? Many additional diagnostic questions can be asked to identify what precise aspect of a company's management systems (or of top managers' behavior) could be causing the difficulty.

    If a management team wants to be thorough, it can systematically consider how each category of management system and management behavior could be adding to problems in its innovation system. Unfortunately, there is not the space to discuss all of the ways in which each of the management systems discussed in Chapter 3 can impact an innovation system, but the examples given in this book will hopefully be helpful.

    Once the management team has identified what systems or behaviors could be causing problems, the next question is appropriate.

4. How do we fix the problem? There are examples of how to fix problems in an innovation system highlighted throughout this book, which managers can use as sources of ideas. Once again, I hope to present a more comprehensive discussion of the management tools in a subsequent book.

Executing solutions and evaluating the results

Once managers have come this far, the next step is to execute the solution. In Chapter 5, I will give some general guidelines on how to plan and execute an innovation system improvement program. Once a management team has put its chosen solution into operation, its members should look back to see whether the solution has worked.

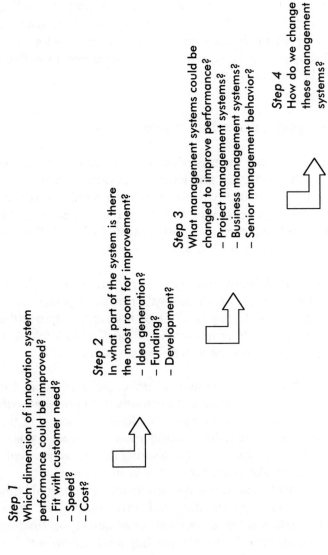

Step 1
Which dimension of innovation system
performance could be improved?
– Fit with customer need?
– Speed?
– Cost?

Step 2
In what part of the system is there
the most room for improvement?
– Idea generation?
– Funding?
– Development?

Step 3
What management systems could be
changed to improve performance?
– Project management systems?
– Business management systems?
– Senior management behavior?

Step 4
How do we change
these management
systems?

Figure 4.9   How to find opportunities for improvement in an innovation system

Are the ideas and products coming out of the system achieving a better fit with customer need? Is the process speeding up? Is it costing less?

When management have elicited the answers to these questions, they may find that the problem has not been fixed, or that there are still problems in the system. If so, it is best to return to the beginning of this list of questions and go through the diagnostic sequence again, focusing on what might have been missed the first time.

It often happens that serious problems in one area mask less serious problems in another. For example, problems in a project funding system can have such serious effects on innovation outcomes that they completely mask problems in idea generation or even development. The latter problems may not be seen until after management has fixed the problems in the funding system.

Identifying opportunities for improvement

Managers often believe that there is room to improve an innovation system even when no particular problems are evident. When this is the case, they can systematically work through a similar series of diagnostic questions as a means of finding ways of bettering the system. Here, a typical sequence of questions would be the following (see Figure 4.9 for a summary):

1. Which dimension of innovation system performance could be improved? Which dimension of innovation system performance does management want to improve? Does it want to improve the resulting products' *fit with customer need*? Does it want to *speed* up the system? Or does it want to reduce the system's *cost*?

2. In what part (phase) of the system is there the most room for improvement? If the management team wants to improve *fit with customer need*, could this most easily be done by improving the quality of *ideas* generated, by making more customer-focused choices in the *funding* process, or by assuring that decisions made during *development* take better account of customer need?

   If the management team wants to *speed* up the system, could this occur by recognizing opportunities and developing *ideas* more quickly? Or by making *funding* decisions more quickly, or funding good ideas more generously? Or by speeding up *development*?

If the management team wants to reduce system *cost*, could it do this by *funding* fewer projects, funding different projects, or reducing the funds given to each project? Or could it be achieved by reducing cost in *development*?

3. The next logical questions are the following. What aspects of the company's *project management systems*, and of the company's *business management systems*, offer the most potential for achievement of the desired outcomes? What facets of *senior management behavior* could be changed in ways that would help to achieve the desired outcomes?

   Once again, if the management team wants to be thorough, it can look systematically at how each category of management system and management behavior could contribute to system improvement, but space precludes a complete discussion here of potential ways to improve innovation management.

   Once the management team has identified what systems and behaviors could be improved, the next question is appropriate.

4. How do we improve? Once again, ideas on how to improve management systems are presented throughout the book. I do not have space systematically to explore the methods for improving each management system, but this discussion will hopefully be presented in a subsequent book.

Once managers execute their chosen solution, they should again look back to see whether the solution has worked. Are the ideas and the products coming out of the system achieving a better fit with customer need? Is the process speeding up? Is it costing less? If their interventions are not improving the system, they may want to reevaluate what they have done and revise their understanding of how their management systems and behaviors are affecting the innovation process. They may perhaps want to go back to the sequence of questions, beginning with question 2, to see whether they really correctly understood what was affecting the dimension of innovation system behavior that they wanted to influence.

On the other hand, if their interventions are actually improving the system, they may not want to rest on their laurels, instead deciding to move forward and find more ways of improving their system. In that case, they should go back to question 1, decide what dimension of innovation performance they want to work on, and proceed with a new diagnostic of how to do it.

The procedures described in this section follow fairly standard procedures of general problem solving. For more detailed discussions of the process of problem solving itself, the reader may wish to refer to Ackoff (1978), Hayes (1989), or Arnold (1992).

This concludes my introduction to how to think about innovation. In the next part of the book, I will look at how to organize a program for improving innovation performance.

Part II

How to Plan and Implement a Program to Improve Innovation Performance

In Part I of the book, I showed that a wide variety of management systems affected innovation performance. I then looked in a theoretical way at three key stages in the innovation process: idea generation, initial funding, and development. In this part of the book, I will build on this material to discuss how change programs can be organized.

Part II of the book is organized as follows. Chapter 5 will discuss some key issues in the overall planning of a change program, considering in particular, what management systems and practices should be changed first, and what changes can or should be delayed until later. In Chapter 6, I will discuss what role managers at different levels can play in an innovation improvement program. In Chapter 7, two paths that typical companies have followed as they have improved their innovation systems over the last fifteen years will be reviewed, Chapter 8 investigating how idea generation, funding, and development systems evolved along these two paths. Finally, in Chapter 9, I will analyze in detail the impact of industry and strategy on the design of companies' innovation systems.

5

Planning and Sequencing Change

Organizing a change program

Readers who have studied Chapters 2, 3 and 4 in detail may by now be feeling a bit overwhelmed. So many different management systems and practices affect innovation performance. If you want to improve the performance of your company, where do you start?

Indeed, this is a question that has faced many managers, most of them working without the benefit of this book, but they have looked at their companies, picked out a few things to change, and moved forward. Sometimes it took them a long time to make substantial progress; sometimes it took them a long time to figure out what was wrong and how to change it. That is where this book can help, as it can give guidance on how to diagnose problems and what to do about them.

The reader may, however, still justifiably ask, 'Where do I start?' I have outlined twenty areas, twenty types of management system and practice, where problems can be found. Each of these twenty areas corresponds to a different set of tools that managers can use to fix the problems. Where should people go first?

Determining what to change

While it is impossible to tell each individual reader what to do, guidelines can be given that you, the reader, can use to determine what to work on first. The process involves three steps, to be repeated in a cycle until you are happy that your company is performing as well as it can:

1. Diagnose what is not working well within the company, using the process outlined in Chapter 4
2. Decide which of the problems identified to begin working on first
3. Do the work, and make the changes.

Then:

Repeat 1. Assess progress, and reassess what is not working
Repeat 2. Decide what to work on next
Repeat 3. Do the work, and make the changes

and so on.

Now suppose, during the diagnostic stage, that you discover that your company has problems in eight different areas. What do you do? Do you work on all of them at once or what? Here, I would recommend in most circumstances that instead of trying to work on them all simultaneously you pick no more than three or four to work on at any one time. Doing more will almost certainly result in cognitive overload and will result in less, rather than more, being accomplished. The exception is when the organization is so frozen that a huge effort is needed to achieve any change at all. In a highly conservative organization, a major, highly publicized effort may be needed to get changes moving. Here, it may be necessary to alter more than three things at once. But a management team that attempts this is well advised to rely on outside help to ensure that the core team does not lose control of the change process once it gets it started. Even here, it is often useful to focus change initially in a few areas so that there will be a few quick wins that can be shown off to the rest of the organization.

Thus, in most circumstances it is better to begin the change program by focusing on three or four areas.

Now, which three? Here I can give some guidance. There appears to be a natural sequence of problems to work on, as identified by drawing on four sources of data:

1. *The behavior of managers.* In the transformation processes I have observed, there were certain management systems and practices that managers consistently worked on first, and others which they postponed until the higher-priority items had been fixed.

2. *Level of impact on the innovation system.* Some management systems and practices appear to have a much greater impact than others on innovation performance. These should reasonably be worked on first.

3. *Ease of changing a management system or practice.* Some management systems and practices are easy to change, others very difficult. Changing the latter can require the coordinated efforts of dozens of managers at several different levels. Companies usually work on the easy changes first, only starting to work on the harder ones when two things have happened: their management team has become more sophisticated about managing innovation, and their management team is mobilized to change the system.

4. *Riskiness of changing the management system.* Changing the way in which a single project is managed carries little risk for the rest of the company, but changing the way in which all projects are managed is riskier. However, the change affects only the innovation projects, so the risk can still be relatively easily managed and contained. Changing systems and practices that affect all units, operating units included, is far more serious. (See Figure 5.1 for a summary of the last three points by intervention type.)

The natural sequence of change is summarized in Figure 5.2. In companies that have not in the past emphasized product innovation, most change programs begin with a change in strategy. For some reason, often competitive pressure, senior management decide that the company needs to innovate more. Then they decide to implement a change program designed to achieve that goal. The change in strategy is not so much part of the change process as the stimulus that gets it started. After the decision to improve innovation performance has been made, the company's management team has to figure out how. Which management systems and practices need to be changed? How should they be changed? And which changes should be applied first?

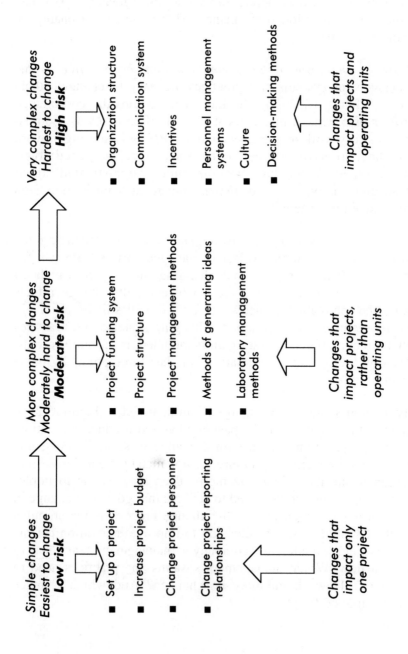

Figure 5.1 Impact, ease of change, and riskiness of various tools

Simple changes
Easiest to change
Low risk

More complex changes
Moderately hard to change
Moderate risk

Very complex changes
Hardest to change
High risk

- Set up a project
- Increase project budget
- Change project personnel
- Change project reporting relationships

- Project funding system
- Project structure
- Project management methods
- Methods of generating ideas
- Laboratory management methods

- Organization structure
- Communication system
- Incentives
- Personnel management systems
- Culture
- Decision-making methods

Changes that impact only one project

Changes that impact projects, rather than operating units

Changes that impact projects and operating units

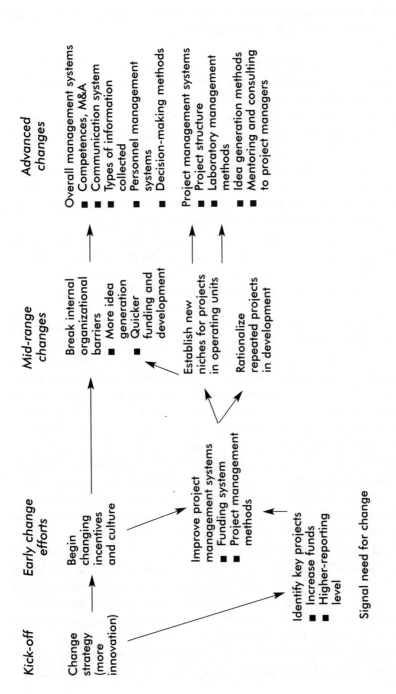

Figure 5.2   General sequence of change efforts

Early change efforts: when a company is just beginning to worry about innovation performance

If the company has never before worried about product innovation (as was the case with MGE), the first steps usually focus on project funding. This work can proceed on two levels. First, managers would do well to collect information on their existing innovation projects, and to determine whether they are being funded properly. Often, when companies do not emphasize innovation, they starve the projects they have, not giving them enough money to make progress quickly enough to have a reasonable chance of conquering a new market. So the first step is to make sure that existing projects are receiving sufficient funds to have a chance of winning.

Some companies may be rich enough to increase the funding of all their projects. Industrial Chemicals had few projects and was able to increase the budgets of most of them, but not all companies have it so easy. Companies often find that the only way they can get enough money to increase the budgets of key projects is by cutting that of others. But what if the company decides that all the projects need more money, but there is not enough money to go around. Tough decision will then have to be made; someone will have to choose which projects will be dropped, and which will have their budgets increased.

Northern Pharmaceuticals ran into this problem very quickly when it began looking at project budgets. Its projects needed much more money to progress quickly, but the company was not rich enough to increase all its budgets at once. Thus, some projects had to be dropped. The decision of which project to drop was political enough and difficult enough that Northern Pharmaceuticals brought in 'unbiased outsiders,' that is, consultants, to help to make the decision.

It should be noted in passing that when senior management begin taking responsibility for project budgets, they change the way in which projects are supervised. The projects whose budgets they review will doubtless have reporting relationships to someone lower down in the company. By reviewing funding decisions made lower down, senior management are, in effect, adding another layer of supervision to the system: projects that formerly had only one supervisor now have two. Employees may still report to their former supervisor, but if senior management review their budgets, they also have an (at least) dotted line reporting relationship to senior management.

Senior management may decide at this point that more systematic changes in project supervision are needed. They may set up a system whereby, as a rule, key projects report to someone in senior management. Alternatively, this change may be made much later.

Once project budgets have been brought into line with need, management teams can usefully begin looking at the project funding system as a whole. Sometimes, as at Northern Pharmaceuticals, this work begins while the project budget review is still underway. There are advantages to looking at the overall funding system just after the review of project budgets has been completed, the main one being that the budget review will have familiarized the management team with key funding system issues.

The management team may have noticed that certain projects have been underfunded. They can begin asking questions about these projects. Why were they underfunded? Was it simply a matter of lack of money? Or had the project funding system been set up in such a way as to discourage the funding of particular kinds of project? If so, how can the system be changed so that it produces more appropriate funding decisions?

Having uncovered the answers to these questions, management may go ahead and reform the project funding system, before proceeding to other issues. A common next target is project management. What are the project managers doing with the money? Are they using it effectively? Are they running the projects well? Senior management may not have the experience to answer these questions at first, as none of them may have experience in project management. They may, however, note that some projects have been proceeding rapidly despite limited resources, while others with greater resources have been floundering. Investigating, they may find that the skill of the project manager may be part of the difference.

Observations such as these may lead them to replace some of the project managers, or to put them through training programs. If they find, or fear, that project management problems are widespread, they may design a more systematic fix, inviting in consultants or academics who are 'experts' in project management to set up a training program for project managers.

As in the case of project funding, managers may go back and forth between working on individual projects and working on systems that affect all projects. In the case of funding, they can, by looking at individual project budgets, obtain the background information necessary for later reforms of the project funding system. Similarly, by looking at how individual projects are managed, they can begin to learn what project managers need to know, and what kind of systematic reforms in project management (for example, training programs) might be necessary.

With so much going on with individual projects and project management systems, management teams may fail to initiate work in some other key areas. Incentives, including promotion patterns, and culture have pervasive influences on people's behavior. Both factors can encourage people either to support innovation, or to discourage it. If the company has not previously emphasized innovation, it is very likely that incentives and culture are encouraging other behavior (for example, a focus on short-term profits), and discouraging innovation.

Very early in the change process, senior management should begin thinking about how to change incentives and culture. People who innovate, in fact all people who work on projects, should be rewarded rather than discouraged. Just as importantly, business unit heads and other leaders should be rewarded for supporting innovation and not for discouraging it.

Culture can slowly be changed by two means: what senior managers do, and what senior managers say. Who gets promoted is a very important part of what senior managers do. If project members, project leaders, and people who support innovation begin to receive promotions, people will start to think that corporate priorities really have changed. This may take a long time, five years being not unusual, so it is best that senior management start doing things differently as early as possible.

What senior managers say about people, particularly who is made a hero, is equally important. If senior managers treat innovators and those who support them as heroes, this will go a long way towards embedding the ethic of innovation into the company. Others will start to imitate their behavior. If they continue making heroes of those who produce short-term profits while ignoring innovation, people will continue to consider that to be the behavioral norm.

Changing incentives and changing culture are much trickier than the other changes so far mentioned. There are two reasons for this. One is the fact that their impact goes far beyond innovation projects, extending to operating units as well as projects. As a result, managers will be reluctant to implement significant changes in either unless they have had a chance to think carefully about how the changes will affect operating units.

The second reason derives from the first. Changes in incentives and culture are difficult to design and implement. It is very hard to get it right. Managers who have been working in a system that does not emphasize innovation may not be successful the first time. Nonetheless, incentives and culture have such pervasive effects that managers should start as soon as they can, using outside help if necessary.

To emphasize the point, changing a project's budgets, adding a new reporting line, or replacing a project manager has little impact beyond the individual project affected. Managers often make these changes early on because the needs are clear, the solution is clear, and it is virtually risk-free. This is all quite sensible.

Their next steps are equally sensible. Having seen the problems that past funding methods have created (for example, projects with too little funding to have a chance of success), they develop ways of reforming the funding system to avoid these problems. Having seen what happens to key projects when they do not receive any attention from senior management, they revise the supervision system. Having seen the result if the quality of project management is low, they develop better ways of selecting and training project managers. In each case, they have direct experience of the problem, thanks to their analysis of the problems of individual projects. And their solutions do not carry much risk. The changes impact on innovation projects, but not operating units.

However, a problem develops at the next step. The changes made so far may move the company forward. But if they are not supported by changes in incentives and culture, resistance will be greater than it needs to be, and progress will be less than that which is possible.

The problem with altering incentives and culture is that they involve high-risk changes, affecting the behavior of people in operating units as well as innovation projects. Managers may not be comfortable changing incentives and culture when either (a) they are not sure of the impact that the changes will have on operating units, or (b) they think that the impact will be negative.

This is one reason why companies sometimes isolate innovation activities into 'skunk works,' sites some distance away from the rest of the company's operations. The skunk works can be operated with quite different incentives and a quite different culture from that of the rest of the organization. As long as people in the rest of the company do not have much contact with the skunk works, they will not be influenced by the different culture.

There is, however, a price to isolating innovation projects from the rest of the company. The work done in the skunk works may not be taken seriously. Xerox's skunk works, PARC, invented the PC, but Xerox never marketed it. Instead, five years later, Steve Jobs and Steve Wozniak launched the Apple, using, in part, ideas they had acquired from PARC personnel (Smith and Alexander, 1988).

If managers want to avoid this problem, they need to link projects to operating units. But then, to assure that the projects get sufficient support, they need to change the incentives and culture. Here is where some innovation system improvement efforts fall down. The management team may not see the need to effect this change, or they may not have the knowledge and experience necessary to manage the change effectively. Seeing that the incentives and culture (the unwritten rules of how to behave) are still the same, many people in the operating units will continue behaving in the old ways. They will decline transfers to innovation projects; they will not support projects when this gets in the way of the daily business of the operating units – and the change effort will stall.

Mid-range changes: fixing ongoing performance or alignment problems

Some companies have already taken care of the basic issues discussed in the previous section. Once a company has begun to deal with basic issues in funding and development, the focus usually changes. What happens next depends on the industry of which the company is part and on the exact configuration of its innovation system.

Companies in some industries manage very large projects. Sometimes these projects are repetitive, that is, the tasks in one project are very similar to those performed in the next. Other companies have more diverse sets of projects. The next steps in the typical company's evolution depend on which group the company fits into.

Rationalizing repeated projects in development. Some companies have very large innovation projects involving tasks that are repeated from one project to the next. A pharmaceutical company, for example, has development projects that involve several hundred people and cost several hundreds of millions of dollars. Although each project will focus around a different compound, all the compounds will have to be run through the same series of regulatory tests. First come the initial tests for evidence of effectiveness, followed by tests for toxicity in animal models. Next are tests for toxicity in humans, and then those for effectiveness in humans. Finally, tests for effectiveness within specific treatment regimes in humans can be carried out.

As a result of this commonality of tasks, the work plans of each project will be broadly similar, many tasks being repeated from one project to the next. This consistency allows for the creation of a standard project plan, as well as for specialization on the part of individuals performing the tasks. Once the project plan has been created, it will very likely be reengineered to shorten the time needed to bring the product to market.

Motor vehicle companies also have projects that involve several hundred people. Such projects can be even more expensive, costing between several hundred million and several billion dollars. In the larger projects, the entire design of an existing model may be reviewed and updated, essentially creating a new car. In rare cases, the design may be started from scratch. In either case, the project work plan is largely determined by the architecture of the car.

The project work plan can be described as a hierarchy of tasks related to the vehicle's major assemblies, subassemblies and components. One part of the project team will update the design of the body, another the design of the chassis. Still another part of the team will look at the engine and drive train. Each of these larger assemblies has subassemblies and parts; thus, subteams will look at the subassemblies, and individuals or small teams will review the components. Another key part of the team will look at how all the pieces fit together. These individuals will be charged with achieving the overall design objectives assigned to the vehicle.

All the work on the components will have to be performed in a coordinated sequence so that the subassemblies into which the components fit can be assembled and tested on time. Initial work on the subassemblies has to be completed early enough that their fit with other subassemblies and their overall impact on the car's performance can be tested. The design of the whole car will have to be coordinated with the design of the manufacturing process, and both of these will have to be completed soon enough for parts to be ordered and the manufacturing equipment to be put into place in time for the scheduled launch.

With so many tasks being determined by the architecture of the vehicle, one vehicle development project will end up following much the same work plan as the previous one; some automobile companies have therefore developed standard vehicle development plans. As in the case of pharmaceuticals, these plans, as soon as they have been written, are reengineered to reduce the time needed to develop the vehicle.

It should be noted in passing that some projects in automobile companies involve 'freshening' a vehicle's design rather than undertaking a complete redesign, these former costing much less than the latter. They are, in effect, special cases, but they still fit the model. Rather than following the whole work plan, they follow an abbreviated version of it, involving only some of the tasks. Since they carry out a small number of the tasks involved in the generic work plan, they can normally squeeze even more time out and finish the vehicle in less time than is needed for a full redesign.

In summary, once funding and other basic issues have been resolved, the next step for companies with large, repetitive projects is to rationalize the project management system. Such companies develop standard project plans and then squeeze as much time and cost out of these plans as they can.

Described in this way, the process may sound easy, but it is not. I will describe what happens in more detail in the next chapter, but it should be realized that a key part of what happens is that people begin to work across functional boundaries. This process is not at all simple. If badly managed, it may disrupt normal operations without any resulting benefit. Some companies have failed to establish effective cross-functional coordination despite years of trying.

As a result, these changes are riskier than simple budget increases, changes in supervision, or changes in project management training. The need for speed and reduced cost in development is obvious, but the method of achieving it is difficult to execute, and there is the danger of disrupting ongoing work.

Breaking internal barriers and creating new niches for projects. Automobile and pharmaceutical companies are very large, single-industry businesses, all their products being designed in the same way, manufactured in similar factories, and distributed through similar channels. As a result, their innovation projects look very much alike.

Many large companies are not like this. They are more diversified, serving several related or unrelated industries, or several very different niches in the same industry. Their products may vary across a number of dimensions. They may deal with very different manufacturing processes and different distribution systems. As a result, the tasks performed during one innovation project may be quite different from the tasks performed during the next.

Unlike automobile and pharmaceutical companies, such companies cannot develop detailed standard project plans that can be applied across all projects. Projects can be planned, and the plans rationalized, but the effect may not carry beyond one project.

Rather than 'rationalizing' project management, these companies deal with other problems, for example the location of projects in the organization structure and the integration of projects with operating units. They also deal with breaking down barriers between units, but the barrier breaking is more complex than in pharmaceutical and automobile companies. In these latter areas, it is mainly barriers between functions that are attacked; in more diverse companies, geographic and business unit boundaries matter too. In addition, the barrier between innovation activities and ongoing operations will come increasingly under attack. More diverse companies can begin by creating a number of different niches in the organization into which innovation projects can be fit. They will, increasingly, adapt the organization to the project rather than the reverse.

Prior to reform, many companies will attach projects to the R&D department. Alternatively, if projects originated in a business unit, they will be managed in their business unit of origin. Neither location is necessarily best for the project.

Reforms that occur may include attaching R&D-managed projects to business units, attaching some projects to several business units, or setting up some projects as independent units reporting directly to group or higher levels. These decisions will be based on what the project needs. If it needs resources from a business unit, it will be attached to the business unit. If all the resources it requires lie in the central laboratories, it will be attached to these. If it falls between the charters of various business units, or if it must appropriate many resources from the outside, it will be set up as an independent project with a budget directly from a division, or from corporate management.

These reforms will work only if the incentives and culture have changed enough that people within business units will support projects, even at some cost to the ongoing operations of the business unit. If such a change has not already occurred, it will have to happen now.

Some companies go further to break barriers, investigating the source of idea generation and discovering that ideas often originate across organizational boundaries. When people with different competences, knowledge bases, and perspectives meet, the resulting conversation often generates new ideas on how the company's competences can be used to serve customer markets.

If a company is organized functionally, management may decide to set up business units or cross-functional coordinating committees. If a company is organized in business units, new links may be set up between them, based on technical or customer commonalties. Alternatively, management may set up cross-functional links within business units to break down functional boundaries.

Such new links tend to stimulate idea generation, as well as smoothing operating problems and facilitating the integration of innovation projects into business units. Again, all these changes work only if people's behavior supports innovation. The structural alterations and changes in communication system work only if incentives and culture support cross-functional communication, cross-functional work, and other innovation-supporting activity.

What is common about all companies going through mid-range changes is that barriers inside the organization are being broken down. In pharmaceutical and automobile companies, barriers between different development functions will be broken down to facilitate faster work. In addition, barriers between development, manufacturing, and marketing will be removed, not only to speed work, but also to ensure that the work done effectively addresses consumer need. In more diverse companies, the primary barrier being displaced is that between innovation activity and ongoing operations. In the process, barriers between functions, business units, and geographic areas are likely also to be attacked.

Diversified activities within automobile and pharmaceutical companies. Automobile and pharmaceutical companies have areas within them that are highly diverse. If an automobile company develops new technology, its new technology development area will resemble the R&D area of a more diverse company, possibly with a wide variety of different projects. Similarly, the discovery area of a pharmaceutical company – the area where ideas for new compounds are generated and tested – can be diverse. Projects in a discovery area tend to be more varied than those in downstream development.

As a result, automobile and pharmaceutical companies may apply some of the same kinds of reform that occur in more diverse companies, breaking down barriers between different units in order more effectively to integrate R&D into ongoing operations. They may also stimulate idea generation by creating links between units that have something in common but do not normally work together.

Automobile and pharmaceutical companies typically first focus on rationalizing their large, repetitive projects. Once they have squeezed large amounts of time out of these projects, however, they look at other aspects of their operations and try to improve them as well.

Advanced changes: fine-tuning the system

As in so many things in business, details matter when you are managing innovation. The difference between highly innovative companies and less innovative ones is not so much a matter of overall structure, but of how they manage the details. In addition to what has already been discussed, nine types of detail matter. Five of these are aspects of overall company management:

1. The components of the company
2. The communications structure
3. The types of information collected
4. Personnel management systems other than incentives
5. Methods of decision making.

Four are aspects of innovation project management:

1. Project structure
2. Methods of laboratory management
3. Methods of idea generation
4. Mentoring and consulting for project managers.

Each of these will be discussed below.

Companies completing the mid-range changes may address one or several of these issues. There is no logical order here; choosing which to address is a matter of figuring out where there is the most need and the most potential for change.

Components of the company. The most innovative companies in my sample were not single-product businesses, but collections of small companies built around a related set of technologies and customer groups. There was a willingness, even a desire, to learn and/or develop new technologies, and to extend the company's reach into new customer groups. Ideas arose within existing business units, at the boundaries between units, and at the edges where the companies were developing new activities.

By contrast, the less innovative companies were either single-industry companies or less dynamic collections of small businesses. There was either less potential for cross-fertilization between competences and new development around the edges, or less effort to exploit the potential.

This suggests that less innovative companies can be enlivened by examining the competence mix in the organization and adding new competences that promise to make the mix more dynamic or more productive. This can be achieved via merger, hiring, or encouraging internal people to learn a new competence. Alternatively, management may take a less directive route and simply broadcast its willingness to let people lower down bring new competences into the organization.

Communications structure. Exploiting the potential inherent in a competence mix is often a matter of improving communication across internal barriers. If people live in functional silos, or in organizational boxes of any kind, the potential for cross-fertilization among them will be lost.

In the more innovative companies in the study, people talked constantly. Cross-functional teams ran most businesses and projects. They typically met weekly or bi-weekly, and team members frequently rubbed elbows between meetings. Whenever a problem, idea, or opportunity arose, it could quickly be discussed with colleagues.

Other links also existed. Everyone belonged to one or more professional networks, which met several times each year. Contacts between meetings were frequent. When someone saw a problem or opportunity that he could not address locally, he would quickly tap into his network(s) to find a solution. Senior people in technology and marketing disciplines functioned as network nodes, knowing who was working on what, and who could answer what question. When people had problems or saw opportunities, they could usually direct them very quickly to someone who could help to develop a solution.

One aspect of these highly innovative companies was that it was easy to form new communication links. When someone had a problem, the person who could help him could be on the other side of the world. Finding her and communicating with her would be impossible in a company that did not encourage communication, but the highly innovative companies encouraged people to look for help wherever they could find it within the company. They also had methods of helping them to find the right person. Once the person had been located, she would undoubtedly cooperate, since everyone in the company was expected to give help when asked. As a result, employees could, when they needed help, find it via a new communications path with relative ease.

Less innovative companies had less communication across functional boundaries, and fewer networks crossing business unit boundaries. Such companies could become livelier by increasing communications between functions, and by establishing networks that crossed other boundaries.

Less innovative companies also had far more difficulty in establishing new communications paths. In many cases, communication with strangers was discouraged, even when they carried the company's business card. In some cases, there was no one to go to for help in finding the right person to consult. No one, not even laboratory managers, knew what was going on in other laboratories. Such companies could become more dynamic by setting up networks among laboratory managers, so that they, at least, would learn what was going on throughout the company. They should also make it clear that people should give help to others in the company when asked. The rule should be not to hoard information, but to share it.

Types of information collected. The more innovative companies collected a wider range and depth of information about their customers than did the less innovative ones. Some of the less innovative companies relied on the customer to come and tell them what he needed. Sometimes the messages were ignored, even when they came. Technology companies particularly seemed willing to ignore messages passed through sales people and marketing departments. These departments do not rank very high in the pecking order of a technology company, and messages passed through them can easily be discounted. As the less innovative companies improved, they began listening to their customers and salespeople. They took these messages to heart, but were not very proactive about figuring out what the customer might want or need next.

The most innovative companies were much more proactive. 3M, an industrial products manufacturer, forms multi-level links with its customers. As in any company, the sales representative talks to the buyer, but at 3M there are other links as well. The technology representative and the R&D department talk to the customer's manufacturing and R&D functions. The marketing department talks to the customer's marketing department, even to the customer's customers. Finally, 3M management talks to the customer's management.

With all these contacts in place, 3M has a thorough picture of what the customer and his customers are thinking about. 3M does not have to rely simply on what the customer, or his buyer, says, as do some of the less innovative companies. As a result, 3M is in a much better position to see several years ahead and to begin the development of a new product or feature before the customer himself publicizes his need.

ConsumerCo deals with distributors and final consumers, in most businesses its primary customer being the final consumer. Like most consumer products companies, it studies its consumers in every way imaginable, but it relies more than most on direct contact. Its sales people talk with customers daily. Its marketers and managers talk with customers at least several days each month. The company invites anthropologists and sociologists in to study its customers' behavior. No one in management is allowed to lose touch with the customers.

Some ConsumerCo marketers are equally obsessed with competing products. They monitor everything appearing on their marketplace. They buy the products, use the products, and keep samples around their offices. They talk to customers about competing products. They are open to whatever customers have to say about both their own products and those of their competitors.

Both of these highly innovative companies collect a wide variety of information. One interesting finding is that they are open to the unexpected. They do not set up a standard questionnaire and collect only the information specified on the questionnaire. Rather, they pursue a large number of direct conversations with customers in which anything can, and does, come up. They listen to these unexpected signals and use them to generate ideas for new products, new features, new marketing campaigns, or other improvements in their product offerings.

Companies that are trying to become more like 3M and ConsumerCo should do two things. First, they should develop more and deeper links with their customers and their customers' customers. Second, they should open their information-gathering efforts to the unexpected, pursuing more open-ended conversations with customers and others, and searching for unexpressed and unexpected trends and opinions.

Personnel management systems. Innovative companies look for creative people when they hire. An unusual career path or education can be a plus, not a minus. They also look for people with practical experience; being smart is not enough. Having a down-to-earth attitude and experience doing things, rather than just thinking about things, is a bonus.

The innovative companies also move people around. The rotation of managers is almost a religion at ConsumerCo. Anyone who wants to move up will regularly move between functions, across business unit boundaries, and into new countries. All this movement builds variety of experience, increasing the likelihood that the individual will see some new connection that no one else before has ever seen. It also increases the variety of experience on any team. A five-person management team can easily include people who have worked in seven different countries, in every function (most of them in several functions), and in a dozen different business units. With such a variety of experience on each team, many different ideas will be proposed, and many perspectives used to evaluate them.

3M is not as religious about moving people around. Their movement of technical people is needs-based. If a laboratory or business unit needs a new skill, and that skill is available somewhere else in 3M, someone from the laboratory or business unit will go to where the skill is available and learn it. He may stay six months, such rotations rarely being for less than six months, or a year – whatever is necessary.

Managers in all functions move between business units. They do not move between countries as often as ConsumerCo managers. But, since many of 3M's businesses are regional or global rather than national, movement between countries would anyway have less impact.

Some of the less innovative companies hardly rotate people at all. The MGE divisions did not practice rotation of any kind in the 1980s and undertook little of it through the 1990s. Movement across functional boundaries at EurAuto was impossible, at least in the mid-1990s.

The less innovative companies could become more innovative if they:

- focused more on creativity in hiring
- rotated people more freely across functional, product line, and geographic boundaries.

Methods of decision making. ConsumerCo has an explicit policy about decision making: no significant decision should be made by one person alone. This rule is interpreted as requiring consensus decision making within management teams. Consensus is required across functional boundaries and across levels of the hierarchy. Marketing, for example, needs the consent of manufacturing and development to introduce a new product. In addition, a boss needs his subordinates' consent to implement a decision.

In companies where everyone was out to make an individual mark, such a consensus-based system would never work. But people at ConsumerCo are selected for their willingness and ability to discuss issues and reach agreement with their colleagues. If an employee cannot function effectively and efficiently within this consensus system, he will certainly not be promoted, possibly even being fired.

Nor would the consensus system work in a company where people were not willing to confront each other with different opinions. If people sat quietly in meetings and let a few dominate, the consensus system would be meaningless. If they agreed with everything the boss said, it would also be useless. As a result, there is another rule at ConsumerCo: a manager can never agree 100 percent with anyone, not even with his boss, not even with the CEO.

As a result, people are expected to voice differing opinions, to discuss them, to pick what is useful from each, and to arrive at a joint decision on what is best for the company. By and large, this happens. Such thinking and working together is not for everyone, but it is effective for ConsumerCo and for its managers.

The effect of ConsumerCo's decision-making system on innovation is that people are forced to express and confront varying opinions. Different viewpoints are expressed, discussed, analyzed, and considered before decisions are made. A wider range of data, interpretations, and opinions are considered than might otherwise be the case. This leads both to variety in the avenues considered, and to a more intelligent choice among them.

3M does not have rules about consensus decision making, but most decisions at the business unit level are the product of extensive discussion and consensus. People from different functions discuss problems together and generally find a consensus position before acting. Business unit heads or project managers may not even be involved in a decision if the function heads are in agreement. They may be informed to be sure that they consent, but the discussion often occurs among team members involved in the action on the ground.

Decision making at ConsumerCo similarly stays close to the ground. This is achieved in two ways. Business units are small, and functional heads within business units are still involved in day-to-day contact with customers, manufacturing, and/or technology. In addition, business unit heads stay in contact with the market. They are required to go out with sales representatives and talk with customers regularly. Within the business unit, they are 'first among equals', rather than distant bosses.

Less innovative companies in the study tended far more often to give an individual sole responsibility for each decision. This makes it simpler to assign and identify responsibility, but it also makes it easy for people to make decisions without communicating. They can make decisions without ever considering viewpoints other than their own. This limits the richness of avenues considered, restricting the number of perspectives brought to bear when considering an option. As a result, fewer options are likely to be considered, and less intelligent choices will tend to be made among them.

The less innovative companies could, perhaps, become more like ConsumerCo if they began (a) requiring consensus decision making, and (b) requiring individuals to express divergent viewpoints. Whether this could be achieved in the less innovative companies is highly doubtful. ConsumerCo has strong norms for how to conduct an effective discussion. People at ConsumerCo do express divergent opinions. Groups at ConsumerCo do reach consensus. People rarely feel a need to hold out or appeal to a higher authority. Would this be the case at some of the less innovative companies? This is not clear. At the very least, people at the less innovative companies would have to learn new skills. They would need to learn how to participate in or lead cross-functional discussions. They would also need to learn how to express and defend opinions that differed from those of the boss and their colleagues.

Project structure. Project teams at 3M and ConsumerCo are formed around tight, cross-functional groups. These teams have extensive, weekly links with customers, suppliers, internal laboratories, manufacturing, and other internal functions. They are led by project leaders with cross-functional experience. Team members at 3M are co-located. At ConsumerCo, they may also be co-located. If not, representatives of each function will meet several times a month, and a liaison person will be appointed to assure that the functions continue working effectively together in between meetings.

Project teams at less innovative companies do not have such tight cross-functional links. A Lawn & Garden manager said that, at his company, development could talk to international marketing, and international marketing could talk to regional marketing, but development could not talk to regional marketing. They simply could not understand each other; they did not speak the same language. The same phenomenon repeated itself elsewhere. Functions that did not have day-to-day contact with each other simply did not understand each other.

Project teams at less innovative companies also have fewer links with the outside. The LC49 development team at Lawn & Garden never spoke to customers, and had few conversations with distributors. While it had contacts with suppliers, these were relatively simple, involving ordering components of the product.

To become more like the innovative companies, the less innovative companies would need to develop a greater number of cross-functional links within their project teams. They would also have to develop a greater number of extensive links with customers, distributors, and, when relevant, suppliers.

Methods of laboratory management. Technical personnel at 3M are famously allowed to spend 15 percent of their time working on any personal project they want to work on, as long as the project shows some possibility of doing something good for the company. This gives the technical people some flexibility. They can choose for themselves what they work on for at least a part of their time. Some do this, and develop such products as the *Post-It*™ note. Others focus on required work, of which there is always plenty to go around, and do not use their 15 percent allocation.

Eastman Chemical has developed what it believes is an improved version of the 3M system. A percentage (approximately 10 percent) of the overall R&D budget is reserved for speculative investigations, to be used at the initiative of bench-level technical people. Anyone who wants part of this fund for a project he has thought of can apply for it. As of the mid-1990s, plenty of money was available relative to the number of applications received. Some applicants end up spending 15 percent of their time working on their own projects, much as they might at 3M. But some, those with larger or particularly interesting projects, use much more than 15 percent of their time in this way. Since many people do not apply for any of these funds, enough are left over for some people to receive allocations that exceed 15 percent of their time.

ConsumerCo also allows laboratory people some freedom in the use of their time, with some supervision. Each year, laboratory heads negotiate with technical people on what their personal projects will be. But each laboratory person has, in theory, a speculative research project that he has proposed and/or agreed to undertake that could, at some point, produce something of benefit to the company.

None of the less innovative companies in my sample had a system anything like this. Laboratory people at MGE and the development area of Northern Pharmaceuticals were expressly forbidden to work on personal projects, their time being 100 percent allocated to corporate projects. By the mid-1990s, there was some talk of instituting a 15 percent rule at MGE, but no one was willing to reduce the time allocated to corporate-approved work.

EurAuto people, similarly, had no time to pursue personal projects. As one development manager told me, development projects were so constrained by time and spending goals that there was no time even to consider anything speculative. If a technology was not proven, a development team could not afford even to consider it.

Obviously, the less innovative companies could become more like the innovative ones if they gave more freedom to their technical people. Whether they have the resources to do this is another question. The results would presumably pay for the investment, were the companies able to exploit them effectively, but the results might be a long time coming. Whether these companies would be willing and able to wait is an open question.

Another issue in laboratory management, besides time allocation, is whose ideas are taken seriously. In the 1980s in Northern Pharmaceuticals' discovery laboratories, it was the laboratory directors' ideas, and only their ideas, that were taken seriously. They decided who worked on what, not necessarily asking laboratory personnel for their ideas. This changed in the early 1990s with the appointment of a new head of R&D. This new head reduced the laboratory directors' power and encouraged discovery laboratory personnel to submit ideas and work on ideas that they found interesting. This revolution in laboratory management shocked some laboratory directors so much that they had to be moved to off-line positions.

Methods of idea generation. In a detailed study of idea generation practices at the eight primary sites, I identified more than two dozen specific methods of stimulating idea generation. The most innovative companies, 3M and ConsumerCo, each used at least eighteen of these. The less innovative companies, the MGE divisions, Northern Pharmaceuticals, and EurAuto, used between three and six. Little more need be said.

Mentoring and consulting. At 3M, project managers have mentors, people they can go to for help or advice on how to run their projects. At ConsumerCo, virtually all management personnel have been involved in innovation projects at some point, so virtually anyone can give advice. At Eastman Chemical, each project head reports to several layers of managers, at least one of whom normally has project management experience.

Little mentoring occurred at MGE. There were no senior people around who had project management experience; the concept of a full-time project manager was too new. In addition, the low status given to project managers had discouraged any of the current leadership from taking roles in innovation projects. As a result, there was no experience base on which to draw. EurAuto was in a similar position: the concept of a strong project manager had been introduced too recently for senior members of the management team to have had any experience with project management.

To become more like the innovative companies, the less innovative ones would have to hold onto the people who have run projects and have them mentor new project managers once they had gained experience. Building up this kind of experience base will take them at least five to ten years. It will be several decades, at best, before their management teams have as much experience with innovation as the teams at 3M and ConsumerCo.

Sequencing the changes, planning the change process

If a management team wants to improve innovation performance, it is necessary to know what needs to be changed and what sequence of changes to follow. This is, however, not enough: other things must also be taken into account. In particular, what people know, how and when they must be trained, and how the changes will affect them must be considered. (See Figure 5.3 for an outline of this section.)

Changes that are simple and can be implemented from the top. For the purpose of understanding these aspects of organizing change, it is convenient to classify changes into four groups. The first group includes changes that are simple, changes that can, in fact, be implemented by fiat from the top. Changing the budgets of individual projects is the best example. A CEO can give more money to a project, or take money away, with little effort. No training is needed.

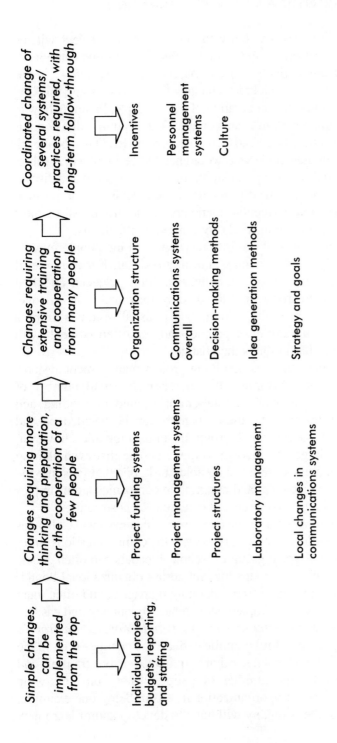

Figure 5.3 Knowledge, complexity and the change process

No cooperation is necessary. Only the people in the project will be affected. Most alterations to individual projects fall in this category.

Changes requiring thinking, preparation, and the cooperation of a few people. The second group includes changes that involve some thinking and preparation, and/or the cooperation of a few people. Planning how to operate a new funding system is an example. The head of a division, his R&D head, the business unit heads, and perhaps the R&D heads of each business unit are all the people who would need to be involved. A subset of this group could develop a proposition for the new system and discuss it with the whole group, or the division head could devise the proposition with a few of the more influential members of the group. All or most would need to cooperate to make the system work effectively.

Changes like this can still run into resistance. Some people may be affected negatively by the change, and may resist it. For example, if business unit managers have the power to fund projects, and that power is being taken away or diluted, they may resist the change. Such resistance can be quite strong, but it usually comes from a limited and identifiable group of people, and can often be dealt with by the small group that initiates the change.

In most companies, changes involving project management systems fall into this category. Assuming that a relatively small number of people are involved in managing laboratories, and in funding and managing innovation projects, these changes can be decided on and implemented by a relatively small group. In some companies, however, R&D areas are so large and involve so many people that even altering the project management system is a complex task, one that falls into the next category. Pharmaceutical and automobile companies are examples of companies that have such large and complex R&D structures.

In smaller and mid-sized companies, some business-wide changes come under this heading. Simple variations in the communications structure are an example. A small group of technical leaders can often decide to create technical interest groups that cut across organizational boundaries. If there is no opposition from operating managers, and often there is not, such a change can be implemented relatively quickly and easily.

Changes that involve extensive training and cooperation from a large number of people. More complicated are the changes seen in the third group, these being changes that require extensive training and cooperation from a large number of people. Many business-wide changes fit in this category, organizational reform being one example. People throughout the company will have to develop and/or learn new roles. New communications paths will have to be established, and new power relationships may need to be developed. A large number of new people will have to be trained to operate the new system, most of whom will have to cooperate, or the change will fail.

Implementing this kind of change requires extensive planning. Where and when will the people be trained? Who needs to be trained first? How will we train them? How will they be affected by the change? What kind of resistance might arise? How can we deal with this?

In some cases, it is best to conduct an open discussion of this kind of change with the managers affected. Several hundreds, even several thousands, of managers may be affected. If feasible, however, it is still useful for them to have a chance to discuss and adapt the change program before implementing it. If they do this, if they make the change program their own, there is less chance that they will resist it.

Of course, extensive discussion and adaptation beforehand are not always possible. Sometimes the management team is simply not ready for it; sometimes they do not see the need for change. In this case, the top management team must try to implement from the top. But they should recognize that training will be necessary and that they have a selling job on their hands.

Areas where the coordinated change of several systems and practices and long-term follow through are required. Finally, the fourth group includes changes that require the coordinated alteration of several systems and practices, along with long-term follow through, to be effective. What is required here is not just planning and training, but consistent effort over many years. Changes in incentives, personnel management systems, and culture fall into this category. These three types of change are linked. If management wants to alter one, they will often have to alter all three. Doing so effectively is a task that may take years.

Industrial Chemicals management tried to change incentives in the early 1990s. They announced that, from then on, successful innovation project managers would be rewarded, being given good jobs heading the company's operating units. The problem was that most managers found it difficult to believe that senior management would follow through on this commitment.

Up to that point, no project manager had ever been promoted to any good job outside R&D. No one in the business units had any experience running innovation projects. Would that really change? Would senior management break precedent and promote someone who had no experience in business units to head one? Would such a business unit head be accepted by other business unit heads? Would they be able to run a business unit effectively? None of the people in the business units could believe that it would really happen, and for a number of years, it did not. Management kept saying that they would promote successful project managers, but since no examples were forthcoming, no one was convinced. Insiders estimated that it would take five to ten years for anyone to believe that this change was really happening.

Similarly, management tried to change the incentives for business unit heads, saying that they should, henceforth, support innovation more fully. They should be willing to take risks. They would be rewarded if they did. Once again, however, it was not clear that management really meant it. Top management still expected business unit heads to produce high, and consistent, operating profits. The fact that innovation project expenses could cut into operating profits was not reflected in the evaluation process. The culture, all the unwritten rules, still said that the best way for a business unit head to get promoted was to play it safe. Do not invest in anything risky. Just produce steady profits. Top management did not make a serious effort to understand the roots of this culture, and they were not very effective in changing it.

To be successful at changing incentives (the written rules), cultures (the unwritten, but not necessarily unspoken, rules), and personnel systems, management needs to think through the origins of key management behaviors within the company. They next need to develop a change program that addresses these issues at the root. Achieving change may then require sustained effort over five, ten, or even twenty years.

General Electric under Jack Welch provides a very public example of successful long-term change. From a company 'with its face to headquarters and its ass to the customer', in Welch's famous phrase, Welch has created a far more responsive and effective company. Wall Street has rewarded his efforts with a substantial increase in share price. But it took more than ten years to achieve the change.

Ease of change. Changes in the first group are easy to implement. At the extreme, top management can think about them for a few days and then implement them by fiat. Changes in the second group are somewhat more difficult, but they can still be implemented by a small group within a few weeks or months. Changes in the third group are markedly more difficult. They may require many months of planning and preparation, and weeks of discussion and/or training may have to occur prior to implementation. The whole program may require many months, or even several years, to implement it. Finally, changes in the fourth group may require deep thinking, coordinated planning, and years of sustained effort. Managers should take these lead times and training/discussion requirements into account as they plan their change programs.

Why change programs differ

No two companies are alike; as a result, no two change programs are the same. This is not a random effect: differences between companies drive differences between change programs. As managers often take other companies as examples, it is useful to look at the reasons why change programs differ, so that they do not mistakenly adopt practices that are good for another company but not for their own. (See Table 5.1 for a summary of this section.)

Industry and strategic context

Industry. Industry differences drive a large number of differences in change programs. In fact, they drive so many differences that I will devote an entire chapter to exploring this area later in this book, citing only one example at this point.

I have already noted that automobile and pharmaceutical companies devote great effort to developing standard project plans that they then reengineer to reduce the time needed to get products to market. This has been the greatest focus of effort for these companies in the past fifteen years. Companies in other industries do not devote so much effort to rationalizing development. Their efforts often focus more on idea generation, or on links between projects and operating units.

This is a difference driven by industry-level factors. Automobile companies have very large projects because they build a large, complex product. Each project team performs tasks similar to those which the previous project team performed. This is because the architecture of the product is consistent from one model to the next. As a result, all projects have many tasks in common, and a standard project plan can be developed. Once developed, the plan can be rationalized. The resulting reengineering is worthwhile because the time needed to complete a project is significant, and time reductions can bring the benefit of being early to market with new features or styling that pleases customers.

Table 5.1   Reasons why change programs differ

Reason	Explanation
■ Industry	■ Different innovation system configurations required for different industries (see Chapters 7–9)
■ Company strategy	■ Different strategies require different innovation system configuration (see discussion of diversification and focus strategies in Chapters 7–9)
■ Urgency, speed of change desired	■ A management team facing a more urgent situation will push changes faster
■ Company's skill at innovation	■ Companies that are not good at innovation may have to make changes that better innovators implemented years before
■ Willingness to use help from outside	■ Use of outside expertise can speed change
■ Ability of top managers to gain control	■ Resistance from below may block change
■ Willingness of top managers to surrender control	■ Unwillingness to give up centralized power may block needed decentralization

Almost exactly the same logic applies in pharmaceuticals, but the reason for the large projects is different. In pharmaceuticals, it is the necessity of doing many regulatory tests that makes projects large, and the consistency of the regulatory regime from one year to the next that causes projects to resemble each other. The expiration of the patent life, as well as competitor entry, drives companies to bring new compounds to market as early as possible. But in both cases, the standard product plan makes sense. Reengineering the plan to reduce the time needed also makes sense.

In many other industries, this logic does not apply. Products and regulatory regimes are simpler, so projects are neither so long nor so complex. Thus, rationalizing and reengineering a product plan has less payoff. Products may be different enough that projects do not resemble each other very much. As a result, a standard product plan may not exist. On the other hand, companies outside automobiles and pharmaceuticals may have trouble finding ideas for new products. In particular, if they sell simple commodity products, they may have trouble figuring out ways to add value to them. They may therefore invest far more effort in ways of generating new ideas than may companies involved in automobiles and pharmaceuticals.

Company strategy. Some companies make the choice to stick to one product area. They will try to strengthen their position in that product area without building the capacity to diversify. Other companies make the choice to pursue diversification opportunities, building up their capacity to diversify. This obligates them to do a number of things differently from the way in which a more focused company would. One thing they will need, for example, is a more flexible organization structure. I will discuss other factors in Chapters 7 and 8.

Urgency of situation, and speed of change desired. When Northern Pharmaceuticals decided to improve its innovation performance, management was in a hurry. They changed budget allocations and the project funding system within a few months. Within a year, they began altering the ways in which projects were managed, using consultants and hired-in management talent to help them advance more quickly.

Industrial Chemicals was not in such a hurry. When MGE senior management decided to increase their emphasis on innovation, project budgets rose very quickly, but no change in project funding systems occurred until a year and a half later. No one took a serious look at the way in which projects were being managed, or at the skills that project managers needed, until two years after the change process had begun. There was no effort to hire outsiders. For nearly four years, management made changes without looking for outside help.

Why was Northern Pharmaceuticals in a bigger hurry than Industrial Chemicals? Northern Pharmaceuticals management had a greater sense of urgency. This was in part because they were in the pharmaceutical industry, where patent lives, and thus product lives, are fixed. They could see that the long duration of their development process meant that they could benefit from only a few years of patent life. The age of the company's existing products may have also lent urgency to the problem of finding ways in which to improve the new product development process.

At Industrial Chemicals the situation was more ambiguous. Patent protection was not such an issue, and there was no prospect of losing revenue because of patent expiration. Some product markets had been lost because of the entry of new competition, but it was not clear whether this would continue: perhaps the tide had turned. In any event, it is clear that Industrial Chemicals management did not feel the same sense of urgency that Northern Pharmaceuticals management did. As a result, they did not move as quickly.

Company history

How good a company is at innovation. 3M and some of MGE's units fall into similar industries, but 3M has been focusing on product innovation for eighty years longer than MGE. It is also far better at it. Nonetheless, 3M is just as interested in improving its innovation processes as MGE, perhaps more so. 3M, however, will not have to go through the same changes. It already has incentives, personnel management systems, and a culture that support innovation. It does not have to build them. As a result, it can concentrate on other things.

No one knows what 3M's next move will be. There may be a further diffusion of R&D resources, or the development of new competences through basic research. MGE could do these things as well, but it has more pressing problems to take care of.

Power and control issues

Willingness to use help from the outside. Northern Pharmaceuticals management began looking for outside help as soon as they became concerned about innovation performance. In fact, they used outsiders' help extensively throughout the process. First, they brought in consultants to help them think through how to improve the process overall. These consultants recommended cutting the number of projects and giving far more money to those which remained, the purpose of these changes being to speed up development. Northern then hired in a number of outsiders to help to improve its management methods, and to speed the process up. Industrial Chemicals did not use outsiders until three years into the process. Then it brought in consultants to help it think through a reorganization.

As was noted above, Northern Pharmaceuticals moved much faster than Industrial Chemicals in making changes. It was in part able to do this because it sought outside help. People on the outside had some insight into the problem of how to run the innovation process more effectively, so why not bring them in and take advantage of their expertise? The attitude at Industrial Chemicals was different. There, the 'Not Invented Here' syndrome seemed to prevail, and managers relied on themselves to figure out what was wrong and how to fix it. This process of learning on their own was slower than Northern's process of finding experts on the outside and taking advantage of their expertise.

There was a cost to going faster. Some of Northern's middle-management team could not handle the pace or direction of change, and had to be removed to nonline positions. Industrial Chemicals moved more slowly, but its managers were better able to keep up.

Ability of top managers to gain control. Some top-management-led change programs slow or stall because senior management cannot take effective control of the organization. Their lieutenants either do not see the need for change, or feel threatened by impending change and block it.

This could have happened at Northern Pharmaceuticals. Laboratory managers were used to running their own laboratories much as they saw fit. They had long controlled the resource allocation process, each getting a share of the pie to allocate to his favorite projects. They had equally long resisted attempts to centralize funding decisions.

Northern Pharmaceuticals management worked around this block by bringing in outside consultants. These outsiders were viewed as unbiased since they were not part of the system. They could identify the best projects, regardless of who supported them. The consultants were seen as being able to make unbiased decisions about which projects were most promising for the company's future. Given the urgency of Northern's financial situation, the laboratory managers agreed to abide by these decisions.

Willingness of top managers to surrender control. At other companies, progress is limited by top management's unwillingness to surrender control. In diversified companies, investment and development decisions are best made by people close to the markets and technologies involved. These people are inevitably several, sometimes many, levels below top management.

In companies where much decision making is centralized, however, top managers may not be willing to give up control. They may persist in making decisions about innovation investments and innovation project management themselves. If they do, they will block an important change: the devolution of power to those best able to make good decisions.

This is exactly what happened at Lawn & Garden for three years. Division management managed innovation projects and retained the control of many other key decisions. Progress at improving the company's innovation system was virtually blocked until management was, finally, willing to give up control. Then change proceeded very quickly, and performance soon began to improve.

All these dimensions can have an influence on the exact shape of a company's change process. Managers should think about them and take them into account when planning and executing the change process. If they do so, they are more likely to achieve the goals they desire.

What an individual can do to improve an innovation system

Up to this point, I have focused on what senior managers can do to improve innovation performance, in particular, on what people who lead whole companies, divisions, or business units can do. I have focused, in short, on relatively senior people in the organization.

But what about the others? Can people who are not top managers initiate or achieve changes without the support of senior management? The answer is, in almost all cases, 'Yes!' Junior technical representatives or salespeople may not have the same level of power as a senior general manager, but they almost always have some power over their immediate environment. At the very least, they can choose what they talk to other people about and how they talk to them. They can talk about innovation and the need for it, or not. They can support risk taking, or criticize it. They can discuss and share potential interesting ideas, or ignore them.

Normally, they also have some flexibility over what they work on. They can pay attention to the interesting and unusual detail that might lead to an innovation, or they can ignore it. If they pay attention to it, they can seek someone to talk to about it. They can look for support in investigating it.

Additionally, junior people can document the problems that they see around them in the company's innovation system. If the company does not care about innovation, this may not make them very popular with their superiors, but they may gradually win their point. And if the company's direction changes, as happened in most of the companies in my sample, they will be well placed to help management to push the company in a new direction, one more supportive of innovation.

6 Different Managers' Roles in Implementing Change

In a large corporation, it is unlikely that any one manager will be in a position to know how the company is managed with respect to all the dimensions identified in this book. It is even less likely that any one manager, even the CEO, will be in a position to change all the dimensions of management that may need to be changed for the company to have an optimally effective innovation system. Implementing a change program in a large company is inevitably a cooperative effort among a number of managers at different levels in the company.

In this chapter, I will give some guidance on what kinds of role different types of managers should play. I studied how eight different companies improved their innovation systems over ten-year periods. In four of these cases, I worked with managers to determine which of the actions they had taken had worked, and which were errors. In all four cases, managers were quite forthright in admitting that at some point they had made mistakes. They had sometimes failed to respect the limitations of their roles within the company's management hierarchy. By looking at what worked and what did not work in these four histories, it is possible to develop guidelines for what roles managers at different levels should play.

In order to be able to discuss and present these guidelines clearly, I will use a framework, part of which I am borrowing from previous work. Bower (1970) and Burgelman (1983) looked at the roles played by different kinds of manager in resource allocation (Bower) and strategic change (Burgelman). I will borrow the classification they use for different levels of manager. But, since my work focuses on innovation management, rather than resource allocation or strategic change, I will have to develop a new framework for describing the different types of managerial role.

A framework for understanding managers' roles

The different levels of manager

Bower (1970) and Burgelman (1983) identified four different levels of manager in their work on resource allocation. These will be described here before outlining the different roles they play.

Corporate management. Corporate managers generally include the CEO and any other senior managers who work closely with him. In a diversified company, they are typically responsible for several groups of business units. These business units may compete in different industries. There may be some variance in management structures, systems, and processes across different divisions or groups. In a large company, corporate managers will not be familiar with each division's business problems, nor will they be intimately familiar with the management structures, systems, and practices in each division.

Division or group management. Large diversified companies often have managers who sit below the corporate level, but above the business unit level. These managers are typically responsible for groups of business units. All of the business units within any one group will usually compete in the same or similar industries. These groups of business units may be called 'divisions' or 'groups,' or they may have some other name. In the rest of this discussion, the title 'divisions' will be adopted.

In most cases, the same management structures, systems, and practices will be used in all business units within any one division. As a result, division managers will be familiar with the management systems in use throughout their division. They will also be familiar, in general, with the business issues in each business unit in their division, but they will rarely be cognisant of all the details of the marketing and technological problems facing the business units and innovation projects in their division.

Business unit heads. Each business unit will have a manager in charge of it. These business unit heads will normally be intimately familiar with the business problems facing their own unit. They will also be intimately familiar with the management structures, systems, and practices in use within the business unit. They will be more acquainted than division management with the technology and marketing problems facing their business unit, but they will not usually know these problems as well as the functional specialists and others further down do.

While business unit heads understand how their own business units are run and what problems they face, they will not necessarily have any knowledge of any other business units in their company. Their expertise may be entirely limited to their own business unit.

Business unit and project team personnel, including project chiefs. All business units and innovation projects have people who actually carry out the work. These front-line people will be more knowledgeable than anyone about the technical and marketing problems facing their units. They will also be intimately familiar with the management structures, systems, and practices in use in their unit, since they face them every day.

What managers do during a transformation

In Chapter 3, I introduced the dimension of *scope* of a manager's action. Along this dimension, managers sometimes intervened in individual projects (narrow scope), sometimes changed the entire project management system (moderate scope), and sometimes made changes that impacted on not only innovation projects, but also operating units (wide scope). I will continue to use this dimension in this section, while adding several others as well.

First, for this purpose, I must break the 'single-project' type of intervention into two groups. In some cases, senior managers actually took control of projects, making operational decisions that would normally have been made by the project team. This type of action was quite different in its effects from engaging in routine supervision, mentoring, or the other single-project interventions. So I will place it in a separate group.

Second, senior managers sometimes signaled the importance of innovation without actually changing very much. Some interventions were much more important for signaling senior managers' intentions and desires than for what they actually did. Bower and Burgelman called these 'signaling' activity, and I will borrow this term here.

Third, I talked in earlier chapters about another type of intervention, the 'stimulating reflection' intervention. I will not, however, use this classification here. Why? – because any manager can stimulate reflection within his domain at any time. There was no distinction in the study between managers at different levels in terms of who could and who could not stimulate reflection. For the other types of intervention, there were differences, and it is those differences which I will talk about.

This leaves five types of action that the different levels of manager can adopt during an innovation improvement effort. I will describe these five types of action before describing who undertook them successfully and who did not.

Taking control of a project. This involves making operational decisions, such as pricing, product configuration, or distribution, for the project. Senior managers who did this were, in effect, taking over the role of project chief.

Creating, funding, or supervising a project. Actions in this category include budgetary and other supervisory decisions related to the project. They involve general managers not taking control of a project, but simply supervising it.

Changing the project management system of a division. These are actions that alter structures, systems, and practices that are part of the project management system. Examples of such structures/systems include the project funding system, project management methods, and the communication system within laboratories or other dedicated R&D areas.

Changing the way in which operating units, as well as projects, are managed. These are actions that alter strategies, structures, and systems that are part of the management system of the entire division or business unit. The key is that these actions impact not just projects, but also business units. Examples of such strategies, structures, and systems include the following: the overall organization structure; the incentive system and other aspects of the human resource system; the communications system linking business units with laboratories, projects, customers, and each other; corporate and business unit strategies; and the methods used to define them.

Signaling the need for change. This type of action involves sensing trends or changes in the environment that imply that the company's strategies, structures, or systems are no longer in line with the environment, and will need to be changed. Those who sense the need for change are not necessarily those who implement the change. Business unit managers, for example, may be able to feel the need for change without themselves being able to implement it. Thus, it is identified as a separate role.

The framework of four managerial levels and five roles is summarized in Figure 6.1. In the next section, I will use evidence from four cases to identify which types of manager can most effectively perform each role.

	Operational control of a project	Funding and supervising a project	Changing project management systems	Changing business management systems	Signaling the need for change
Corporate managers					
Division/group managers					
Business unit managers					
Project managers					

Figure 6.1 Framework of management levels and roles

How managers performed the roles

In this section, I will briefly recount four case histories of companies trying to improve their own innovation performance. These case histories are drawn from four different and independent units of the diversified European manufacturer MGE. I will discuss the roles played by different levels of management during each case history, and then, in the next section, summarize the analysis and draw out the lessons it has for managers at other companies.

Industrial Chemicals

The reader has met the Industrial Chemicals division before with regard to the CR project, whose tale was told in Chapter 2. I will thus not recount the story in detail here, but instead remind the reader of some key events and of how different levels of manager were involved in this story.

The CR project had been going for four years when corporate management decided that MGE, and Industrial Chemicals, had to improve its innovation performance. When corporate management decided to change strategy, they initiated a long series of changes in individual projects, in project management systems, and later in division-wide management systems.

The first changes were made by corporate managers and involved changes in project budgets and reporting relationships. These interventions in effect signaled to skeptical managers lower down that corporate management was interested in change. A few months later, division-level managers began altering project management systems, and several years later, division-level managers began changing division-wide management systems. Business unit level managers were not involved in making changes.

Managers familiar with the history of these changes felt that some mistakes had been made. Interestingly, no one felt that division-level managers had made any significant mistakes as they changed the division's innovation systems. But some managers felt that corporate management had made mistakes along the way.

The mistakes they pointed to were the following. When corporate management discovered the CR project, they effectively increased its budget authority by a huge factor. For all practical purposes, there was no limit on how much money the project team could spend. Even the project chief thought that this had led to a lack of discipline on the part of the project team.

Later on, corporate management set excessively high performance expectations for the CR team. The team found it dispiriting to be faced with expectations that they knew they could not meet.

Third, corporate management set up financial incentives to reward certain project managers for successfully completing their projects. But at least one project manager thought that the rewards were too high and too skewed in his favor (as his team had no comparable incentives). The incentives were high enough to cause resentment among business unit managers and, potentially, towards the team.

Fourth, some corporate managers tried to encourage division and business unit level managers to take more risks, but unfortunately, their efforts to do this did not work. They would say, in speeches, that they wanted their people to take more risks, but the effect of the speeches, as one business unit manager put it, was to inspire more fear. No one was willing to stick his neck out.

Fifth, corporate managers decided, in order to shore up MGE's stock price, to publicize the CR project before the project team felt that it was ready. The effect was, however, to alienate CR's potential customers when it turned out that the project had not progressed as far as corporate management had indicated.

The overly high budget and the excessive performance expectations were single-project interventions that went wrong. The financial incentives that were granted to some project managers were also single project interventions that went wrong. The attempt to increase risk taking was an attempt at a business-wide change (a change in culture) that was not working. In each of these cases, corporate management did not know the territory, or the projects, well enough to bring about change effectively. By contrast, division-level managers made many efforts to change project and business management systems, all of which worked. They were much more intimately familiar with the people, management systems, and practices in their division, and they were able to bring about change more effectively.

By recounting corporate management's errors like this, I may inadvertently be leading the reader to the conclusion that they should have left the job of improving innovation performance to division-level managers. That is, indeed, one lesson I would draw from this story, but this lesson must be carefully qualified.

Had corporate management not done anything, it is not clear whether the innovation system improvement effort would have got off the ground at all. They may have gone too far in some of their interventions in the CR project, but from their perspective they had to do something. Division management was not mobilized to improve innovation performance at the beginning of the story. Corporate management wanted to mobilize them. Just saying, 'Improve innovation performance' may not have been enough.

Rather than just talking about innovation, corporate management chose to act. They searched out interesting projects and gave them a large amount of support. In effect, they showed everyone in the company, by their actions, that they were very serious about putting more emphasis on innovation. Without the concrete signal of their action, the message would not have been as strong; words alone might not have been enough.

The premature publicity given by corporate management to the CR project reveals another difficult aspect of their job. Looking at what happened from the perspective of the project, it can be seen that publicizing CR as early as they did was clearly a mistake. But the corporate managers who publicized it were not just thinking about the project: they had to think about the company's public image as well. In particular, they had to think about its image to its stockholders.

The stockholders wanted some reassurance that the company had reasonable plans for growth. From the corporate manager's point of view, not telling the stockholders about all the investments the company was making in innovation would have been irresponsible. Unfortunately, the stockholders' need for information on the company's investments was in direct opposition to the project's need for time to develop outside the public eye. Corporate management thus chose to inform the stockholders at the cost of harming the project. Had they not done so, they would have protected the project at the possible cost of the stockholders' loss of faith in the company.

To summarize, two lessons can be drawn from this case. The first is that division managers were more effective in changing the division's management systems and practices than were corporate managers. The second is that corporate managers had conflicting responsibilities that division-level managers did not have to worry about. Corporate managers had to choose between (a) fully informing the stockholders about the company's new investments in innovation, or (b) protecting projects from premature publicity. They could not do both.

In addition to these two lessons, I will note one fact that will assume importance when we look at the next case: the fact that Industrial Chemicals division managers let the CR project team run the project on their own without interference. When they were unhappy with the project manager's performance, they replaced him. But they made no attempt to change his decisions while he was in charge or to take control of the project outright, as occurred in some other cases (see the Lawn & Garden story, below). Division management recognized that the members of the project team knew more about the CR technology and markets than they did. But senior managers were not always as generous, as the next story will indicate.

Lawn & Garden

Like CR, the LC49 project began as a chemist's idea. Both projects suffered from neglect for several years as their chemist-champions worked to find resources and advance their projects in the face of corporate indifference. Both projects were 'discovered' by corporate management shortly after they had decided to put a much greater emphasis on innovation performance. Both projects received much greater support after they were thus discovered. There, however, the similarities end.

While Industrial Chemicals' management left the job of running CR to the project team, the opposite was the case at Lawn & Garden. Division management in Lawn & Garden thought that they could make a significant contribution to LC49. Senior division managers had spent their whole careers in the lawn and garden market, and thought that they knew that market well. They believed that they understood the technical side of the product from occasional conversations with laboratory scientists. Unfortunately, however, these assumptions turned out to be wrong.

Senior division managers made decisions about how the product should be configured, when it should be launched, who should sell it, how and when it should be advertised, how it should be distributed, and how it should be priced. All of these decisions were later recognized as errors, even by the senior managers involved. Senior management was quite excited about the project, but the market had changed since they were younger and more directly involved in it. The technology was not as predictable as the laboratory scientists supporting it had led them to believe. As a result, they promoted and launched the product too early and at too high a price. They chose a questionable product configuration and distributed and sold it through what were arguably the wrong channels. As a result, the results of the launch were very disappointing.

To their credit, division management recognized their errors soon after the launch. They resolved to limit their future intervention in projects. Also to their credit, they proposed reforms of the division's management systems soon after the failed launch. One aim was to decentralize power in the division by giving much more power to regional marketing groups. They proposed to involve regional marketing groups in new product development decisions in order to bring current information on market conditions into the product development decisions. These proposals were discussed and developed by mid- and junior-level managers in the division for several months. When implemented, they became a great success, and the division's results noticeably improved over the next few years.

The lessons of this case are complementary to those of Industrial Chemicals. At Lawn & Garden, division managers found the limits of their power and expertise. While they had enough power to take over the management of a project, the results were not very good when they did that: the managers were not as familiar with the technical and market questions involved as were their subordinates. Project management was thus better left to those who specialized in it full time.

By contrast, division management at Lawn & Garden did a very good job of proposing and implementing changes in the division's management systems. This was the territory that they knew well: the management of the division as a whole. Here, their interventions were successful, in sharp contrast to their interventions at project level. Their subordinates, business unit, and project managers also made significant contributions to these reforms.

Northern Pharmaceuticals

The innovation improvement process at Northern Pharmaceuticals moved more quickly than at Lawn & Garden and Industrial Chemicals. There were also many fewer errors made in the change process than at the two other divisions, for several reasons.

First, the Northern Pharmaceuticals management recognized the need to improve innovation performance before corporate management did. Thus by the time corporate management became interested in innovation, Northern Pharmaceuticals was already two years into a reform program that was having a noticeable effect on its innovation processes. There was little obvious need for corporate to intervene, which eliminated one potential source of errors, that of corporate managers intervening at the division level simply to get the change process started. Division management was already mobilized, which was not the case in the other divisions.

Second, none of the members of corporate management came from the pharmaceutical business. Had they originated from this background, they might have been more willing to intervene in the change process, even several years into it. They did so in Advanced Materials, as we shall see shortly. In this case, however, none of them felt confident enough to argue with Northern's management team, which was made up of people who had spent their lives in pharmaceuticals.

Third, division management did not intervene in the management of individual projects. They changed the project funding system; they pushed all the project teams to develop accelerated work plans involving a large amount of cross-functional cooperation; but they made no effort to delve into the detail of the individual projects. Beyond giving the general goal of 'speeding up', they left decisions pertaining to each project in the hands of the project manager.

Fourth, the extensive use of consultants and the extensive hiring from other pharmaceutical companies doubtless helped Northern Pharmaceuticals to avoid many simple mistakes. More than any of the other divisions, Northern Pharmaceuticals made use of outside expertise. This paid off as management made few errors. In addition, reforms in Northern Pharmaceuticals proceeded much more quickly than those in other companies.

With no one acting outside his area of competence, and with the extensive use of outside expertise, Northern Pharmaceuticals' managers made relatively few errors. While speeding up development and increasing cross-functional work were difficult, everyone recognized the need to achieve this. Some mid-level managers were not able to keep up with the changes, but even they (or at least those to whom I talked) agreed that the changes were necessary.

Advanced Materials

The innovation system improvement process at Advanced Materials followed much the same script as that at Industrial Chemicals. Corporate management signaled the importance of innovation by identifying key projects and increasing their budgets. Division-level managers then took over and improved the division's project funding system. Later, they implemented a series of organizational reforms designed to bring technologists and sales and marketing people into closer touch with each other and with clients.

There were, however, two special features of the story at Advanced Materials that made it different from that at Industrial Chemicals. First, several senior corporate managers took a great interest in how one of the innovation projects at Advanced Materials was being run. This was Safety Materials, a project housed in the Advanced Plastics business unit. Corporate management regularly second-guessed the Safety Materials project team on issues such as pricing, publicity, and distribution.

The team viewed many of corporate management's suggestions, in particular requests to increase price, as misguided. On the issue of price, they documented the reasons for their disagreement in considerable detail. They saw the interventions from corporate as needless distractions from the business of getting on with the project.

It was not just the project team who resisted corporate management's attempts to influence the project. Frank Kelly, the head of the Advanced Plastics business unit, supported the project team on virtually every issue. The way in which he played his role was the second factor that distinguished the Advanced Materials from the Industrial Chemicals story. Kelly was the project manager's supervisor, and he acted to protect the project team from corporate management. Thanks to this protection, the team was able to get on with its business in spite of many requests for changes from senior management.

To summarize the lessons of this case, Frank Kelly demonstrated that a business unit manager can play a positive role as a consultant and supervisor to a project team. Corporate management's actions in this case demonstrated once again that more senior managers start having difficulty as soon as they begin to usurp the project manager's role. When they try to interfere in decisions related to the operations of the project, they rarely have enough information or background knowledge to contest the decisions of the project team sensibly.

Managers' roles in a diversified company

Building on the lessons of the four case studies just presented, we can identify which level of management is in the best position to play each role. Since management's roles are somewhat different in a diversified company than they are in a focused company, I will consider the diversified company case first. A summary of the discussion is presented in Figure 6.2.

Corporate management's role

Corporate management can fund and supervise projects without creating any serious problems. MGE corporate management supervised the CR project and arranged for division-level funding. Division-level managers also supervised the CR project. The additional reporting to the corporate level cost some time, the project manager spending an hour or more with corporate managers each month. However, the high-level report had the benefit (for the project) of signaling that corporate management believed the project to be one of the most important in the company. This eased access and resource problems. Virtually everyone in the company was willing to help the project, assuming that they had time.

Corporate-level intervention in project management created far more problems. Members of MGE's Executive Committee tried several times to influence the operational decisions of the Safety Materials project team, in particular urging them to increase price. This intervention met with resistance from the team, who viewed corporate management's knowledge of the situation as being inadequate to make such decisions. Corporate management backed their opinion up with a consulting report, but the project team responded by pointing out flaws in the consulting report. In the end, corporate management had no influence on project pricing.

Corporate managers were more effective when they played a normal supervisory role. Paul Thomas, one member of the Corporate Executive Committee, pointed out some shortcomings in the Safety Materials project manager's performance. In particular, he thought that the project manager did not have enough time to devote to the project (being also the Advanced Plastics R&D director), and that he was not promoting the project aggressively enough. Thomas eventually succeeded in having the project manager replaced, probably to the project's ultimate benefit.

	Operational control of a project	Funding and supervising a project	Changing project management systems	Changing business management systems	Signaling the need for change
Corporate Managers	Dangerous	Secondary role		Change incentives and culture	Possible role
Division/group managers	Dangerous	Secondary role	Core role	Core role	Possible role
Business unit managers	Consultant or mentor	Core role	Contributions and exceptional cases	Contributions and exceptional cases	Possible role
Project managers	Core role		Contributions	Contributions	

Figure 6.2 Managers' roles in a diversified company

Corporate management's key role at MGE was signaling the need for change. It was corporate management who picked up signals from a variety of markets and from stockholders, signals that indicated the requirement for the company to put more emphasis on developing new products. It was corporate management who carried the word to the divisions and the business units, first by picking projects to support, and then by pushing division managers to adapt and improve their innovation management systems.

In no case, however, did corporate-level managers actually participate in the design and implementation of new management systems. The Lawn & Garden division head discussed his proposed changes in division management systems with the CEO, who approved them. Others may have checked out proposed changes with the Executive Committee before implementing them. But each division manager said that it was the division-level management team who designed and implemented changes in project and business management systems. This was consistent with the fact that division management knew divisional systems and the divisional environment better than corporate management did.

Corporate management did manage one type of system-wide change. MGE's incentive and promotion system was run on a company-wide basis. Only corporate managers could set incentives for business unit heads and above, which they did. They sent signals, which they thought were clear, that innovative behavior would be rewarded. The problem was that it took some time for them to convince lower-level managers that they were serious about this change in the incentive system. They had to 'prove it,' through their actions over time, before lower-level managers would believe that risk taking, rather than playing it safe, would be rewarded.

Division/group management's role

Like corporate managers, division/group-level managers can also fund and supervise individual projects. All four MGE projects studied received support and supervision at this level, but problems arose when supervision became control. This was most clear in the LC49 project at Lawn & Garden.

Division management ran LC49 for several years, although they understood neither the market nor the technology as well as they thought they did. They received many signals from the project team and others that they were making mistakes. But they maintained control of the project, setting prices and making distribution decisions against the advice of those lower down. When the product was launched, it was evident to everyone that many of their decisions had been wrong. At that point, they returned control of the project to the project team.

Division managers elsewhere did not try to run projects. What they did do, in all the cases studied, was to restructure project and business management systems. In Industrial Chemicals, division-level managers identified and fixed problems in project funding and project management systems. The same thing happened at Advanced Materials.

At Lawn & Garden, it was division management who proposed changes in divisional management systems after the disappointing LC49 launch. While lower-level managers had considerable input into the design of the new systems, it was division management who managed both the design and implementation of the new systems. At Northern Pharmaceuticals as well, it was division management who proposed changes in division-wide systems, and who managed their implementation.

Business unit management's role

Business unit managers throughout MGE funded and supervised projects. Problems arose in Industrial Chemicals when they had monopoly control of project funding, since they would not fund projects that did not fit within their business units. But even in the reformed system, business unit managers continued to have some control of project funding. This assured that projects (such as Safety Materials) that could benefit from access to business unit technology and market knowledge would have easy access to such knowledge.

The Advanced Plastics business unit funded the Safety Materials project from the start. The project needed technological resources that were available within the business unit's laboratory, as well as market contacts that the business unit could easily provide. The fact that the business unit was funding the project meant that it had easy access to these resources. This example confirms that business unit-level funding has a useful role in an innovation system.

The supervisory role can go beyond providing funding. In the Safety Materials case, Kelly, the business unit manager, was familiar enough with the project's technology and market to act as a consultant to the project team. He also participated in the team's work, in effect, by using his hierarchical weight to solve access problems that the team faced. Presumably division- or corporate-level managers could do the same. Corporate-level managers helped CR to get access to internal resources, for example.

There was, however, no evidence in any of the cases that business unit managers could make good operational decisions for project teams. Kelly did not try to make decisions for Safety Materials. He simply acted as an advisor to the project team and left the control of operational decisions in the hands of the project manager.

Business unit managers did not normally have control over project management and business management decisions at MGE. Kelly, for two reasons, succeeded in maintaining both a culture and management practices that were different from those at other MGE business units. First, his unit was acquired, and most management systems of the acquired unit were left in place. Second, Kelly's unit was profitable, giving senior managers no reason to interfere in its management. In some companies, business unit managers may have more influence over the management systems used in their units, but at MGE this was the exception rather than the rule.

Project manager and team member roles

Most ideas for projects are generated by people below the level of business unit manager. When people at this level have access to resources, they can sometimes pursue their ideas without seeking funds elsewhere. But once a project needs significant resources, the project team will need to look to higher levels for support.

Project team members are usually the experts in the operational problems facing projects. Most project teams in the four cases studied remained under the control of project team members throughout. Whenever higher-level managers made operating decisions that were contrary to the team's judgement, the results were uniformly bad for the project. The clearest role for project managers and project teams, then, is to maintain control of their projects.

People below the business unit manager level rarely have any opportunity to influence corporate management systems. The head of the Lawn & Garden division did involve project managers in the discussion of changes in the project management system, but this was exceptional. Project managers were not involved in similar changes in other divisions.

Summary of management roles in a diversified company

Senior managers could quite effectively make changes in division-wide project management and business management systems. Corporate managers at MGE were responsible for corporate-wide promotion and other incentive systems. No one objected to them changing these systems. They were most knowledgeable about how the people in the company were being rewarded and how this fitted with the long-term strategies of senior management.

Division managers were responsible for division-wide management systems. No one questioned their ability to change these systems. In almost every case, the changes they made were viewed as appropriate by others in their divisions. Division managers had more knowledge than anyone else of how their management systems worked and what effects they had on innovation systems, so it is not surprising that they would make fewer mistakes than anyone else in changing these systems.

Senior managers encountered a vast amount of trouble when they tried to run projects. Here, they had little expertise, while the project teams themselves had much. Running projects is better left to project managers and project teams.

Business unit managers rarely had the responsibility for project and business management systems. They could play a role in supervising projects, consulting to project teams (when they had expertise in relevant areas), and mentoring project managers. When asked, they could contribute usefully to the reform of division management systems. Project and functional managers were primarily responsible for managing projects. But they could also, when invited to by senior management, contribute usefully to management system reforms.

Management roles in a focused company

In the last section, I discussed the roles that different levels of management should play in improving the innovation system of a diversified company. I assumed that each division of the company had a set of business and project management systems that were consistent within the division, but which differed from those of other divisions. Since management systems differed across divisions, corporate managers were not in most cases in a position to change management systems. Unless they had themselves worked in a division, they would not have enough expertise to identify what kinds of management system it needed, nor would they know a division well enough to be able to manage a change process.

If a company were to focus on one business, or a few closely related businesses, corporate management might be much more knowledgeable about how management systems in each division worked. They might also be in a position to have far more influence on management system changes in each division. In fact, if management systems are uniform across the entire company, corporate management may be the only ones authorized to change them. This apparently was the case in the companies that Bower (1970) and Burgelman (1983) studied.

Figure 6.3 summarizes how managers' roles in a single industry company would differ from those in a more diversified company. The key distinctions made in the discussion of diversified companies are still valid. It is still appropriate for senior managers to make changes in company-wide (or division-wide) project and business management systems, and still dangerous for them to try to micro-manage a project.

The key difference between the single-industry company and the diversified company is the following. It is appropriate for corporate management in the single-industry company to change project and business management systems, since these systems are the same company-wide. In the more diversified company, these systems are likely to differ from one division to the next. Corporate management may not be familiar with all systems; it is also unlikely that they will know the market and technological environments of all the divisions. As a result, it is reasonable for the responsibility for project and business management systems to rest with division management in more diversified companies. It is equally reasonable that such responsibility rest with corporate managers in single-industry companies, since in the latter case, corporate managers are likely to be familiar with internal systems, technologies and market environments throughout the company.

	Operational control of a project	Funding and supervising a project	Changing project management systems	Changing business management systems	Signaling the need for change
Corporate managers	Dangerous	Funding	Core role	Core role	Possible role
Division/group managers	Dangerous	Funding and supervision	Possible role	Possible role	Possible role
Business unit managers	Consultant or mentor	Supervision	Contributions and exceptional cases	Contributions and exceptional cases	Possible role
Project managers	Core role		Contributions	Contributions	

Figure 6.3   Managers' roles in a focused company

7 Two Common Paths of Innovation System Evolution

Why innovation systems follow different evolutionary paths

If you read the literature on innovation, you will find that there are many books and articles on how to improve an innovation system. The problem is that they do not all address the problem in the same way, and the solutions they propose are not completely compatible. For example, a variety of writers on the automobile (for example, Womack *et al.*, 1990; Clark and Fujimoto, 1991) and pharmaceutical (for example, Spilker, 1989) industries have described how the innovation process can be made more efficient (quicker, and less costly). Other writers (for example, Schroeder *et al.*, 1989; Van de Ven *et al.*, 1989; Garud and Van de Ven, 1992; Brown and Eisenhardt, 1998; Meyer, 1998) offer quite different prescriptions. Looking at projects in a variety of industries, they describe methods of diversifying and managing the proliferation of ideas. Are these prescriptions compatible with each other? Should all companies adopt both prescriptions? If so, how? If not, which prescriptions are valid when?

When I looked at what eight companies had done between 1984 and 1995 to improve their innovation systems, I found that they were not all pursuing the same goals. Some were focusing on improving their ability to diversify, that is, their *diversification capacity*, building their capacity to create new businesses, and to create products different from those previously produced. Others were focusing on improving *innovation system efficiency,* decreasing the time needed to develop a product, and the cost of its development. In effect, the former were implementing the solutions proposed by Brown and Eisenhardt (1998) and others, solutions that focused on new ideas and diversification. The latter were implementing the solutions proposed by Clark and others (Clark and Fujimoto, 1991), which focused on innovation system efficiency.

In this chapter, I will describe the change paths followed by these companies. To give the reader a more concrete idea of what the changes were, I will look in more detail at the evolution of two companies: Industrial Chemicals, which increased its diversification capacity, and Northern Pharmaceuticals, which improved its innovation system efficiency. I will also explore the reasons why the two companies' paths differed.

In Chapter 5, I briefly discussed seven reasons why management teams follow different paths as they work to improve their companies' innovation performance. Here, I will focus on two of these: industry and company strategy. These two reasons explain most of the differences between the companies that focused on innovation system efficiency and those which focused on diversification capacity.

Here, I will summarize the thrust of this chapter, repeating part of what was said in Chapter 5, since it is also key to the argument of this chapter.

In more stable industries, the amount of uncertainty involved in innovation projects is relatively low, as the tasks that must be performed to develop a new product can be foreseen. In addition, they are consistent from one project to the next. As a result, standard project plans can be developed and improved as time goes on, each new project following the standard project plan, or an adaptation of it. Managers can improve the performance of the system by working to improve the standard project plan. Improvements usually involve shortening the amount of time involved, or reducing the cost of development. It is in these industries that managers work on improving innovation system efficiency. It is here that they develop standard project plans, and here that they work most assiduously to reduce the amount of time needed for development.

In less stable industries, it is sometimes not possible to foresee what tasks an innovation project team will have to perform. Unstable markets or technologies may make it impossible to foresee what tasks an innovation team will have to perform more than a few months, or even weeks, in advance. Uncertainty is also high when a company tries to develop a new business. Even if the business is new not to the world, but only to the company, the company may not know enough about it to be able to predict what its new business development team will have to do.

In these unstable or new businesses, project leaders will not be able to predict what their teams will have to do more than a few months, even weeks, in advance. Worse still, previous projects, if any exist, will not necessarily be a guide to what has to be done. As a result, a standard project plan, if one existed, would have to be so vague as to be unhelpful in managing everyday operations. Reengineering a project plan to reduce the time needed for development is difficult when no one knows what will have to be done. Teams in such businesses are much more concerned with reacting effectively to change than with reducing the time needed to execute a standard project plan.

On the other hand, companies in new or unstable businesses have far more opportunities to pursue new paths. They are far more likely to have a variety of ideas for new businesses and for new products that do not fit existing molds. It is in these industries that managers worked to increase their companies' diversification capacity. It is here that they looked at how to create and develop a proliferation of ideas. It is in these that they developed management systems capable of handling a wide variety of projects.

To fill in the argument, I will discuss several examples in more detail. The tasks involved in developing a pharmaceutical compound are largely driven by the regulations governing the industry. As a result, the tasks are much the same from one compound to the next. Since these tasks are predictable and are repeated from project to project, the innovation process can be planned and rationalized.

The situation is similar, although not identical, in the automobile industry. Here, the tasks involved in developing a new vehicle are largely driven by the complex but stable architecture of the vehicle. For each new vehicle, a variety of parts must be redesigned and refitted into an overall system. Again, most of the tasks are predictable and repeated from project to project. As a result, the innovation process can be planned in advance and rationalized.

By contrast, companies operating in less stable businesses have different innovation problems, as do companies diversifying into new businesses. Such companies tend to have a variety of projects, few of which are alike. Such companies cannot rationalize innovation tasks as much as companies in more stable industries, since the tasks vary from one project to the next. Rather, they have to develop management systems that can effectively support a variety of projects.

For the sake of convenience, I will put labels on the two types of innovation system. I will call systems designed to focus on one type of project in a stable industry *Focused* systems, and those designed to work in unstable industries, or in companies wanting to diversify, *Flexible* systems. I will call older systems that are not well adapted to either situation *Traditional*.

As mentioned above, I will in this chapter discuss the evolution of eight companies: MGE's Industrial Chemicals, Advanced Materials, Lawn & Garden, and Northern Pharmaceuticals divisions, EurAuto, Eastman Chemical, 3M, and ConsumerCo. In 1985, only one of these eight organizations had a Focused system, and only one a Flexible system. The other six possessed Traditional systems that were not well adapted either to focusing effectively on one product area or to diversifying into new areas.

By 1995 this had changed. Four had Flexible or Advanced Flexible systems, four had Focused or Multi-focus systems, and no Traditional systems had survived. There were evidently pressures on all companies to leave the Traditional system behind and to become either Focused or Flexible. In this chapter, I will look at what these pressures were, and how they forced the innovation systems to change.

Innovation system types

Differences in organization structure, project structure, and communications

The innovation systems of the eight companies differed on many dimensions. Since I cannot cover all of these, I will focus on the three that describe the largest changes made by these organizations in the period 1984–95: (1) *organization structure*, (2) *communications structure*, and (3) *project structure*. Conveniently, these three dimensions cover the most important changes recommended in the innovation literature discussed earlier in this chapter.

In the area of organization structure, many of the eight companies altered the way in which projects fitted into their organizations over the ten years. Several also altered their basic organization structure. In the area of communications, several companies set up new horizontal links between functions, within their laboratories, or between laboratories, projects and business units. Several also improved communications links between their business units, laboratories and projects on the one side, and their customers on the other.

Focusing on these three dimensions, I will describe five types of innovation system that could be observed in the eight companies:

1. *Traditional system.* A central laboratory or design area controls most or all new product development projects. Business units may independently fund projects, without necessarily coordinating their work with other business units. The work the functions do on projects is usually carried out sequentially; that is, one function will start working on a project only when the previous function has finished with it. Project management, if it exists at all, is weak.

2. *Focused system.* A central laboratory or design area still controls most projects, but the functions are now performing their work in parallel. It is no longer necessary for one function to finish its work before another starts. Strong project managers begin to appear.

3. *Multi-focused system.* The central laboratory or design area has been broken up into product-related units to increase the efficiency of the development process. Within each product-related group, the different functions continue to work in parallel. Project management is clearly more powerful than the functional dimension.

4. *Flexible system.* Operating units have control of most projects. Many different types of organizational niche for projects begin to appear. Project management begins to be as powerful as functional management, and different functions work simultaneously.

5. *Advanced Flexible system.* Permanent project teams have begun to appear in some areas. These teams are continuously adapting and extending existing product lines, as well as developing new ones. Project teams, including the technical side, have direct links with customers.

The first type of innovation system, the Traditional one, is neither Focused nor Flexible. Rather, it is the sort of undifferentiated, low-performance system that many companies had before they evolved to become Focused or Flexible. In effect, the Traditional system is the starting point for two evolutionary paths. Some companies that start with Traditional systems become Focused; others become Flexible. Some of the Focused systems move on to become Multi-focused, while some of Flexibles move on to become Advanced Flexibles. (See Figure 7.1 for a graphic depiction of the two paths.) In the rest of this chapter, I will describe each of these five systems, also outlining how companies evolve from one to another.

At several points in the chapter, I will use charts that summarize the typical structures and workflows used in each system. In these charts, projects are represented by a P with a number after it ('P#'), business units with 'BU#', group- or division-level administrations with 'Group,' and functional groups within laboratories by an 'F#'. Hierarchical (structural) relations will be shown by solid lines. Workflow patterns will be shown by dashed lines (see Figures 7.2 and 7.3, below).

The Traditional system

Six companies started with a Traditional system. The main (essentially the only) feature of such a system is a central laboratory or design area that is detached from the company's operating units. Most project work is undertaken within this laboratory. Project work done here is carried out sequentially. That is, different technical functions work in sequence, rather than in parallel, on each project. This type of laboratory organization existed in Industrial Chemicals, Lawn & Garden, Advanced Materials, Northern Pharmaceuticals, EurAuto and Eastman Chemical in the early 1980s. By the early 1990s, it had disappeared.

In these laboratories, there was, at best, a weak project structure. Formal projects existed in some cases, but responsibility for them was passed from one function to the next. The project manager, if she or he existed at all, was a weak figure relative to the function heads. People in the laboratories were rewarded for the quality of functional work performed. There were no rewards for finishing a project quickly, nor for the successful implementation of a project. Functions worked on projects slowly, their priorities and resource allocations being determined by the functional hierarchy.

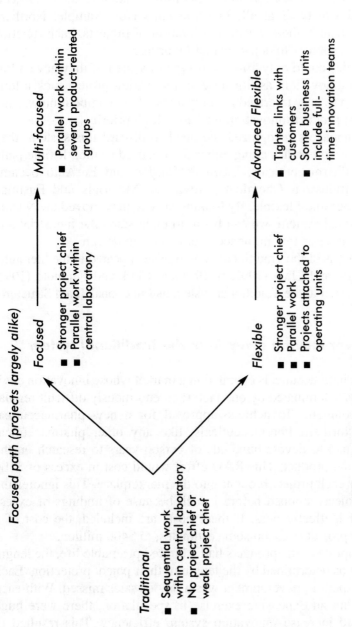

Figure 7.1 Evolution of innovation systems: general sequence

Focused path (projects largely alike)

Multi-focused
- Parallel work within several product-related groups

Focused
- Stronger project chief
- Parallel work within central laboratory

Traditional
- Sequential work within central laboratory
- No project chief or weak project chief

Flexible path (many types of projects)

Flexible
- Stronger project chief
- Parallel work
- Projects attached to operating units

Advanced Flexible
- Tighter links with customers
- Some business units include full-time innovation teams

Projects were passed from one function to another without much communication. Distortion and mis-communication resulted. Projects progressed slowly, if at all. In some units (for example, Northern Pharmaceuticals), there was a proliferation of projects, each function allocating resources to departmental favorites.

Companies could only afford this type of system if they gave a low priority to innovation, as finishing an innovation project took a long time. This was only tolerated in companies where competition was not intense and product innovation was not a high priority.

When managers recognized the need to discard this system, they moved their companies along either the Focused or the Flexible path. Northern Pharmaceuticals, Lawn & Garden and EurAuto became Focused; Industrial Chemicals, Advanced Materials and Eastman Chemical became Flexible. By looking at why they moved away from the Traditional system, we can begin to understand the industrial and strategic pressures that influence overall system design.

Descriptions of the Traditional system have appeared in the literature. Wheelwright and Clark (1992, p. 191) and Clark and Fujimoto (1991, p. 254) referred to the Traditional system as Functional Team Structure.

Reasons for moving away from the Traditional system

Northern Pharmaceuticals operated in a market whose innovation environment was dominated by one factor: an enormously difficult regulatory environment. To achieve approval for a new pharmaceutical product, Northern Pharmaceuticals, like any other pharmaceutical company, had to devote hundreds of person-years to research on the effects of the product. This R&D effort would cost in excess of $100 million for each project brought into the marketplace. This ignores the cost of projects stopped before launch because of findings of excess toxicity or ineffectiveness. If these costs are included, the cost of a successful project rises, on some estimates, to $400 million.

Once approved, the products had a limited profitable life, the length of which was determined by the length of their patent protection. Each extra day spent in development was a day of sales missed. With each project being an expensive exercise in speculation, there were huge pressures to increase innovation system efficiency. This resulted in efforts to speed the development period up and to cull unpromising projects as early as possible.

Three factors put increased pressure on pharmaceutical companies in the 1980s. Markets began to globalize, increasing competition. Governments and third party insurers became increasingly concerned with the cost of medical care, leading to an increased pressure on prices. In addition, generic pharmaceutical products came into increasing use, putting additional pressure on price, particularly for products going off patent.

Northern Pharmaceuticals' managers reacted to these pressures by abandoning their Traditional innovation system. In theory, perhaps, Northern's innovation system could have evolved in either a Focused or a Flexible direction, but the choice of a Focused system was in fact, ordained by the characteristics of the pharmaceutical development process.

First, the high cost of bringing a compound through the regulatory approval process assured that no company would push more than a few compounds through approval at any one time. Thus, the possibilities for diversification were limited.

Second, the repetitive nature of pharmaceutical development process, the fact that each compound went through the same series of regulatory tests, meant that substantial efficiency gains were available to companies who could speed up or rationalize this process. Thus, companies could gain much time and money by pushing for efficiency. However, wide exercise of creativity, if that meant wide diversification within pharmaceuticals, was prohibitively expensive.

Companies that went for efficiency gains did not ignore the issue of diversification. Northern Pharmaceuticals was working on some unusual drugs, but it worked on diversification only at the beginning of the process, at the point where it selected compounds for development. Once a promising compound entered development (this being where most of the money was spent), the goal was efficiency in development, rather than diversification or creativity.

Industrial Chemicals faced pressures similar to those facing Northern Pharmaceuticals. Declines in transportation cost and trade barriers led to the globalization of many of Industrial Chemicals' markets. Increased price pressures in the newly globalized markets forced its managers to move away from a focus on low-price strategies toward increased value added and diversification. Since no one could forecast how new value could best be added, however, Industrial Chemicals was forced to explore a number of new and unfamiliar paths. In developing the capacity to explore these varied paths, the company developed a Flexible system. Since projects in Industrial Chemicals were, in general, far less expensive than those in pharmaceutical companies, the division could afford to explore a number of new and risky areas.

Methods of moving away from the Traditional system

One of the first moves managers made when they moved away from a Traditional system was to set up a formal project structure, complete with formal teams and a project manager. Typically, the project manager was at first considerably less powerful than a functional head. In most cases, project managers became more powerful over time. At the same time, project management methods became more formalized and professionalized.

Managers in some companies saw reason to take projects out of the laboratories and attach them to operating units. At Industrial Chemicals, for example, business units were knowledgeable about their markets and the technologies used to serve them. Projects designed to serve the same markets could benefit from this knowledge by being linked to business units. At the same time, integration with a business unit could make the ultimate implementation of the project easier.

Industrial Chemicals managers later realized that not all projects fitted well within existing business units. Some used the competences of several business units, others exploring areas that were entirely new to the company. These projects were eventually freed not only from laboratory control, but also from business unit control, and were attached directly to division-level management. With this proliferation of places where projects could be located, Industrial Chemicals began moving down the Flexible path. By creating a variety of ways in which to support projects, management increased the variety of projects the system could support and thus its *diversification capacity*.

Managers at other companies, such as Northern Pharmaceuticals, saw no need to move projects out of the R&D laboratories. In effect, the competences needed to create and develop pharmaceutical products existed only in the laboratories and nowhere else. Thus, at Northern Pharmaceuticals, projects remained under the control of the laboratories, but it was obvious that the efficiency of the work performed by the laboratories left something to be desired. It was clear that the old, sequential patterns of work had to be altered. Parallel work patterns were established to replace the much slower sequential work patterns of the Traditional system, which greatly increased the *efficiency* (speed) of the system.

To develop parallel work capability, the functional people had to change their ways. Used to working alone, Northern's functions had different methods of tracking and planning projects. Each function had its own set of milestones. Each function tracked different aspects of a project's development. This was not a problem when the functions worked sequentially on the project, as each function could track whatever it needed while the project was under its control. When it finished working on the project, it could relinquish control and stop tracking the project.

Independent tracking no longer worked when the functions progressed in parallel. Suppose function B cannot begin its work until function A has finished task X. In the parallel work system, function B needs to know when function A will finish task X. Under the old system, however, function A may not have cared when it finished task X. It simply was not important to track when X was done, since X was merely one task in a long sequence of tasks performed by function A.

But once a parallel work system is in place, it becomes very important for function B to know when function A completes task X. For the parallel system to function optimally, function A has to learn what milestones are important to other functions and how to track them. It then needs to develop a system for tracking and reporting these milestones. Function B and all the other functions need to do the same.

At Northern Pharmaceuticals, since the functions had never worked in parallel, they did not have a common vocabulary, even for tracking milestones. Before function A could track task X, it had to figure out what function B meant by 'X', as function A called it something else. In effect, members of each function had to learn much about the vocabularies and concerns of the other functions before they could work together effectively (see Dougherty, 1992, for a more theoretical discussion of this point).

Once the functions had learned each other's vocabulary, they had to determine which milestones were crucial for the system and which they all needed to track. They then had to develop a common tracking system. Much management time went into establishing these new tools.

The Focused system

The most commonly discussed successor to the Traditional system is the Focused system, which was observed in motor vehicles (EurAuto), pharmaceuticals (Northern Pharmaceuticals), and consumer and industrial products businesses operating in heavily regulated areas (for example, Lawn & Garden).

The key distinguishing features of the Focused system can be summarized as follows. Large R&D structures exist in the form of independent laboratories or design areas. As in the Traditional system, the laboratories are hierarchically separate from the company's operating units. But in a Focused laboratory, the development and design functions work in parallel, rather than in sequence. Project managers exist to coordinate projects.

Like Northern Pharmaceuticals, Lawn & Garden and EurAuto moved from Traditional to Focused systems between 1984 and 1995. The reasons for these transformations were much the same, each company wanting to increase the speed and efficiency of its innovation processes.

Part of the innovation literature has focused on the development of Focused systems. In particular, work on the automobile industry (Womack *et al.* 1990; Clark and Fujimoto, 1991), and on pharmaceuticals (Spilker, 1989) has focused on the development or optimum design of such structures. Wheelwright and Clark (1992) discussed in detail how to move from a Traditional system to a Focused system. The Heavyweight Team Structure (Clark and Fujimoto, 1991, p. 254; Wheelwright and Clark, 1992, p. 191) was the typical project team structure in the Focused systems in my sample.

Figure 7.2 compares the Focused system with the Traditional and Multi-focused systems. In the next few paragraphs, I will describe Multi-focused systems and how they developed in greater detail.

The Multi-focused system

After developing a Focused system, Northern Pharmaceuticals' managers continued to look for ways in which to improve their innovation system. Later changes they implemented included the following.

First, management found a way to increase the gains available from specialization within the laboratories. Unified functional groups had

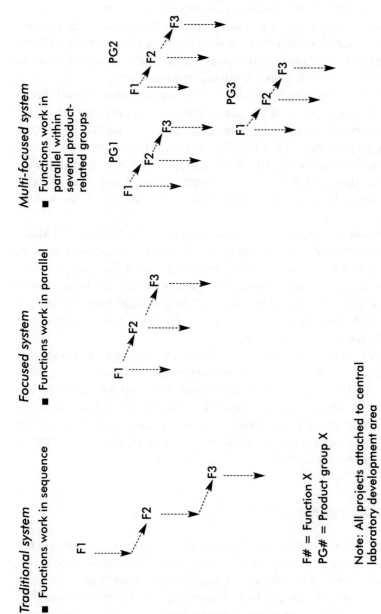

Traditional system
- Functions work in sequence

F1

F2

F3

Focused system
- Functions work in parallel

F1

F2

F3

Multi-focused system
- Functions work in parallel within several product-related groups

PG1

F1

F2

F3

PG2

F1

F2

F3

PG3

F1

F2

F3

F# = Function X
PG# = Product group X

Note: All projects attached to central laboratory development area

Figure 7.2 Evolution of workflows and organization in Focused systems

previously managed functional work for each project, but then management broke the functional administrations up into product-related units. They next grouped these smaller functional units together by product to form product-focused development groups. Each of these smaller, product-focused groups was capable of managing several development projects within a narrow therapeutic area.

Management believed that this new organization would bring greater efficiency gains, these gains arising from two sources. First, specialization within the laboratories would increase the efficiency of task performance. In addition, with multiple projects being carried out, in essence, by the same specialized team, working relationships within and between laboratories would not change after each project. This would mean that less start-up time would be necessary.

The second change involved a reduction in the laboratory chiefs' power. Fundamental research areas, or 'discovery' areas, were seen as the seed bed of ideas for new pharmaceutical products. The power of laboratory heads in these areas was greatly reduced. People lower down were given license to use some of their time to seek and pursue ideas on their own, ideas for which the laboratory head would not necessarily have given approval.

The third change involved a substantial increase in horizontal communication links between laboratory personnel. Northern's R&D head believed that horizontal communication would facilitate the emergence of interesting new ideas. He wanted all of his laboratory scientists to be aware of each other's work. To achieve this, he set up twice-yearly science fairs, as well as a variety of interest groups to facilitate horizontal contact.

The Flexible system

At the end of the section on Traditional systems, I described what happened when a company moved away from this system to go down the Flexible path. As mentioned, managers first sensed a need to make someone responsible for the fate of each project. Then, responding to this need, they set up formal project structures, complete with formal teams and project managers.

I have also mentioned that projects began to move out of the laboratory, and be attached to operating units. Some projects could be attached to a single business unit. These were, in effect, 'business unit-managed projects'; they needed market and technological competences that were available within a single business unit.

Other projects did not readily fit into business units. They needed competences housed in several business units, or they had to develop competences that were not available within the company at all. These projects were attached directly to group-level management, where they could benefit from the support of higher-level managers. They were, in effect, 'independent projects'.

This new system provided several things that its predecessor, the Traditional system, lacked. One was early business unit involvement, the other multiple places within the organization to place projects.

Under the old system, all projects were supervised by the same laboratory people and managed in the same way. In the new system, the laboratory could still control projects, but projects could also be supervised by business unit- or group-level managers. Whichever group was best equipped to manage the project could do so. Each project could be placed within the organizational unit where it best fitted. This approach facilitated the proliferation of a variety of projects.

Figure 7.3 graphically shows the Flexible system and compares it with the other two systems on the Flexible path, the Traditional and Advanced Flexible.

A large part of the innovation literature has focused on business unit-managed and independent projects within Flexible systems. Most of the projects studied by Allen (1977), Katz and Allen (1982), Minnesota Innovation Research Project (Van de Ven *et al.* 1989), Dougherty (1992), and others appear to fall into these categories.

As was noted above, Clark and Fujimoto (1991) and Wheelwright and Clark (1992) provide an overview of the evolution of project structure within Traditional and Focused systems. But their descriptions of internal team structures (as distinguished from overall corporate structures) apply in Flexible systems as well. A business unit-managed or independent project could have, in Clark and Fujimoto's (1991, p. 254) words, an Autonomous Team Structure. Alternatively it could be a Heavyweight Team or (less likely) a Lightweight Team. In the case of a Heavyweight or Lightweight Team, this would mean that the project manager reported to an operating unit, while all other members of the project continued to report to their functional hierarchies.

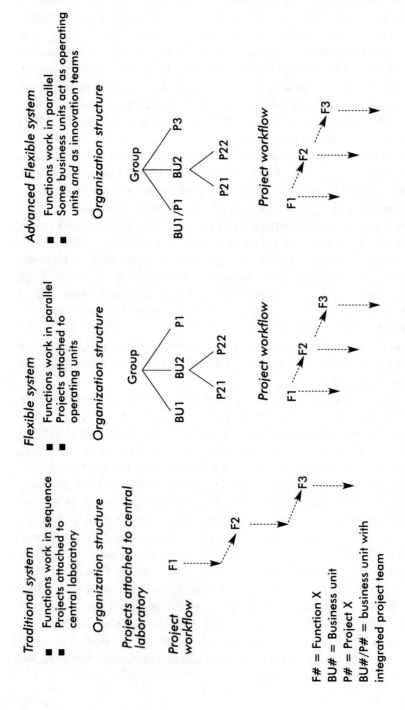

Figure 7.3   Evolution of workflows and organization in Flexible systems

The Advanced Flexible system

By 1994, one company, 3M, had introduced a system that went beyond the Flexible configuration, and three others were moving in that direction. Two key features distinguished the new system towards which they were heading. One is that business units have tighter links with customers: less preoccupied with technology, they invest more energy in understanding their customers. The other distinguishing feature is that some business units in the new system become permanent innovation machines. Such business units devote an unusually large proportion of their resources to innovation.

Business units with Flexible systems were pressured to become more customer focused for several reasons. Managers at Industrial Chemicals thought that they could come up with more ideas for ways in which to serve existing customers if they knew the customers better. They set up multi-functional, cross-business unit teams to manage interfaces with key customers. These new cross-functional links speeded up communication within business units, and facilitated faster innovation. The new cross-business unit links enabled the joint application of multiple technologies to solve customer problems.

At 3M, the establishment of customer-focused business units had occurred by the mid-1980s. But, late in that decade, some business units went one step further. Because of continued client pressure for a fast response on change requests, business units began to accumulate dispersed laboratory resources on their own. One unit I visited set up what I will call a Permanent Project Team. Located in Europe, far from the corporation's central laboratories, it acquired its own laboratory resources in order to serve clients' needs more quickly. The delays caused by the need to communicate with distant laboratories in the United States were eliminated, and the business unit was able to dramatically increase its response capability.

Company configurations

In previous sections, I described two directions in which innovation systems can evolve. In Figure 7.4, I show how each of the eight sample organizations studied evolved over the period 1984–95. The six that began as Traditional systems moved away from this position to become either Focused or Flexible. By 1995, one system was Multi-

Focused path (projects largely alike)

Multi-focused
1984–95

	Traditional	Focused	Multi-focused
ConsumerCo	1984	1990 → 1995	
Northern Pharmaceuticals	1984	→ 1995	
Lawn & Garden	1984	→ 1995	
EurAuto	1984	→ 1995	

Flexible path (many types of projects)

Advanced Flexible
1995

	Traditional	Flexible	Advanced Flexible
3M	1984	→ 1995	
Eastman Chemical	1984	1988 → 1995	
Industrial Chemicals	1984	1992 → 1995	
Advanced Materials	1984	1992 → 1995	

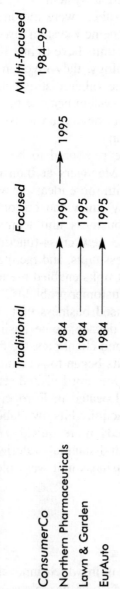
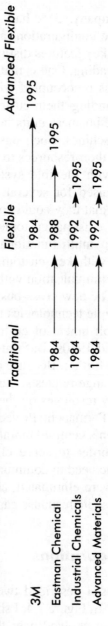

Figure 7.4 Evolution of eight companies: 1984–95

focused, one more was moving in that direction, and two others were Focused. On the Flexible side, one system was an Advanced Flexible, and all three of the others were moving towards the same end. The Traditional system had entirely disappeared.

The reasons for this evolution pattern have been discussed throughout the chapter. Single-product companies in relatively stable industries (for example, pharmaceuticals and automobiles) could foresee the tasks involved in development projects well in advance. This low level of uncertainty, combined with the high level of task consistency across projects, allowed these companies to plan and rationalize development project tasks in an effort to build innovation system efficiency.

In effect, these companies developed innovation systems that were specialized to run one or a few specific types of innovation project (a Focused system). As time went on, these companies developed even more specialized innovation structures (Multi-focused systems) in an effort to increase innovation system efficiency.

By contrast, more diversified companies, particularly those operating in unstable industries or exploring new ones, could not foresee the tasks involved in innovation projects, nor could they expect one project to be similar to the next. The high task uncertainty of individual projects, combined with the dissimilarity between projects, meant that these companies could not plan and rationalize innovation projects to the extent that the companies with Focused systems did.

Given their diverse portfolios of projects, these companies found it more effective to provide a variety of potential slots for projects. As a result, they established Flexible systems. As time went on, companies with Flexible systems tended to proliferate the number of slots they had for projects, while simultaneously establishing closer ties with customers. These closer ties allowed them to increase both idea generation and the speed with which they could turn ideas into projects. The most advanced company in this group, 3M, also began to establish permanent innovation teams in many business units. These steps marked the move from a Flexible system towards an Advanced Flexible system.

Both Focused and Flexible systems can be relatively effective at developing new products, but they are configured quite differently. As Figure 7.5 illustrates, all the various functions in a company with a Focused system are 'focused' on producing one type of product. By contrast, the various functions in a Flexible system may pair up

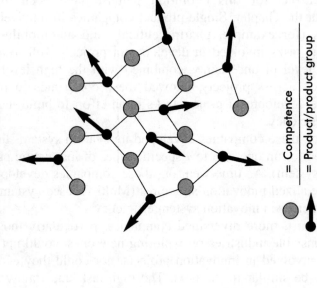

Focused system:
one-product company

Flexible system:
diversified manufacturer

● = Competence
↑ = Product/product group

● = Competence

↑ = Product/product group

Different idea generation methods

Different funding systems

Different development problems

Figure 7.5 Focused innovation system and Flexible innovation system compared

with each other in many different ways. In fact, some of the most important innovation in a Flexible system may occur as a result of new pairings. One example is when a salesperson in a Flexible system discovers a market that can be served with a technology available in a different part of the company. The people who serve the market will have to link up with a new technology group to develop the new product.

The Multi-focused system differs from the Focused system represented in Figure 7.5 in that there are several parallel arrows. The functions of the Focused company divide to form several product development groups, each focusing on one type of product. The Advanced Flexible system differs from the Flexible system of Figure 7.5 in the way in which the competences are organized, and in where they are located. The control of competences is likely to be even more decentralized in an Advanced Flexible than in a Flexible system.

This completes the first half of my discussion of the two common paths of innovation system evolution. In this chapter, I have looked at how the overall structure and workflow of innovation systems in eight companies evolved from 1984 to 1995. In the next, I will take a more detailed look at how the idea generation, funding, and development systems of these companies evolved.

The Evolution of Idea Generation, Funding, and Development Systems

In the last chapter, I looked at how the innovation systems of eight companies evolved from 1984 to 1995. I focused on overall structures and workflows, and identified two evolutionary paths that these companies followed. Single product-line companies in relatively stable industries focused on increasing innovation system efficiency, rationalizing the innovation process and developing Focused systems. Companies that wanted to diversify, particularly those exploring unstable or new industries, focused on increasing diversification capacity. They found ways in which to proliferate the number and types of project they could deal with. In the process, they developed Flexible innovation systems.

In this chapter, I will continue to look at the evolution of companies' innovation systems, but focusing more narrowly on the evolution of idea generation, funding, and development (project management) systems. I will consider how these systems have evolved in typical companies since the mid-1980s. I will look in particular at how company strategy (for example, one-product focus versus diversification) affected the evolution of idea generation, funding, and development systems.

Before beginning the discussion, I will note parenthetically that a one-to-one correspondence between focus strategies and Focused innovation systems does not exist. Focused systems occur in companies with focus strategies, but not all companies with focus strategies can have Focused innovation systems. Some focus-strategy companies may be in industries with high uncertainty, where idea sources and project tasks vary too much for the company to be able to establish a Focused system. These companies are likely to have Flexible innovation systems.

Managing idea generation

Generating ideas in companies with Focused or Flexible innovation systems

Managers in focused companies often localized idea generation in a few areas of the company. Northern Pharmaceuticals chose and screened compounds in its research (discovery) area, the research units being charged with the task of finding new compounds to screen. No one expected the development area to come up with new compounds. Its function was to test the compounds research had initially screened. The compounds themselves did not vary once they entered development.

In automobile companies, idea generation is more widely diffused, as a wide variety of automobile components can change. The overall architecture can, to some degree, change as well. In EurAuto, however, as at Northern Pharmaceutical, there was a tendency to freeze idea generation (that is, to freeze changes in the product) early in the development process and to focus the remaining effort on execution.

As a result of splitting the process, idea generation in focused companies is localized. People in a few functions are expected to come up with ideas for new products or variations in products, whereas others have far more responsibility for execution. While no one is completely out of the idea generation loop, some are far more involved than others.

Managers in diversifying companies did not localize idea generation as much. Product development in new areas, being unpredictable, often took unexpected turns. New ideas and new projects could be spun off existing products. People in operating areas, just as much as those in R&D areas, were expected to come up with new ideas. As a result, no one was outside the idea generation loop. All had the opportunity to contribute.

In both systems, managers working to stimulate idea generation believed that useful ideas resulted from the formation of new connections between existing bodies of knowledge. They commonly referred to this as 'cross-fertilization'. A variety of academics (Utterback, 1971; Simon, 1985; Cohen and Levinthal, 1990; Dougherty, 1992) conceptualize idea generation in the same way.

Cohen and Levinthal (1990) summarize the argument as follows:

diverse knowledge structures coexisting in the same mind elicit the sort of learning and problem solving that yields innovation. Assuming a sufficient level of knowledge overlap to ensure effective communication, interactions across individuals who each possess diverse and different knowledge structures will augment the organization's capacity for making novel linkages and associations – innovating – beyond what one individual can achieve. (p. 133)

This conception of idea generation is graphically modeled in Figure 8.1. M refers to bases of market knowledge, held by customers themselves, or by people in direct contact with them. T refers to bases of technical knowledge, held by technical people inside and outside the company. The solid and dotted lines represent links or potential links between competences. The management issues important to managing idea generation (which will be discussed below) are summarized at the bottom of the chart.

The left-hand side of Figure 8.1 represents idea generation in a Flexible system. Links can occur between technical and market-linked units in all parts of the company. On the right, idea generation in a Focused system is represented. Here, most idea generation occurs through new technical links in the research area of the company. The downstream development areas in the Focused system are mainly concerned with the efficient development of ideas generated in the research area.

With this view of idea generation, managers in both focused and diversifying systems use two types of tool to improve innovation performance. First, they build useful bodies of knowledge. Second, they make sure that links between different bodies of knowledge are made. I will discuss each of these types of tool in the next sections. (See Figure 8.2 for a summary of the tools used.)

Having the right competences

A company's innovation performance is partly a result of its mix of competences. It may have a rich mix of competences, pregnant with many possibilities for new combinations, or a poor or limited mix, with few possibilities for interesting, new developments. Recognizing this, managers sometimes make efforts to bring new competences into their

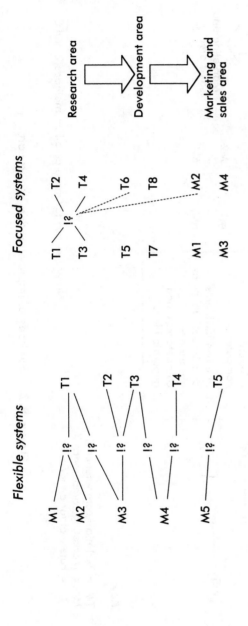

Flexible systems

New, often unexpected links between technical
and market competences lead to new ideas

Focused systems

Targeted search for new ideas occurs upstream,
feeds downstream development

Key:

T# = Technical competence X
M# = Marketing competence X
!? = Potential for an idea

Figure 8.1 Types of idea generation system

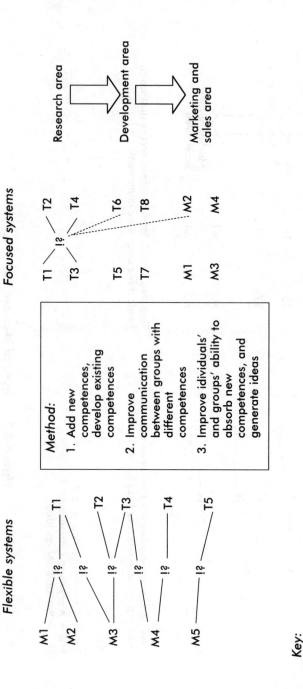

Figure 8.2 Methods of improving idea generation

companies. They can do this top down, or they can allow it to be done from the bottom up. The top-down method will be described first.

At MGE and elsewhere, top managers sometimes identified specific competences that the company needed to learn in order to improve or maintain its competitive position. Northern Pharmaceuticals, for example, acquired a biotechnology capability to supplement its traditional pharmaceutical skills. In effect, management made a speculative bet that biotechnology would be useful in the development of new pharmaceutical compounds. Eastman Chemical went as far as to carry out a thorough inventory of its skills and to identify areas that needed to be supplemented with new expertise. In both companies, these resulted in top-directed investments in new competences.

In some companies, managers also allowed people at lower levels to invest in new competences – the bottom-up solution. By allowing the *ad hoc* importation of new competences, managers allow their employees to take advantage of opportunities that top management have not foreseen. They give people lower down the opportunity to act on opportunities not noticed by those at the top.

At Lawn & Garden, a research scientist named Bill Marshall came up with an idea for a new project. This idea arose because Marshall had invested heavily, without company direction or approval, in new competences (the full Lawn & Garden case is recounted in Christiansen, 1997). Looking at this experience and similar ones elsewhere, some MGE units loosened the rules for their laboratory scientists in order to allow them a little more flexibility to invest in new competences. 3M and Eastman Chemical routinely allow people to make such investments, if they wish. Many companies encourage their technical people to maintain contacts with outside scientists in order to keep abreast of potentially relevant technologies.

Assuring that new links are made

All companies of any size contain multiple bodies of knowledge (competences). Additional competences exist within the companies' environments. Managers used five types of intervention to increase the linkages between different competences.

By 1995, most companies had (1) set up cross-functional units and work groups, which, in effect, involved permanent links between different competences bases. Several of the organizations also (2) set up permanent communications links, such as liaison people (or committees), trade fairs, or seminars of technical specialists. 3M, a famous diversifier, was particularly good at (3) facilitating the *ad hoc* creation of new communication links, when people on the ground sensed potential new opportunities.

ConsumerCo (4) practiced rotation, regularly moving people across functional, geographic and business unit boundaries to create new mixes of competence within each unit. Finally, ConsumerCo regularly attempted (5) to directly stimulate people's creativity. It used brainstorming sessions, off-site seminars and creativity training seminars to encourage people to rethink and recombine the knowledge they already had.

Managing project funding

A summary model: four types of funding system

Managers in both focused and diversifying companies were concerned with two key dimensions of funding systems. First was their ability to make appropriate decisions, that is, how well they selected projects that fitted customer need, while minimizing waste. Second, they were concerned with their ability to make decisions quickly. Focused companies were primarily concerned with making the right decisions. Diversifying companies also emphasized speed in decision making.

In 1984, most of the eight companies had undifferentiated funding systems. They were not particularly well adapted for either a focused or a diversifying company. By 1995, however, most focused companies had much more centralized funding systems. Diversifying companies, meanwhile, had dispersed their resource allocation responsibility, consistent with their desire to diversify their product offerings.

The key differences between funding systems are summarised in Figure 8.3. The four zones in this figure represent four types of funding system. The 'Fs' represent funding sources, the 'Ps' potential projects needing money, and the 'Hs' hierarchical levels not authorized to make funding decisions. The solid lines are normal hierarchical links, while the dotted ones link projects with funding sources.

The first zone on the left represents a non-innovative organization, the second a somewhat more innovative one. The third chart area

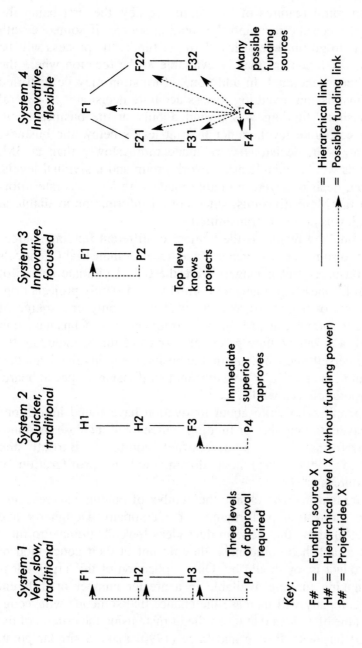

Figure 8.3 Types of funding systems

Key:

F# = Funding source X
H# = Hierarchical level X (without funding power)
P# = Project idea X

——— = Hierarchical link
·······▶ = Possible funding link

System 1
Very slow, traditional

F1 ——— H2 ——— H3 ——— P4

Three levels of approval required

System 2
Quicker, traditional

H1 ——— H2 ——— F3 ——— P4

Immediate superior approves

System 3
Innovative, focused

F1 ——— P2

Top level knows projects

System 4
Innovative, flexible

F1
F21   F22
F31   F32
F4 ——— P4

Many possible funding sources

describes an innovative (state-of-the-art) system in a focused company, while the fourth exemplifies an innovative (state-of-the-art) system in a diversifying company.

Two structural features of the charts are key, the first being the distance between the idea and the funding source. If someone with an idea has to go up several levels to get funds, the process will be slower than if funds are readily available at the location where the idea has been generated. In addition, information may be distorted during transmission, resulting in less accurate decisions. At several MGE divisions, funding was provided only at the business unit, group, or corporate level, rather than at levels below the business unit. As a result, decisions were made more slowly than at 3M, where funds were available at the work group and individual levels. In addition, decisions were probably made with less accurate information at the MGE divisions, since not all information available at the lower levels could be transmitted.

The second key feature is the number of different funding sources accessible to someone who generates an idea. In Industrial Chemicals in 1985, business unit managers were the only legitimate source of funding. A business unit manager normally funded only projects originating in his own unit, so any given idea had only one source of funding. By contrast, at 3M, an idea originating in a business unit could have a dozen or more potential sources of funds, including the individual herself, the work group, the business unit involved, another business unit, the particular division, another division, a special board, or the corporation as a whole.

Other people who write about innovation have found indications that increasing the number of funding sources will increase the innovation performance of a diversified company. Bartlett and Mohammed (1994, 1995) have documented the proliferation of funding sources at 3M.

There are reasons why raising the number of funding sources stimulates the innovation performance of a company. Dougherty and Heller (1994) argue that new product ideas look illegitimate to most people in established companies: they do not fit their conception of what a product is, or should be. One implication of this argument is that by making funding available in a greater number of different places, a company will increase the chance that someone will recognize the value of an idea that looks illegitimate using the criteria of the established business. Pearce and Page (1990) make a similar point.

They argue that centralized, rationalized funding systems rarely support radically innovative ideas. They recommend that a number of individuals be empowered to support such ideas, regardless of their fit with any preordained criteria (in effect encouraging a proliferation of funding sources, from one to many).

There is a chronological progression in Figure 8.3. A company with a system such as system 1 could move forwards by moving towards system 2 if it has small projects. It could move toward system 3 if its projects are large enough that top management involvement is deemed essential (as seen, for example, with the typical pharmaceutical company). Diversified companies with system 2 could move toward system 4 as they increased the number of funding sources available to any potential project.

Tools used to improve funding systems

Managers can use five types of intervention in order to improve the performance of their funding systems. They can (1) shorten the communications paths between idea sources and funding sources. This has the effect of speeding decisions and reducing information distortion (thus increasing decision quality). In addition, they can (2) alter who makes funding decisions. By broadening functional representation on funding boards, Lawn & Garden assured that a wider variety of viewpoints would be heard. Companies could also (3) change the types of information used in the decision, typically broadening the range of information used. Managers of diversifying (Flexible) systems can (4a) increase the number of funding sources, which will allow a wider variety of projects to be funded. Managers of Focused systems may, by contrast, want (4b) to eliminate certain funding sources to ensure that product development will be focused on the one or two areas selected by senior management. Finally, managers can (5) change the incentives of those who make the funding decisions. Typically, they give people incentives to fund more risky, long-term investments. (See Figure 8.4 for a summary of methods of improving funding.)

**One funding
source**

F1

P2

Method:

1. Shorten communications
   paths; eliminate levels

2. Change who makes
   funding decisions (more expertise)

3. Change the types of information
   used in the funding decision

4. Increase (or decrease) the
   number of funding sources

5. Change the incentives of the
   decision makers

**Many possible
funding sources**

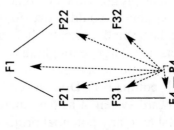

F22

F32

F1

F21

F31

F4 — P4

Key:

F# = Funding source X
H# = Hierarchical level X (without funding power)
P# = Project idea X

——————— = Hierarchical link
- - - - - ▶ = Possible funding link

Figure 8.4   Improving funding systems

Managing development

Distinguishing between different project types

Two of the projects I observed at MGE (at Northern Pharmaceuticals, and at Lawn & Garden) were organized quite tightly. Work plans were set up several years in advance, and people's task assignments were clear. The project manager was concerned with finishing the project on time (or more quickly), and on budget (or more cheaply). In these projects, most potential pitfalls could be foreseen and prepared for. The main concern was completing the project on time and within budget.

The other two projects (CR and Safety Materials) were quite different. In these, project organizations were relatively loose. Unexpected events could cause work plans to change overnight, and people's task assignments could alter just as quickly. The project manager's main concern was to develop a product or business system that worked. What it would take to do that could not be fully foreseen. As a result, his main job was to react effectively to unexpected events, and to move the project toward completion despite the unexpected obstacles that arose. Budget and speed were important, but could not be planned in advance in the way in which they could in the more predictable projects.

Not surprisingly, the tightly organized projects were found in divisions with focus strategies and Focused innovation systems. Here, uncertainty was relatively low, and project tasks could be foreseen, tightly organized, and rationalized. The loosely organized projects were found in divisions with diversifying strategies and Flexible innovation systems. Uncertainty was relatively high: work plans sometimes needed to be changed overnight. As a result, reacting effectively to the unexpected was more important than sticking rigidly to a prearranged plan.

Project management literature does not always recognize that there are two distinct types of project. Many writers (for example Lock, 1977; Archibald, 1992; Randolph and Posner, 1992) propose tools that, they say, can be used to improve the management of all projects. The careful identification and rationalization of tasks, the careful planning and sequencing of tasks, and the identification and shortening of the critical path are all proposed as management methods applicable to all projects.

This is doubtless to some degree correct. However, the extent to which tasks can be foreseen and rationalized varies considerably across projects. It is hard to foresee what the critical path will be if you do not even know what you will have to do in six months. Rather than finding the critical path, the issue in a project with high uncertainty is to track the sources of uncertainty and, if possible, reduce them.

Projects involving the development of a new or follow-on product in an existing, stable industry will usually involve low uncertainty. Projects involving the development of an entirely new business, or a new product in an unstable industry, are likely to involve high uncertainty.

Focused systems exist mainly in existing, relatively stable industries. They are, by definition, designed to handle low-uncertainty projects (those in which the tasks can be foreseen well in advance). Managers in Focused systems must, as a result, know how to manage low-uncertainty projects. Flexible systems involve the exploitation of a variety of opportunities, some of which may involve the development of new businesses or new products in unstable businesses. Thus, managers in Flexible systems must know how to manage high-uncertainty projects. Some opportunities in Flexible systems may, however, involve repetitive development of follow-on products, or of minor variations in existing products. So managers in Flexible systems must also know how to manage low-uncertainty projects.

Muzyka (1989) and Eisenhardt and Tabrizi (1995) argued that high-uncertainty projects must be managed differently from low-uncertainty ones. In my interviews, the methods that managers reported using did indeed vary depending on whether they were dealing with low- or high-uncertainty projects. The differences were broadly consistent with those identified by Muzyka (1989) and Eisenhardt and Tabrizi (1995).

Managing low-uncertainty projects

A low-uncertainty project involves a number of tasks, each known in advance, which must be performed in order to reach a predetermined goal. The project can be planned in advance and then executed largely as planned. Figure 8.5 presents a very simple example of such a project graphically. All tasks, as well as their interrelationships, are known in advance and can be plotted on a flow chart, such as the one in Figure 8.5.

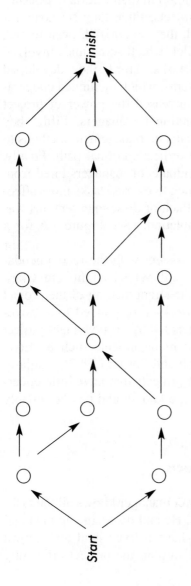

Start

Finish

Key:

○ = Event (for example, the end of a key task)

⟶ = Task

All tasks can be foreseen and planned in advance
Rationalization of tasks and project plan possible
Key issues:
  Eliminating unnecessary tasks, combining tasks
  Finding critical path
  Reducing time to complete process

Figure 8.5   A low-uncertainty project

At Northern Pharmaceuticals and EurAuto, general managers performed six different types of intervention in their efforts to improve the management of low-uncertainty projects. First, they set goals for the overall time to completion. Second, they authorized, even forced, the functions to perform tasks in parallel, which sometimes involved combining or eliminating duplicated tasks. Third, they developed tools, such as joint project tracking systems, which facilitated cooperation between functions. Fourth, they increased the power of project managers compared with that of functional managers. Fifth, they trained project managers and project teams in management methods to help them to identify and reduce each project's critical path. Finally, they brought in outsiders, such as consultants or managers hired from rival companies, to identify ways in which to overlap tasks more effectively and to speed their performance. Each of these interventions was focused on reducing the time to completion. (See Figure 8.6 for a summary of these methods.)

These interventions were largely consistent with the recommendations of Clark and Fujimoto (1991) and Wheelwright and Clark (1992). In Clark and Fujimoto terms, the strengthening of the project manager and the increase in parallel work corresponded to a movement from Traditional projects to projects led by Heavyweight project managers. Other literature on project management, such as Lock (1977), Archibald (1992), and Randolph and Posner (1992), similarly deals with the efficient management of projects that have little uncertainty, that is, of projects whose tasks are known and can be reliably planned in advance.

Managing high-uncertainty projects

In the low-uncertainty project, the project manager knows all the tasks necessary to reach the goal in advance. He and his team can plan and rationalize their activities. Since they have a fixed goal and known tasks to reach it, their main issues are to plan the project efficiently and perform the tasks effectively.

High-uncertainty projects are different. In these, the project team knows the goal in advance, but they do not know what tasks will be necessary to reach it. In addition, they may have to choose between several different paths, either one of which may, or may not take them to the goal. There may be several technical configurations to choose

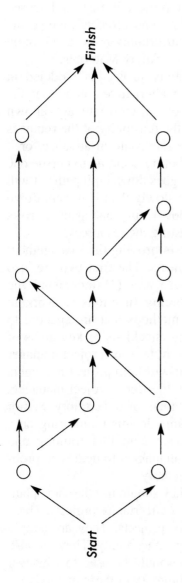

Methods:

1. Set goals for time to completion
2. Force functions to perform tasks in parallel (including combining or eliminating duplicated tasks)
3. Develop tools, such as joint project tracking systems, to facilitate cooperation
4. Increase the power of project managers
5. Train project managers and team members in methods to reduce critical paths
6. Bring in outsiders to help find ways of reducing critical paths; manage projects more effectively

Figure 8.6 Methods of improving the management of low-uncertainty projects

from (see, for example, Garud and Van de Ven, 1992), or several potential customer groups that the product could be designed to serve.

These choices may be made under considerable uncertainty. The team may have no way of knowing which path is best, or even whether either is feasible. This type of project is rare in Focused systems. But in Flexible systems, where some projects involve the creation of whole new businesses, high-uncertainty projects are more common, as seen for example with CR and Safety Materials.

A simple example of a high-uncertainty project is modeled in Figure 8.7. In this figure, there are two alternative routes that the project team can take. Not all tasks on either route are known (symbolized by dotted-line arrows), and the feasibility of the routes is unknown. The project team may choose one route in advance, or it may proceed part way down both routes before deciding to pursue one (and only one) to completion. If the team goes down both paths, it will spend more resources and/or move more slowly than if it went down only one path. However, if it moves down only one path, it risks choosing the wrong path and entirely wasting the resources.

Managers have four main methods of improving the management and supervision of high-uncertainty projects. The first two are also used for low-uncertainty projects. These are: (1) increasing the power of project managers, and (2) forcing functions to work in parallel. In addition, there are two key methods that are specific to high-uncertainty projects: (3) developing checklists of key areas of potential uncertainty, and (4) developing systems of project manager training, mentoring, and supervision that will help project managers and their teams to deal with uncertainty. In effect, project managers can be trained to identify and monitor areas of uncertainty. Senior managers should ensure that project teams do this monitoring on a continuous basis. They should also make sure that training and supervision are designed to help project managers to deal with problems and opportunities that arise unexpectedly.

In addition, *to the extent possible*, (5) they should use the same planning and rationalization tools used for low-uncertainty projects. These tools are not invalid for high-uncertainty projects. They are simply more difficult to use in a situation of high uncertainty. They are also prone to having a lower payoff, but they should be used to whatever extent is possible. (See Figure 8.8 for a summary of these methods.)

Of the four diversifying companies in my sample, 3M was most attuned to the management of high-uncertainty projects. 3M's training

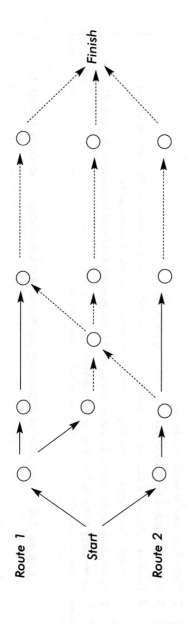

Route 1

Start

Route 2

Finish

Several possible routes to the goal may be visible
Not all tasks can be foreseen on any route
Not clear which route, if any, will work
Key issues:
  Define and monitor sources of uncertainty
  Resolve uncertainty as early as possible
  May need to follow several routes to see which
  works best

Key:

○ = Event (for example, the end of a key task)

→ = Known task with foreseeable time frame

┈┈▸ = Unknown area: not clear how to do task
        and/or how long it will take

Figure 8.7   A high-uncertainty project

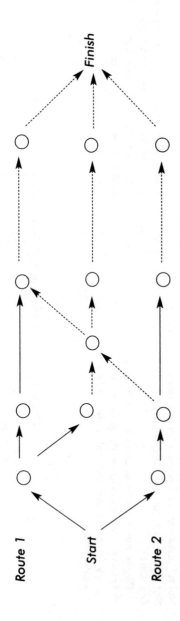

Route 1

Start

Route 2

Finish

Methods:

1. Increase the power of project managers
2. Force functions to work in parallel
3. Develop checklists of key areas of potential uncertainty
4. Develop systems of project manager training, mentoring, and supervision that will help project managers and teams to identify, monitor, and react to areas of uncertainty
5. In addition, to the extent possible, set goals for completion time and rationalize tasks, as for low-uncertainty projects (see Figure 8.6 above)

Figure 8.8 Methods of improving the management of high-uncertainty projects

and supervision systems helped people to learn to deal with uncertainty effectively. Eastman Chemical had also made great progress in orienting its training and supervision systems in this direction. Industrial Chemicals and Advanced Materials were in a more ambiguous situation. MGE managers had not yet fully grasped the difference between low- and high-uncertainty projects.

Part of the problem at MGE was that some senior managers wanted all projects to be run like low-uncertainty projects. They wanted all project teams to produce detailed plans, showing how and when they would bring their project to completion, but this was not successful. Project teams could produce detailed plans, if required to, but the plans would have to be rewritten a few months later when something unexpected came up.

In general, efforts to manage high-uncertainty projects as if they were low-uncertainty projects did not work well. Setting goals for overall time to completion could put pressure on the project team. But when the team could not foresee what would have to be done to bring the project to completion, such goals had little meaning.

In a low-uncertainty project, if a team missed a reasonable goal, it was almost certainly the team's fault. But, in a high-uncertainty project, it was difficult to see in advance what goal would be realistic. Punishing a team for missing a goal, when the goal was missed for reasons beyond the team's control, would be viewed by the team as unjust.

Similarly, while functions should work in parallel in a high-uncertainty project, the kind of reengineering of project plans that occurs in automobiles and pharmaceuticals is difficult in high-uncertainty areas. Attempts to identify and reduce the critical path may come to naught when tasks take far more (or far less) time than anticipated, or when unforeseen but urgent tasks emerge. Unpredictable task length is less of a problem in a low-uncertainty project. Wholly unforeseen but urgent tasks are also rare.

Summary of system evolution

In the last two chapters, I have analyzed how the innovation systems of eight companies evolved over ten years. I also looked at what the managers of these companies did to improve their innovation systems. In the last chapter, the evolution of structures and workflows was traced, showing that the organizations' innovation systems developed in either of two directions: toward increased specialization and a focus on one type of innovation (a Focused system), or towards a Flexible system capable of handling a wider variety of innovations. I argued that the differences were related to the industry in which the company was competing and the strategy being pursued in that industry. Generally speaking, companies pursuing focus strategies in relatively stable industries developed Focused systems, whereas companies pursuing diversification strategies developed Flexible systems.

In this chapter, I explored the implications of company strategy on the way in which the company managed idea generation, funding, and development. Improving idea generation in all systems involved increasing communication links between different competence groups. But in Focused systems, idea generation was more localized. Different research functions, for example, would be linked more extensively in an effort to improve research productivity. Downstream development and operating units focused on the execution of ideas generated in research areas. Idea generation in Flexible systems tended to be more diffuse. Anyone in any function was treated as a potential idea source. Increasing idea generation involved increasing and tightening links all across the company.

Funding systems also varied. Focused funding systems were highly centralized. In the cases of companies with high-cost projects, decision making was typically centralized near the top of the company or division. In companies with Flexible innovation systems, funding systems were more decentralized, any idea having multiple potential funding sources. In either type of system, shortening communications paths and changing the type of information used in decisions were additional methods of improving performance.

Development systems varied depending on their mix of low- and high-uncertainty projects. Focused systems managed low-uncertainty projects. Improving the management of these projects involved developing a parallel work capability, as well as other methods of increasing project speed. Flexible systems managed mostly high-uncertainty projects. Improving the management of these projects involved training and supervising project managers in ways that helped them to deal with high uncertainty.

The Impact of Industry and Strategy on Innovation System Design

9

Not all companies have the same kind of innovation system, nor should they. Very effective innovators, such as 3M and ConsumerCo, have very different innovation systems. Why? In part because their industries and strategies require them to do different things when they innovate.

So how do industry and strategy affect the configuration of an innovation system? I have already given part of the answer. In my discussion of development methods, I noted that some projects face much higher levels of uncertainty than others. In the case of low-uncertainty projects, such as those in the automobile industry, most of the tasks that will need to be done can be foreseen at the beginning of the project. The vast majority of the work to be carried out during these projects can, as a result, be planned in advance, and the plans can be rationalized. For high-uncertainty projects, this is not the case. The tasks that will need to be completed cannot be foreseen more than a few months, or even weeks, in advance. For these projects, long-term planning is much less useful.

In some industries, most projects involve low uncertainty. Projects may even be very similar one to another, just as automobile design projects resemble each other. In these industries, innovation systems will feature much planning and rationalization. There may be a standard project plan that nearly all projects use. The plan will very likely have been reengineered several times in the 1990s, as the company tried to bring new products into the market more and more quickly. The automobile and pharmaceutical industries in particular have followed this pattern.

In other industries, nearly all projects involve high uncertainty. Or the projects may just be different from one to the next. At 3M, there is no standard project plan. Rather, each project is new. In companies in these industries, there will be no standard project plan. Project leaders will instead be trained how to recognize and deal with important unexpected events.

But why, you might ask, do companies have projects that differ so much? There are two answers to this. One is that companies' industries differ. The other is that companies' strategies differ. I will spend the bulk of this chapter discussing how industries differ. At the end of the chapter, I will briefly explore how companies' strategic choices affect their innovation systems.

Industry differences

In a search for differences between companies' innovation systems, I carefully analyzed the innovation systems of eight companies in five industries: chemicals, pharmaceuticals, consumer packaged goods, automobiles, and diversified industrial products. I also, more briefly, looked at the innovation systems of companies in computers, consumer electronics, telecommunications equipment, financial

I.	How ideas and opportunities differ
	1. Scarcity or abundance of new ideas
	2. Cost of ideas relative to company resources
	3. Complex or simple products
	4. Availability of diversification opportunities
II.	**How companies' environments differ**
	5. Extent of competitive pressure
	6. Length of product life
	7. Extent of regulation
III.	**The stability and predictability of companies' environments**
	8. Level of uncertainty
	9. Frequency of radical transformation

Figure 9.1   Industry differences listed

services, cement manufacture, optics, food processing, and industrial machinery. Variations among these thirteen industries were quite substantial. At least nine different factors, which I have classified into three groups, drove differences in their innovation systems.

Four of the factors relate to the differences in the ideas or opportunities that companies in these industries typically encounter. Three relate to features of the companies' environments, and the last two to the stability or predictability of the companies' environments (see Figure 9.1 for a summary).

How ideas and opportunities differ

The opportunities available to companies in different industries vary across a number of interesting dimensions. First, they may be scarce or abundant. Second, they may be inexpensive relative to the resources of the average company, or they may be very expensive. Third, they may involve very complex products, processes or services, or very simple ones. Fourth, they may, in almost all cases, relate closely to existing businesses, or they may frequently involve the creation of new businesses. I will discuss each of these dimensions in turn (Table 9.1).

Table 9.1   How ideas and opportunities vary

Dimension of variation	Impact
Scarcity or abundance of new ideas	■ Affects methods of searching for ideas (see also joint effects with cost, Figure 9.3)
Cost of ideas relative to company resources	■ Affects generosity of funding, and willingness to explore new areas (see also joint effects with scarcity/ abundance, Figure 9.3)
Complex or simple products	■ Complex product architecture may force new development projects to revisit each aspect of architecture, leading to a large, complex, but relatively predictable project
Availability of diversification opportunities	■ To create new businesses, organization, communication, funding, and incentive systems must all be appropriately adapted (see text)

1. Scarcity or abundance of new ideas

2. Cost of ideas relative to company resources

These two dimensions need to be discussed at the same time, as they interact with each other, in effect forming a two-by-two matrix (see Figure 9.2). Along the scarcity/abundance dimension, ideas can be either few or numerous. Along the cost dimension, the ideas on one end are cheap relative to the company's resources. In this case, no individual project would cost enough that its failure would threaten the health of the company. At the other end of the cost dimension, projects are very expensive, such that the failure of any one project could cause serious damage to the company's health. When we cross these two dimensions, we come up with the four cells of a two-by-two matrix. Ideas can be few and cheap, numerous and cheap, numerous and expensive, or few and expensive. I will discuss each of these cells in turn.

Ideas are few and cheap. Cement, as a product, has hardly changed in the past hundred years. R&D budgets are low in the industry, and ideas for how to improve the product do not come along very often. In addition, when they do, they are not that costly to pursue, being well within the resources of the average international company. As a result, the cement business falls into the *few/cheap* quadrant of the matrix.

When companies in this quadrant want to develop better products, they need to carry out directed searches for new ideas. They may target technical areas where they think some ways may be found to improve the product. Or they may identify niches where customers will value customized products. Alternatively, some companies in this kind of industry may give up on the idea of product innovation and focus instead on process improvement. Various international cement companies have pursued each of these options.

Companies in commodity chemicals and other commodity businesses are often found in this quadrant. Few ideas come along, and when they do, they are relatively cheap to pursue. Such companies typically have low R&D budgets, and relatively stable product lines, and they are not known as outstanding innovators.

Ideas are numerous and cheap. Diversified manufacturers who master a number of related technologies often find themselves in this quadrant, particularly if the relevant technologies are useful in a number of different markets. 3M is the classic case of a company in this quadrant. 3M excels in a number of technologies, chiefly in the

	Numerous and cheap Pursue many ideas; diversify (diverse industrial and consumer products businesses)	Numerous and expensive Focus on area with clear competitive advantage (pharmaceuticals)
Few ideas	Few and cheap Directed search for new ideas (cement, commodity chemicals)	Few and expensive Join the race to get there first with the best (memory chips, consumer electronics)

Many ideas

Abundance of ideas

Low   High

Cost relative to resources

Figure 9.2 Scarcity of ideas and cost of investigating them

areas of materials and coatings. It has applied these technologies to numerous markets. There appears to be no end in sight for the number of additional new products that 3M can develop, building on these core technologies. ConsumerCo also falls into this quadrant, although its technologies are more tightly focused around a few consumer product specialties.

Companies in this quadrant typically have innovation systems that encourage the generation of a large number of ideas. They possess funding systems that allow people to pursue a large proportion of the ideas with little review. They let them go far enough to see whether their ideas are winners. Thus, they need effective means of identifying winners, through market tests or actual entry into the market. Successful companies in this quadrant (for example, 3M, ConsumerCo, and Rubbermaid) often acquire reputations as effective innovators.

Ideas are numerous and expensive. The pharmaceutical industry today lies in this quadrant. It was less securely in this quadrant ten years ago, when some companies had trouble finding enough promising ideas to pursue. But with the advances that have occurred in chemistry over the past ten years, there has been an explosion of techniques for creating new pharmaceutical products. As a result, pharmaceutical companies have a wide array of ideas to choose from.

Pursuing any one option, however, costs a lot. Taking a compound through all the testing required by customers and regulators costs well in excess of $100 million. As a result, pharmaceutical companies cannot afford to 'try everything to see what works', in the way a company such as 3M can. They have to choose carefully among the potential options and pursue those which show the greatest promise of success.

Companies in this quadrant have quite different funding systems from those in the *numerous/cheap* quadrant. While 3M gives quite junior people the power to fund projects, high-level corporate boards make such decisions in pharmaceutical companies. While 3M has many sources of funds, there is usually in pharmaceutical companies a single central board that decides which projects will be funded.

The logic behind these differences is easy to explain. Companies in the *numerous/cheap* quadrant can afford to let junior people make decisions about funding projects because the projects are cheap. They allow many different people to make funding decisions since (a) they can afford it (because projects are cheap), and (b) they want to encourage variation. Letting different people fund projects tends to encourage variation, since they will use different criteria to make their choices.

Companies in the *numerous/expensive* quadrant cannot afford to fund a large number of projects because they are too expensive, so they must choose the projects they do fund very carefully. As a result, a single, high-level board usually makes the choice. Since each project represents a major investment of corporate resources, the board does not usually encourage variation. Rather, it uses a single set of criteria, uniformly applied across all projects, to determine which projects are most likely to turn out to be profitable for the company.

Companies in the *numerous/expensive* quadrant need to have three things for their funding systems to work effectively. First, they need communications systems that bring good information on opportunities to a high-level funding committee quickly. Second, they need good information on market interest and on competitor investments and capabilities in order to make judgements on the likely profitability of each investment. Third, they need clear and widely accepted criteria for choosing projects.

Ideas are few and expensive. Companies in this quadrant have little trouble choosing which ideas to invest in, since there are few attractive ideas on the table. However, if competitors have the same ideas (as they often do), all the competing companies may enter a race to be first in the market with a new product, or with an improved version of an existing product.

Examples of this can be found in the electronics business, the best example perhaps being that of memory chips. USComputers builds such chips. For the past thirty years, the goal in this business has been the same: a larger, faster, cheaper (per unit memory) chip. All the players in this industry have pursued this goal, and the winners, consistently, have been those who first develop the next-generation chip. The goal for the next round – to develop another larger, faster chip – is known to everybody, companies racing each other to achieve this first.

The biggest problem for companies in this quadrant is usually the speed of development. Companies will focus and organize their efforts to get the product out the door as quickly as possible. Efforts at improving the product innovation process usually revolve around cutting the time of development.

It is in this type of market that Andy Grove's famous statement, 'Only the paranoid survive,' (Grove, 1996) is most true. People in companies in the *numerous/cheap* quadrant are, in my experience, rarely 'paranoid'. They do not need to be. When people at 3M are inventing a new business, there is generally no threatening competitor on the horizon to fear. Competitors will come, if the idea succeeds, but often there is no one else working on the idea until after 3M enters the market.

By contrast, when 3Mers or others are in a competitive business and are running neck and neck with their competitors to develop the next generation of product technology (that is, when they are in a race), they start showing signs of fear. Companies in electronics, where a few well-known ideas are pursued by many competitors, also have reason to be paranoid.

3. Complex or simple products

Complex products. Companies producing complex assembled products, such as automobiles, major appliances, airplanes, or mainframe computers, usually have innovation systems that look quite different from those of companies that make simpler products. Complex assembled products have hundreds, if not thousands, of parts, these parts usually being organized into subassemblies. The process of redesigning the parts, the subassemblies, and the entire product takes a long time. To make things more complicated, there are often many complex interactions between the parts. For the design to come together quickly and effectively, the whole process must be planned carefully and executed according to plan.

New technologies may result in design changes for a few parts or several modules, but they rarely result in radical transformations of the product as a whole. Developments in electronics result in changes in the automobile's electronic systems, but automobile bodies, chassis, and engines (save for the electronic parts) change only at the margins. Developments in materials technology may result in changes in the materials used for certain parts, but the functions of the parts remain the same.

As a result of this stability in overall design, one development project may look much like the next. At an automobile company, for example, each new vehicle development team must look at the design of the body, the chassis, the engine, the drive train, and all their subassemblies and parts. When the parts and subassemblies have been redesigned, all interactions between parts must be checked, and the performance of the overall result must be evaluated. Most of this process can and must be planned in advance so that it can be completed expeditiously.

Since the process is long, there is usually considerable pressure to reduce the time needed to complete it. As a result, many innovation system improvement efforts in companies making complex products have focused on speeding up product development times.

Simple products. No product is simple in the eyes of those who design it, but most designers will admit that some products are less complex than others. Few products use as many different parts or draw on as many different technologies as an automobile or an airplane, for example.

Less complex products take, on average, fewer person-hours to design. Fewer tasks are involved. Fewer complex coordination problems arise. As a result, development planning is a less complex process. Projects in these industries can afford to be somewhat more informal. The products themselves take less time to develop. Since design times are short, there is less benefit to reengineering the process. There is simply less time to be squeezed out.

On the other hand, there is more potential that the product will be substantially affected by a new technology. The transistor and the integrated circuit revolutionized electronics products. They also had an effect on the automobile, but the effect was proportionately less.

As a result, innovation system improvement efforts in these industries have been less concerned with time compression. In industries subject to a rapid advance of technology, developing the flexibility to deal with radical transformations in technology has been an issue. Few companies, however, have found effective formulae for that (Tushman and Anderson, 1986; Anderson and Tushman, 1990; Christensen, 1997). 3M's solution – setting up new organizations to exploit new technologies – is the closest that anyone has come to solving this problem.

4. Availability of diversification opportunities

Some companies rarely or never develop new businesses. They simply develop new products that fit within existing businesses. Other companies develop a large number of new businesses, diversifying into new areas. The diversifiers have innovation systems that are different from the systems of those who stick to one business.

Some industries may be more conducive to diversification than others. I know of no definitive study of which industries are most so, but my best guess is that those most suited to diversification are those in which two conditions hold: that there are numerous niche markets, and that serving those markets demands a mastery of several technologies. Companies in such an industry will need to master several technologies to be able to play at all. The availability of numerous niches, which they can serve with the same or a slightly broader set of technologies, encourages them to begin diversifying. Once they cover a range of niches, the next step, diversification into related industries, is not a large one.

One other thing is clear. Diversification is driven not just by industry of origin, but also by managerial choice. Some companies compete in markets with many niches, and they have sets of competences that would allow them to diversify, although they choose not to. Management prefers to focus on one market niche, which the company defends to the death. Such companies are likely to have Focused innovation systems. Other companies in the same industry may choose to expand continuously into new niches. These companies will have Flexible innovation systems, like those of diversifying companies in any industry.

New business creation. A company that wants to innovate in areas not related to its existing businesses would do well to have an innovation system that features the following. Its organization structure and communications systems will facilitate contact between people from different functions and business units. Its incentive systems will encourage people to communicate and cooperate with people from other areas. Both of these factors will encourage the generation of ideas that lie outside existing business boundaries.

In addition, the companies will have funding systems that encourage variation and diversity. Such funding systems will typically provide many different funding sources. They will also give lower-level people enough resources to fund some projects. Both of these features ensure that the projects selected for funding will vary across a wide spectrum.

The development system should be set up to handle a wide variety of projects. There will be no simple, standard project plan. Rather, project managers will be trained to handle a wide variety of situations. Since new business development projects usually involve much larger uncertainties than product line extensions, project managers should be trained to identify, monitor, and deal with sources of uncertainty.

Supporting this system, the company will need an organization structure that allows for two things: the easy set up of new projects in a variety of locations, and the easy evolution of successful projects into business units. In addition, incentives and the culture should encourage people to invest in risky initiatives when there is a potential for a payoff.

Innovation within existing businesses only. Companies that focus on one or a few niches often limit their innovation activities to those niches. They will have innovation systems that feature the following. Idea generation will be more focused, centralized, and controlled. Such companies sometimes set up permanent product development groups that systematically search for new technologies or other developments that could have an impact on their product. The corporate office will fund directed investigations into promising technologies.

Such companies also need close links with known sources of variation in the industry. Customers may be a source of variation, as may technological development – inside the company, in competitors, in other industries, or in university or other laboratories. Links with customers and with these sources of technical variation will be essential in enabling the company to keep ahead of changes in its market.

Companies will find it useful to make investments in interesting technologies, even before there is a proven use for these technologies in their industry. By investing in the technology, they will build up their familiarity and competence with it. This will make it much easier for them to adapt and build the technology into their products, if and when a real use develops (see Cohen and Levinthal's article on absorptive capacity, 1990).

Project funding decisions will, in all likelihood, be made by a single corporate board. Companies in several niches may have a different board for each business unit. The criteria used for all funding decisions will be the following: 'How will this project help us to defend or develop our niche?' Development projects may be more patterned than those in diversifying companies, since they always deal with the same product family.

More broadly speaking, companies that want to develop innovations in existing businesses would do well to set up goals and incentives for people in the existing business to support innovation. In the absence of explicit goals, supported by senior management, the temptation will be to focus on short-term results, since they are always important, even in a company that wants to innovate.

At the same time, some organizational flexibility may be necessary. If the company ever needs to integrate a dramatically different technology and/or product configuration into its product, it may be necessary to create a new operating unit or to radically transform an old one, in order to manage the transition.

Companies in many industries focus primarily on innovation in existing businesses. This is true of automobile assemblers and pharmaceutical companies to name but two types of company that are frequently used as examples in discussions of innovation practice.

How companies' environments differ

Three things in a company's environment can have a substantial effect on the configuration of its innovation system. Competitive pressure can force it to innovate more quickly, a short product life can have much the same effect. In addition, heavy regulation can cause a company to build a substantial apparatus to deal with that regulation. I will discuss each of these points in turn (Table 9.2).

Table 9.2   How industry environments vary

Dimension of variation	Impact
Extent of competitive pressure	■ High pressure forces companies to innovate quickly
Length of product life	■ Short product life forces companies to innovate quickly
Extent of regulation	■ Heavy regulation can force each project to follow a prescribed set of tasks to fulfil regulatory requirements; this can lead to a complex but predictable project plan

5. Extent of competitive pressure

6. Length of product life

I will discuss these two dimensions together because they have similar impacts on a company's innovation system. Both can have the impact of forcing the company to innovate more quickly.

High competitive pressure, short product life. When a company faces aggressive competitors, when the competitors are there with new products and new features every few weeks or months, the company will have to move quickly to keep up. At the extreme, the company will need to be quick at all aspects of innovation. This means quick opportunity identification, quick funding decisions, and speedy development. Companies can best achieve this by establishing:

- Dense communication networks across functions and business units
- Tight links with leading clients
- Tight links between idea sources and funding sources
- Project management structures and methods designed for speed.

Electronics businesses are famous for high competitive pressure and short product life. It may be here where the pressure to be quick is greatest. Pressure is, however, also high in pharmaceuticals, automobile assembly, and many other businesses. The pressure in pharmaceuticals comes from a product life that is limited by patent law. While the typical pharmaceutical product's patent-protected life of eight to ten years may seem like an age by the standards of the electronics industry, it is still much shorter than the pharmaceutical companies owning the patents would like. Once the patent on any product expires, competitors will enter the market with copies. With the great growth in our understanding of how to alter molecules, they are increasingly able to invent around patents as well.

The pressure in automobile assembly comes entirely from the competitors. With the Japanese in the lead, automobile assemblers have been developing models much more quickly than in the past. As a result, they are able to respond much faster to changes in consumer taste or need. In addition, the shorter design processes are proving to be less expensive.

Low competitive pressure, long product life. If a company is protected from competitive pressure, or if product lives are long, there is less need for speed in innovation. Speed is still useful for the flexibility and additional revenue it brings, but it is less necessary. As a result, companies enjoying low competitive pressure and long product life can still benefit from working on speed, but their need is less urgent.

Companies with a legal monopoly, or with some other form of exclusive access to markets or to a key raw material, and those with a substantial lead in a key technology, are likely to enjoy low competitive pressure. This allows them to invest less in innovation. If they are too slow, however, they risk losing the advantage that gives them the breathing space. Pressure may build to break the legal monopoly. Someone may find a way around their exclusive access. Competitors may catch up in the key technology. Companies that have invested less in innovation, such as many recently privatized European companies, have found that they have to invest substantially in innovation to keep pace with their new competitors.

The breakdown of a cartel can have the same effect. European telephone equipment providers have faced much more effective competition over the past ten years. For many decades, EurTel (a pseudonym) was virtually the monopoly supplier of telephone equipment in its home country. 'Oddly' EurTel's dominance stopped at the borders of its home country, other suppliers dominating neighboring countries. Little real competition existed. This changed in the 1990s when Asian-based competitors flooded the market. EurTel and the other older companies found that they had greatly to accelerate their innovation processes in order to keep up with the new competitors.

Companies in industries with slow-moving technologies will benefit from long product life. Two things drive product life: (1) product maturity, and (2) the level of competitor interest in developing new technologies. There is generally more room for variation and new development when a technology is new, mature products often retaining the same configuration for decades. A new competitor can sometimes find ways dramatically to improve a product offering, even when existing competitors have run out of ideas. An example of this is provided by the automobile industry.

In the post-war period, the leaders of the United States automobile industry made relatively few technical advances. Products stayed much the same, but for styling differences, in the 1950s and 60s. It was foreigners, especially the Japanese, who developed methods of building and selling new types of cars, for example compacts, in the American market.

The Japanese made substantial technical progress throughout the post-war era. In particular, they developed manufacturing methods that were superior to those used by the Americans. Additionally, they were able to design and develop new models much more quickly and cheaply than the Americans. As a result, they brought considerable new life, and considerable competitive pressure, to a market that had not changed much for several decades.

7. Extent of regulation

Some industries are far more heavily regulated than others. 3M prefers to stay out of regulated industries, but other innovators, such as pharmaceutical companies, are in the most heavily regulated industries of all. A company can innovate in either case. But the configuration of a company's innovation system will vary, depending on whether its industry is regulated or not.

Heavily regulated industry. Companies in heavily regulated industries may have to build up a substantial apparatus to be able to deal with regulators. They must:

- Understand existing regulation and how to apply it
- Track changes in regulation
- Have the technical capability to fulfil regulatory requirements
- Be able to manage their relations with regulators in ways that will smooth the acceptance of new products.

In addition, they need to be able to integrate the concerns of regulators into the development process so that technical development, market development, and regulatory approval are all managed within the context of a coherent project plan.

Generally, the more regulation in an industry, the more work the company will have to do to gain regulatory approval. On the positive side, however, regulations in established businesses can be stable for long periods of time. In addition, when they change, they normally change only at the margins, the existing body of regulations remaining in place. As a result, the company can foresee the vast majority of the tasks it will need to perform to secure regulatory approval. These tasks can be planned out long in advance. The plan itself can be reengineered and rationalized to speed completion of the project. If the company produces a number of products subject to the same regulations, much of the regulatory work can be carried out by specialists in regulation, and thus expedited.

The pharmaceutical industry provides the classic case of a heavily regulated industry. Project teams perform hundreds of tests of a new compound to assure regulatory acceptability, the tests being repeated from one compound to the next. Indeed, pharmaceutical companies have invested heavily in reengineering to help them to shorten this process and reduce the expense involved.

Little or no regulation. Companies in unregulated industries have the privilege of being able to innovate without worrying about regulators. In most cases, this means that the innovation process is less complicated and moves more quickly than in a regulated business. Customers are the major source of market demands on the project team in these industries.

Industries whose products do not directly impact the human body or the environment are subject to less regulation than those which do. Most manufacturing companies have some capacity to affect the environment with waste products, but those handling toxic substances, with a high potential for a negative impact, are regulated much more heavily. Service industries are less subject to regulation than manufacturing industries, although, again, service industries that handle toxic substances (for example, waste disposal) are subject to more regulation than those that do not.

Is regulation a problem? The United States has experienced several waves of deregulation in recent decades. Roll-backs of regulations have occurred in some industries. Other industries have attacked environmental regulation and won some victories. As a result, one might get the impression that companies are always opposed to the regulations that affect them. But this is, in fact, far from the truth.

During interviews with several pharmaceutical executives, we discussed their attitudes towards regulations. They distinguished between two different kinds of regulation. They said that the regulations related to product safety and effectiveness are quite natural given the nature of their business. If the regulators did not require all the tests, the customers (doctors) would. In effect, the regulators act as representatives of the customers, as well as guardians of public safety and health, when they write regulations.

Regulations related to the safety of manufacturing practices are somewhat different. The safety of manufacturing operations touches the product, as one aspect of it is maintaining product purity. But one aspect of manufacturing regulation relates to the safety of procedures for handling toxic chemicals. These regulations, designed to protect workers and the surrounding communities, have been strengthened considerably in the past fifteen years.

The pharmaceutical executives I interviewed also viewed this evolution as natural. Pharmaceutical products used to be relatively simple, nontoxic compounds. Little regulation was needed to assure the safety of an aspirin manufacturing operation, for example. Now, however, pharmaceutical companies work with chemicals that are both increasingly complex and increasingly toxic. A complex chemical may require a complex manufacturing process that is harder to manage. The fact that the final product, and its components, may be toxic means that the stakes are high: a mistake can mean lost lives. As a result, much more attention to safety is needed than was the case several decades ago, and the strengthening of regulations can be seen as an unsurprising result of the evolution of the industry.

For companies in heavily regulated industries, regulations can serve as a barrier to entry. Incumbents know the regulations, and produce products that are in conformity with them. They also have infrastructures built up for dealing with the regulators. New entrants need to learn the regulations, design their products in conformity with them, and develop methods and systems for dealing with regulators. All this takes time and effort that slows the process of entry into the market. As a result, incumbents may value complex regulations as a barrier to entry by new competitors.

The stability and predictability of companies' environments

Industries vary in the extent to which they are subject to unforeseen changes in technology, consumer demand, or regulation. An industry subject to frequent, unforeseen changes can be said to be unstable, or subject to a high level of uncertainty. The level of uncertainty can have a substantial impact on the configuration of a company's innovation system.

Even beyond normal uncertainty, companies sometimes have to deal with radical changes in technology that threaten their position in the industry. When such radical changes occur, companies need special skills or assets to maintain their position in the industry.

I will discuss methods of dealing with 'normal' uncertainty first. Technological transformations, which involve the replacement of one technology with another, are a special case that I will deal with as a separate dimension (see Table 9.3).

Table 9.3   How industry stability and predictability vary

Dimension of variation	Impact

Level of uncertainty
– Technology
– Consumer need/
  preference
– Regulation
	■ Different management methods
	needed in high-uncertainty situations
	  – Identify areas of uncertainty
	  – Track change
	  – Adapt products and processes
	    to changes that occur

Frequency of radical transformation	■ Surviving a radical transformation requires considerable alertness and organizational flexibility; may need to start up new unit in parallel with old unit before old one dies (see text for a discussion of how this might be done)

8. Level of uncertainty

Most of the uncertainty that innovation projects face comes from three sources: technology, customers, and regulators. Technologies can evolve quickly. This has been the case in the electronics industry for several decades. Alternatively, one technology can displace another in an industry, as jet engines replaced propeller engines in long-range air transportation. Consumer needs and preferences can change quickly too. Fashion-driven industries such as clothing and personal accessories are famously subject to fickle consumer taste.

In some cases, regulatory environments may change. This can happen in new industries as vague or nonexistent regulations are replaced with a clear set of new regulations. This can also happen when the public learns more about an industry, or when attitudes towards the industry change. The nuclear power industry endured regular strengthenings of regulation during a period when public attitudes toward that industry were turning sharply negative (Muzyka, 1989). Finally, older, heavily regulated industries may experience periods of deregulation if older regulatory regimes are suddenly viewed as irrelevant, ineffective, or a hindrance to progress.

High uncertainty. Companies buffeted by unpredictable events need to have means of (a) identifying areas of uncertainty, (b) tracking change, and (c) adapting their products and processes to any changes that occur. In detail, this means setting up relationships with regulators, customers, and any potential sources of technological change so that changes can be foreseen in advance. A company in a high-uncertainty industry needs to make a judgement about where unexpected changes may come from, and monitor any changes that occur in those areas. In addition, the company must be flexible enough to set up new units to investigate how to exploit or react to changes, and to adapt existing products to changes that occur.

In particular, companies in high-uncertainty industries need to be able to manage innovation projects in a way that takes account of the industry's uncertainty. This requires that several things be done for each project. First, the team should identify areas of uncertainty that might affect the project. Second, they should put into place methods of tracking what is happening in these areas of uncertainty. Third, when it is within their control to resolve the uncertainties (for example, through technical tests, market tests, or discussions with regulators), they should resolve them as early as possible. Finally, project planning and management will need to be flexible enough to allow the team to react effectively to changes.

Chemical companies developing new businesses or new uses for existing chemicals are particularly prone to encountering uncertain regulatory environments. The fact that a business is new means that the regulators have not had time to think about it. Nonetheless, their approval may be needed before the product hits the market.

Consumer products companies of all kinds face uncertainty in the consumer response to new products. New electronics products do not always sell well, even though they may be technically superior to their predecessors.

Finally, all companies with technical research programs have experienced the unexpected failures or successes of new technologies.

Low uncertainty. Companies in more stable environments do not have to invest as much in detecting and monitoring areas of uncertainty. Nor do they have to embed as much flexibility into the planning of their innovation projects.

9. Frequency of radical transformation

Frequent radical transformations. Industries differ with respect to how often the basic technology of the business changes. They are also subject to unforeseen invasions from or displacements by entirely new technologies. When radical change happens frequently in an industry, the incumbents will need considerable flexibility and alertness if they are to survive (Tushman and Anderson, 1986; Anderson and Tushman, 1990; Christensen, 1997). If they have substantial related assets, such as complementary technologies and distribution systems, they will have a better chance of surviving. But even in the best case, survival may be difficult.

I visited a 3M business unit whose product had gone through three changes in technology in fifteen years. A fourth change was on the horizon. 3M had led the first change, as an outsider, and built its position on the basis of a new technology. It had managed to stay on top during the next two changes, by developing the new technologies in separate laboratories and bringing them into the distribution arm when the time came. The business unit's managers were worried, however, that the company would not be able to retain its position if a fourth change came. The company was simply not competitive enough in the new technology that threatened to invade the business.

To survive radical transformations, a company needs a high degree of alertness and organizational flexibility. Links with customers and outside sources of technical development (including competitors) will help the company to detect impending changes early on. The company must be able quickly to fund investigations into any new technology.

Such investigations will need to be managed separately from the existing business unit for a time. In most cases, it is best for the company to set up a new unit to investigate the new technology. The new unit will need to have some new people, people who have not worked in the market before. These people will be in a much better position to develop a new conceptualization of the business and to see how the new technology will fit into it. The new unit will, however, also need some people from the old unit. They will be needed to contribute to the new team's understanding of the market and customer need.

3M has a system for managing such transitions. At 3M, the new unit may be married to the old, in that it will share administrative and marketing resources, while pursuing a different technology. Conversely, it may be set up separately. In either case, if the idea works, 3M's organizational flexibility allows the new project team to grow into a business unit relatively painlessly.

Advances in electronics and, more recently, materials technology and chemistry have meant that some businesses have seen radical technical transformations every few years (Henderson and Clark, 1990). Electronics and telecommunication have probably been the hardest hit, but many other manufacturing industries and finance have also been affected.

Governments can be another source of radical transformation. Deregulations of airlines and trucking in the United States have substantially transformed those industries. Privatizations and eliminations of monopoly privilege have also revolutionized industries, particularly in Europe. Such politically driven transformations are, however, rarely repeated. By contrast, a technological revolution one year may be followed by another one five years later.

No radical transformations. If the technology behind a company's business is stable, and its competitors are quiescent, radical transformations may not occur for decades. The cement industry has not seen a revolutionary product innovation for a century. Cement companies have invested far less in R&D than sectors such as pharmaceuticals and electronics, or even consumer products. They have not needed to invest in speed and flexibility, nor have they had to invest in sensing impending changes in their industry. In short, the special measures to prepare for radical change that need to be taken in electronics and other industries do not need to be taken here.

This completes this discussion of the impact of industry differences on companies' innovation systems; a summary can be found in Figure 9.3.

Other impacts on innovation system configuration

Up to this point, I have looked at how industry-wide factors affect the innovation system of each company in an industry. But not all companies in an industry will have identical innovation systems. Their systems may vary substantially; they may vary in ways that reflect more than just random variation (Table 9.4).

Competence

One source of variation that should not be overlooked is that of competence. Some companies may be blessed with managers who thoroughly understand how an effective innovation system should be run. Others

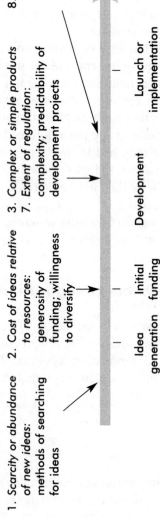

Phase-specific issues:

1. _Scarcity or abundance of new ideas:_ methods of searching for ideas

2. _Cost of ideas relative to resources:_ generosity of funding; willingness to diversify

3. _Complex or simple products_

7. _Extent of regulation:_ complexity; predictability of development projects

8. _Level of uncertainty:_ methods of managing development

Idea generation · Initial funding · Development · Launch or implementation

Issues impacting the whole process:

4. _Availability of diversification opportunities:_ methods of idea generation, funding, and development

5. _Extent of competitive pressure_

6. _Length of product life:_ overall pressure for speed

9. _Frequency of radical transformation:_ level of alertness and flexibility needed

Key: Dimension of variation: Impact

Figure 9.3   Summary of industry differences

Table 9.4   Other impacts on innovation system configuration

Dimension of variation	Impact
Competence	■ A company with a management team skilled in innovation management may have a different system from that of a similar company whose management is not as skilled
Management's level of interest in innovation	■ A management team that wants more innovation will invest more resources into improving system
Management's level of interest in diversification	■ A management team that wants diversification will adapt systems accordingly; their system will be different from that of a Focused company
Product-market strategy	■ Low-cost strategy will lead to process innovation, while focus or diversification strategy will lead to product innovation ■ Specific product-markets chosen will affect competences developed and areas of investment
Company history	■ A company that has been focusing on innovation for decades will look different from one which is just discovering its importance

will not be so blessed. The former company's innovation system may be structured in a far more effective way than the latter's.

Management's level of interest in innovation

Management's level of interest in innovation can have an impact on the amount of resources devoted to innovation and on the general configuration of the system. If management is happy with the company's position, they may devote relatively few resources to innovation and tolerate an innovation system that is far from the industry's best. On the other hand, if management is trying hard to improve the company's status, they may invest far more resources, proportionally, in innovation. They may not rest until they have ensured that the company's innovation system is the best in the industry.

Management's level of interest in diversification

Similarly, management's level of interest in diversification can have an impact on their willingness to tolerate and fund initiatives that could take the company beyond its current area of focus. If management is happy with the company's place in the market, they may be happy to have a Focused innovation system that develops products only in the company's current area of activity. If, on the other hand, management wants to develop new areas of activity, they are much more likely to have a Flexible innovation system.

Product-market strategy

Innovation system configuration also varies with the product-market strategy that the company adopts. Two companies in the same industry might have quite different product-market strategies. This can have a substantial impact on the companies' innovation systems.

Within a single industry, some companies may follow low-cost strategies across a broad range of products, while others go after one or a few niches, and still others pursue high-quality or new feature innovation strategies across a wider range of products. Some may grow by acquisition or consolidation within the industry, whereas others grow by developing new businesses within the same or a closely related industry (Porter, 1980).

Companies following low-cost strategies will put more emphasis on process innovation than those not following such strategies. They will not need the same range and depth of customer contacts that companies following high-quality or new feature strategies will need. Extensive technology networks will prove useful to such companies because they will help to stimulate the generation of ideas for process improvements. Networks linking technologists with marketers will be less useful since the company is not looking for new product ideas.

Companies following high-quality or new feature strategies will place more emphasis on product innovation. Here, developing close links with customers will matter much more. Effective links between marketers and the technology side will be key, since such links will be the means by which the company brings new, high-quality features into being.

Willingness to grow into new businesses is another distinguishing feature (see also the discussion of diversification, above). Companies looking to develop new businesses are likely to have denser networks between different business units than companies that do not want to build new businesses. These inter-business unit networks will help the company to identify any opportunities that lie outside the charters of existing business units. Second, they are also likely to have funding systems that provide funds in a wider variety of places, and from a wider variety of people. Third, incentive systems will encourage managers throughout the company to support innovation. Finally, they are likely to have more flexible organization structures. In the best case, these structures will allow them to easily set up project teams and easily grow these teams into new business units.

Company history

Finally, a company's history can explain much about the position of its innovation system today. Two companies may both put a high emphasis on product innovation. But if company A has been focusing on product innovation unwaveringly since 1920, while company B has been 'asleep' for much of that period, their innovation systems may look quite different. Company A may have a 'best in class' system, while company B may have many anti-innovation practices.

In this chapter, I have shown the reader nine dimensions of variation among industries that drive much variation between companies' innovation systems. I have also noted that management competence, company history, and the company's strategy can have a significant impact on the structure of a company's innovation system. In the next chapter, I will sum up the results and conclude the book.

10 Conclusion

Summary

The past eight chapters have demonstrated a number of points. First, the CR story demonstrated that a wide variety of management systems and practices can affect a company's innovation performance. Part I of the book built on that story to develop a number of definitions and concepts that helped to illustrate two things. First, they showed how the innovation process works during the key phases of idea generation, funding, and development. Second, they showed the key methods of improving the innovation process during each of these phases. Part I ended with a brief discussion of how managers could diagnose problems in innovation systems and how they could identify opportunities for improving their innovation systems.

Part II of the book built on the basic insights of Part I. Chapter 5 discussed the problem of how to organize a program to improve innovation performance. A management team that wants to improve innovation performance may look at their management systems and find that they want to change dozens of different things. Chapters 5 and 6 looked at the questions of what to change first and how, in general, to plan and execute the changes. Then, Chapters 7, 8 and 9 showed how innovation systems differed across industries. They also showed how the problem of improving innovation performance differed across industries.

Conclusions

The main conclusions to be drawn from this book are the following. First, *a wide variety of management systems and practices affect inno-*

vation performance. Business management systems such as strategy and goal setting, structure and process design, people management systems, and culture all impact innovation performance. Specific innovation management systems such as idea generation methods, funding systems, and project management methods also affect innovation performance. Finally, the interventions of senior managers in specific projects can have a major impact on these projects.

The fact that so many factors influence innovation performance has two corollaries. The first is that companies that are excellent innovators differ in a large number of ways from companies that are average or poor innovators. Their management systems may differ on dozens, perhaps even hundreds, of different points. This makes it difficult for the less effective innovators to copy the more effective innovators. There are just too many things to change. Also management teams in less effective companies may find it doubly difficult to change, since they themselves may not be aware of many of the differences.

The second corollary is that organizing a change process, when the goal is to improve innovation performance, is a complex task in itself. If a management team wants to manage a revolutionary transformation, they may have to change dozens of different management practices. They will not, however, be able to make all the changes at once. They may have to plan extensive training or other preparation to be able to execute some of the changes at all.

The second conclusion to be drawn from the book is that *it is possible to improve the innovation performance of virtually any company.* Even the oldest, most conservative company will be open to some kind of change, assuming that the senior management team wants to improve innovation performance.

There are principles that a management team should follow in organizing a change program, including making simple changes first, and taking advantage of the expertise that outsiders can provide to accelerate the change process. Some of the simple changes outlined in Chapter 5 can be made in almost any company. Once the larger management team begins to recognize the importance of innovation (if they have not done so already), more complex changes will become possible, and the company will be well on its way to an improved performance.

The third conclusion that should be drawn from the book is that *innovation systems differ across industries and across companies within industries.* The innovation problem for a pharmaceutical company is not the same as that for an industrial product manufacturer. The innovation problem faced by a company that wants to diversify is not the same as that of a company wanting to focus on one or two product niches.

As a result, managers who want to improve innovation performance should not just blindly apply the first techniques they encounter, nor techniques seen to be successful in another industry or another company. They should determine first whether these techniques are appropriate for their industry and their company. They may find, for example, that they should use not the well-publicized techniques for accelerating development used in the automobile and pharmaceutical companies, but an entirely different set of techniques altogether.

The message to managers

The messages to managers are fairly easy to draw from this discussion. Innovation systems can be improved if the managers running them (a) carefully identify the systems and practices that are not operating optimally, and (b) proceed to change them step by step.

I have given illustrations throughout the book of how various management systems can be run in ways that encourage innovation. I have not had space for a comprehensive discussion of the different tools available, but managers can use the examples given as guidelines for diagnosing their own innovation systems. I plan, in a subsequent book, to provide a detailed guide to how all the management structures, systems, and processes identified in this book can be managed in ways that encourage innovation. Unfortunately, space limitations prevent me from including such a guide in this book. It would have doubled the size of the book.

Once they have diagnosed problems and identified opportunities for improvement in their innovation systems, managers should carefully plan a program for improving innovation performance. In most cases, they should take the simple and obvious steps first. Having taken the simple steps, they may want to pause and see how the system is working after the changes. Having removed superficial problems, they may be able to see more fundamental issues that are slowing or blocking the system. With a deeper understanding, they should then go forward to the next round of change.

Managers can speed up their own learning about innovation system management by drawing on expertise from the outside. Some consultants have extensive experience in innovation management. They can help companies come up to the standard in their industries or even go beyond it. Consultants are particularly useful when a management team wants to plan and implement complex changes. The impact of an organizational transformation is difficult to predict and evaluate, for example, and experienced consultants can help in this area, as well as others.

Most companies also have the option of hiring in expertise from the outside. Unless a company is a clear industry leader, it may benefit by hiring people away from companies whose innovation systems perform better than its own. These outside hires will bring with them a knowledge of management systems and practices that can be applied to transforming their new environment.

In the process of implementing broad changes, managers may need to focus considerable attention on training their subordinates to run the new system. This will be particularly the case if they are trying to change daily work practices, organizational structure, or culture. New practices will have to be learned, and the logic behind them understood, if they are to be implemented correctly. This training and assimilation process may be speeded up by giving subordinates a voice in designing the changes. If they have designed the changes themselves, they will take ownership more quickly, and less training will be necessary.

Most managers automatically pay attention to industry constraints. There are many differences between industries that have an impact on the design of an innovation system. Managers moving from one industry to another should pay particularly careful attention to the conditions in their new industry. They will find that things they learned in their old industry do not automatically transfer to the new industry. Chapter 9 itemized the dimensions of industry variation that have an impact on innovation system design. Managers can use this as a checklist to determine what they need to pay attention to in designing changes in their innovation system.

Within many industries, managers have a choice between several strategies and thus between different kinds of innovation system. Do they want to have an innovation system that is maximally efficient in a few narrow areas, but not adept at exploiting diversification opportunities? Or do they want a system that may be less efficient, but which is capable of developing new product and new business ideas over a wider area?

In some industries there may be no choice. When development is very expensive, there is often no choice but to go the efficiency route. In many industries, however, managers have the choice of focusing on a few narrow niches, or adopting a wider diversification strategy that may lead them into unknown territory. Which route they choose will have a significant effect on the design of their innovation system.

Next steps

So where do we go next? Managers can use the techniques described in this book to improve the innovation performance of their companies. Through their experience, we can learn more about how innovation systems work and how they can be improved.

Scholars, meanwhile, can use this book as a source of information and ideas on how innovation systems work and how managers can act to change them. They can build on the material presented here and increase our understanding of how to manage innovation effectively. This will increase our ability to educate and advise managers.

As a final note, I ask all readers of this book to remember that business is, at its best, about value creation. We earn our living and justify our place in society by increasing the value of the inputs available to us. We will continue to earn our place only as long as we continue to add value. Innovation thus has a key role in our lives. The more we innovate, and the more effectively we innovate, the more value we will create. And the more value we create, the more value will be available to the people around us and to ourselves and our families. So let's work together to innovate more effectively and create as much value as we can.

There is no shortage of needs to be met. Our customers and potential customers today are asking us to solve a number of very difficult problems. Consumers in developing countries want to achieve developed world lifestyles. Consumers in industrialized countries also have a vision of a better life, a vision they would like us help them to achieve. Meanwhile, our technologists and others are constantly inventing new ways to add value, ways consumers are only beginning to dream of.

Our ability to meet customer needs is subject to constraints. Innovation often involves finding ways to do things within the limits of cost or other constraints. Cost factors will continue to be important.

They may become increasingly important in areas where there are environmental limits on our ability to consume more energy, space and materials (see, for example, OECD, 1997a, 1997b).

We can meet these new customer needs at a reasonable cost only if we learn to make more with less, if we learn to provide more and better products and services with fewer material and energy inputs. We have made considerable progress in this direction in the past thirty years. But to navigate the next fifty years successfully, we will have to continue innovating. To achieve what our customers want, we will have to innovate even more quickly and even more often. All of us will have to improve our innovation performance beyond what we have already done. Can we do it? The job will be difficult, but I think we can. I hope that this book will help.

Appendix: Notes for the Academic Community

Virtually all of the data presented in this book were collected in the course of an academic research project sponsored by INSEAD, the leading European business school. Most of the insights presented here were developed during the course of this project. While the book is written to be accessible to the general reader, the data collection and analysis followed rules set by members of the academic community. In this Appendix, I will briefly summarize how the data were collected and analyzed. Readers who want a more detailed discussion of the methods are referred to Christiansen (1997).

Before beginning this research project, I consulted a wide variety of texts on the problems of managing large, complex organizations; the activities of general managers in those organizations; and the problem of improving innovation performance. I cannot list all of the works consulted, but some of the most important were Prahalad and Doz (1987), Ghoshal (1987), and Bartlett and Ghoshal (1989) on the problems of managing large multinationals; Mintzberg (1973) and Kotter (1982) on general managers and leadership; and Van de Ven *et al.* (1989), Clark and Fujimoto (1991), and Wheelwright and Clark (1992) on the problem of improving innovation performance. In addition, Stalk and Hout (1990) convinced me of the importance of time in many business processes, including funding decisions.

A core assumption behind the research project was the idea that managers' actions would be a useful focus of study. In effect, I began the project with a simple model in mind, one that can be summarized in one phrase: general managers take actions that impact innovation performance.

The simplicity of this phrase is entirely deceptive. There are several types of manager who can be labeled general managers.

There are an unknown but large number of discrete actions they can take that will affect innovation performance. In addition, innovation performance itself can be broken down into a number of components. As a result, the issues in the first phase of the research were (a) to begin sorting out the different types of general manager, (b) to determine what types of action they were able to take that would impact innovation performance, and (c) to identify the likely impacts of their actions on innovation performance.

The initial data collection framework

In this section, I will discuss the previous literature on innovation and describe how I used it to construct the initial data collection framework. The reader should recall that there are three key features of this framework. First, there are different types of general manager. Second, there are different actions that managers can take (or different tools that they can use) to influence innovation performance. Third, there are different types of result that their actions can have on the innovation system. I will discuss each of these features of the framework in turn.

Different levels of general manager

The first set of distinctions in the data collection framework involved the different types of general managers. In this area, I borrowed distinctions made by Bower (1970) and Burgelman (1983) in their studies of resource allocation and new venture development. Both identified four levels of manager as having distinctly different management roles. The four levels were functional managers, business unit mangers, middle managers (responsible for several business units), and corporate-level managers.

Different types of general management activity (use of different tools)

Previous work on innovation has identified a wide range of corporate systems and practices that impact innovation performance. The company's communication system, its organization structure, its resource allocation (project funding) system, its personnel management system (especially incentives), and its project management practices all have an impact on innovation performance. Each of these systems can be changed by general managers. Thus, each represents a possible tool for general managers to use as they try to improve innovation performance.

Prior to beginning data collection, I combed the innovation literature to develop as comprehensive a list as possible of methods that general managers could use to improve innovation performance. A short summary of the list developed, along with the principal sources, appears in Figure A.1. A more complete list can be found in Christiansen (1997).

1. Setting goals (goals in the context of project selection are discussed in Schmidt and Freeland, 1992; Wheelwright and Clark, 1992; goals in the broader strategic context are discussed in many works on strategy)
2. Improvements in organization structure and communications within the company (Bower, 1970; Allen, 1977; Burgelman, 1983; Maidique and Hayes, 1984; Van de Ven, 1986; Angle, 1989; Dougherty, 1992; Ghoshal and Nohria, 1992; and others)
3. Improvements in communications between the company and its environment (Von Hippel, 1986, 1987)
4. Improvements in the resource allocation system (Bower, 1970; Burgelman, 1983)
5. Altering incentives (other than communication incentives, mentioned above) (Bower, 1970; Argyris and Schön, 1974, 1978; Roberts and Fusfeld, 1981; Burgelman, 1983; Argyris, 1985; Angle, 1989) and corporate controls (Haspeslagh, 1985, 1986; Goold and Campbell, 1987)
6. Altering other personnel policies (Katz and Allen, 1982; Angle, 1989; Adler, 1990)
7. Changes in culture (A): Broad expectation of innovative activity (Imai, 1986; Zuboff, 1988; Jaikumar and Bohn, 1992)
8. Changes in culture (B): Cognitive maps and responsibility-taking behavior (Barr et al., 1992)

Figure A.1 General categories of methods for improving innovation performance identified in the literature (prior to 1994)

In setting up the initial research design, I did not look in detail at the literature on project management methods, as this had been relatively well studied. Rather, I preferred to focus on corporate-wide or division-wide systems that impacted idea generation and funding, since the latter were less well-studied areas. During the interviews, however, it was impossible to separate project management methods from the other subjects. As a result, I collected considerable material on methods of improving development as well as on methods of improving idea generation and funding. As the research progressed, I added various dimensions of project management, as well as other management tools not foreseen in the initial design, to my list of methods for improving innovation performance.

I used my evolving list of management tools to guide data collection. In order to assure that comprehensive information on management activity in relation to innovation was collected, I asked about each type of management tool within each site.

After collecting the data, I developed a new, comprehensive list of methods that general managers could use to influence innovation performance. I began referring to these methods as methods of 'intervening' in the innovation system, or as 'management tools.' The twenty categories of tool identified were listed in Chapter 3. A full listing of the tools in each category will have to await another book.

Impacts on the innovation process: phases of the innovation process

The innovation process is a complex one. In a large company, a large project can involve many people and run through multiple phases. The management of the project at the beginning will involve dynamics different from those seen at the end.

As a result, I assumed that management interventions might affect different phases of the innovation process quite differently. Some might impact idea generation without impacting development. Others might affect funding without directly influencing any other phase of the process. I therefore distinguished between different phases of the innovation process. I adapted a model developed by Angle and Van de Ven (1989) to identify five distinct phases during which company-wide management systems and practices might have an impact on innovation performance. These five phases are outlined below.

Phase 1: Idea generation. This encompasses Angle and Van de Ven's first two processes: (1) gestation, and (2) 'shocks' triggering innovation. Following Angle and Van de Ven, corporate communications and incentive systems could be expected to play key roles during this phase.

Phase 2: Initial funding. This includes Angle and Van de Ven's planning and funding process (3). Corporate communications and incentive systems continue to be important here. In addition, the structure of the corporate resource allocation system will be crucial.

Phase 3: Development. This includes the eight processes that Angle and Van de Ven assigned to the development period. General managers would be involved in setting up 'management involvement and roles' (9). They could also become involved in the other seven development processes (4–8, 10, 11), or these could be managed by lower-level people.

Phase 4: Decision to launch (implement) a project. This includes part of Angle and Van de Ven's 12th and 13th processes – the decision to implement a home-grown (12) or an imported (13) innovation. It involves, in addition, the termination process (14). This phase would involve, primarily, the resource allocation and incentive systems, the same systems that were involved in initial funding (see above).

Phase 5: Launch (implementation). This includes the remainder of Angle and Van de Ven's 12th and 13th processes (implementation after the decision is made). General management activity during this phase is likely to vary widely depending on the needs of the project.

In pursuing the research, I decided to focus my attention on the first three phases: idea generation, project funding and development.

The overall framework

Having developed these three sets of distinction (types of general manager, types of activity, and phases of the process), I built a preliminary model of the activities that I was studying (Figure A.2). The model included the principal methods identified in the literature by which managers could affect innovation performance. The question marks on the figure represented links to be investigated: 'Who does what type of intervention?' and 'What is the impact?'

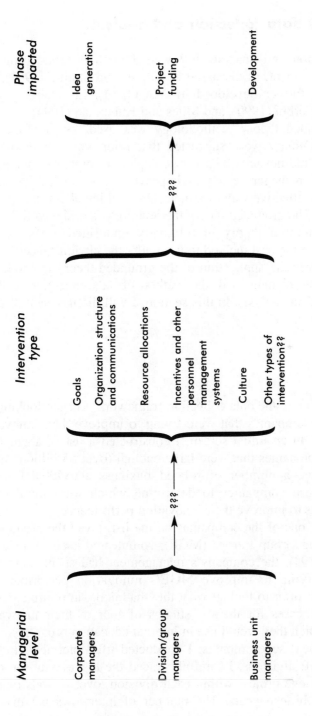

Figure A.2 The preliminary view of general managers' methods of improving innovation performance

Method of data collection and analysis

Data collection and analysis followed a method called grounded theory development, as discussed by Glaser and Strauss (1967). The method was further developed by Yin (1984), Eisenhardt (1989), Strauss and Corbin (1990), and Miles and Huberman (1994).

The grounded theory methodology was used for the following reason. Preliminary work suggested that prior work on innovation management did not provide a very complete or organized picture of how general managers acted to improve innovation performance. Thus, a more effective way of structuring thinking about this activity was needed. The grounded theory methodology is designed to help to develop structured theory in relatively undefined areas. It thus appeared to be the best method to use under the circumstances.

Key issues in the application of the grounded theory methodology are the sample of data used, the method of data collection, and the methods used in analysis. In this section, I will discuss each of these subjects in turn.

The data

After constructing the data collection framework, I began looking for examples of companies that were trying to improve their innovation performance. In an initial screen, I constructed a list of about forty diversified companies that were large enough (over $5 billion annual sales) to have a number of related business activities. I began screening these companies to determine which were involved in serious efforts to improve their innovation performance.

Very soon, one of the companies on the list, given the pseudonym Manufacturing Group Europe (MGE), volunteered itself as a site. At that time (1994), the company's management had spent more than four years trying to improve MGE's innovation performance. I accepted their offer to look at what they had done, in return agreeing to write four cases for them – studies of four of their innovation projects – which they would use in internal education programs.

Over the next seven months, I conducted fifty interviews in four different MGE divisions. I carefully traced the histories of the divisions, and of one project within each division, over periods ranging from ten to thirteen years. The number of interviews per division varied from ten to seventeen. The people interviewed in each division differed in level from a member of the Corporate Executive Committee to members of project teams. Four interviews (those with the most senior managers) covered events in more than one division. The methods used in collecting and analyzing this data will be discussed below.

The reader should note that, at MGE, a division was a cluster of up to a dozen business units. At another company, such a cluster might have been called a group or a sector. Each MGE division had revenues of several billion dollars. The divisions all had their own management team and were managed independently, with only limited supervision from corporate management. Each division was the equivalent of a related-diversified company on its own. MGE had more than four divisions, but only four of these were studied.

MGE's purpose in giving me access was to obtain case studies on the histories of four innovation projects, one in each of the four divisions. As part of these case studies, I collected information on how each division managed innovation. I also collected information on what each divisional management team had done to improve the innovation performance of their division over the previous ten years. Each division was managed by a different group of general managers, although there was some overlap of supervisors at the corporate level. Each division's leadership group followed a different approach to the problem of improving innovation performance. This led to considerable variation in the types of intervention used, although there were similarities in the patterns of change as well.

I coded the information that I collected on general managers' activity in the four divisions as 273 separate events, each of which involved an interaction between one or more general managers and MGE's innovation program. Thirty of these events occurred some time prior to the beginning of the projects. These 30 events were dropped for analyses that focused on events occurring during the histories of the projects themselves. Fifty-four other events occurred after the projects began, but before senior management began to try to improve company's innovation performance. These events were dropped in analyses of the innovation system improvement programs.

MGE was not the only company willing to open its doors. In 1994 and 1995, I conducted fifty-four additional interviews in ten other organizations. These organizations provided many additional examples of the methods that general managers used to improve innovation performance. Four of these organizations provided enough access (between eight and sixteen interviews each) for me to construct ten-year histories of their innovation methods and structures, histories comparable to those of the MGE divisions.

Data collected outside the formal research project

After the initial research project had been completed, I collected additional information via interviews with managers at five additional companies: USAuto, CementCo, USComputers, EurTel, and AmPro. These interviews were conducted primarily to identify further aspects of industry and company variation.

The interviews were less structured than those conducted during the initial research. They focused on three subjects: (1) how these companies managed innovation, (2) how their innovation management systems differed from those in other companies, and (3) how innovation problems in their industry differed from those in other industries. Information from these interviews was used for the analysis in Chapter 9 (on industry variation). Except when referring to Chapter 9, the discussion below on methodology does not refer to these interviews.

My contact with USF occurred during a three-month long consulting project prior to the beginning of the formal INSEAD research project. This contact did not involve structured interviews, but did involve considerable learning about how the company managed and mismanaged innovation. Material from this contact was used in the Introduction and in Chapter 9, but not in any of the other analyses.

Method of data collection

Data collection and analysis proceeded somewhat differently at MGE from the other sites because I had the opportunity to collect information on the histories of four innovation projects at MGE. I was not, however, able to collect project-level data at the other sites.

Interviews lasted from one to three hours, the average being about one and one-half hours. Each interview began with three open-ended questions. At MGE, these questions related to three things. First, I asked about the history of the focal innovation project and the interviewee's role in relation to it. Next, I asked about the interviewee's job and his or her unit's role in relation to the innovation process. Third, I asked what had been done in the past ten years, and what still needed to be done to improve the company's innovation process.

The questions were left open ended to allow respondents to bring up aspects of the company's management practices that they viewed as significant to innovation management but which were not foreseen by the investigator. Follow-up questions were used, to the extent necessary, to ensure that information was obtained on all phases of the innovation process and on all aspects of company management that had previously been identified as having an impact on innovation performance.

In general, the questions asked were complex and numerous enough that no one manager was able, in the time allotted, to answer all the questions. Rather, respondents were selected so that, as a group, they would be able to give a full and detailed history of each project, along with information on all aspects of management previously identified as having an impact on innovation performance.

Interviews at Eastman Chemical, 3M, EurAuto, ConsumerCo, EuroChem, Optico, MachineCo, Admin, ConElec, and Finco followed the same procedures as the MGE interviews. The first open-ended question (on project history) focused, however, on the history of a 'typical' project, rather than on any specific project.

Detailed hand-written notes were taken at each interview. These were transcribed into typewritten form, in almost all cases within forty-eight hours of completion of the interview.

The information contained in the MGE interview notes was then assembled into four detailed project/divisional histories. Information on general management activity related in any way to the innovation process was included in the histories. Each history was verified through criticism from at least two MGE managers familiar with the project (including the project head) and from one co-investigator. Follow-up interviews were conducted to fill in details missed during the first round of interviews. Inconsistencies and errors of fact were corrected until all readers were satisfied that the history constituted a complete and accurate account of events significant to the project's history.

Method of data analysis

After this process of verification had been completed, each MGE project history was broken up into a series of events. Event study methodologies have been used before in the innovation literature (see, for example, Garud and Van de Ven, 1992), but there are two differences between my method and that of Garud and Van de Ven.

First, prior to beginning their research, Garud and Van de Ven constructed a specific list of the types of event they were going to track. They tracked these, and only these, events. No change was made, during the course of their study, in the tracking frame. My list was much more open ended. I gathered information on any event seen (by the participants) as having been important to innovation in the division, or to the history of the project.

Second, Garud and Van de Ven collected their data as the events unfolded. I collected most (80–90 percent) of my data retrospectively, via historical research. While a part of my data could be verified through a consultation of historical documents, much of them could not. The data are, thus, subject to memory bias.

This memory bias is, in part, problematic. Respondents may color their stories to make themselves look better. I was able to minimize this danger by obtaining at least two witnesses to each period of each project's history (with the exception of the first two years of the CR project, for which only one witness was available). In each case, the second witness had personal interests different from (and often opposed to) those of the first witness. This led to the surfacing of differences of opinion in the (rare) cases where one respondent was trying, consciously or otherwise, to bias the story.

In another way, memory bias worked in my favor. Respondents tended to remember events that involved changes in direction, being more likely to omit events that were simply continuations of what had gone before. This bias was actually helpful, given my research design. I was much more interested in events that involved changes in direction than in events that were mere continuations or reaffirmations of the *status quo*. This bias thus helped me to screen out events that did not have any great impact on the division's innovation system or on the history of the project. An example will illustrate this.

Using Garud and Van de Ven's methodology, I would have tracked each time that a funding committee (or a responsible individual) considered the funding of any of the MGE projects. However, as a matter of fact, I was interested not in each funding decision, but only in decisions that resulted in some change in funding level or in the funding system itself. Conveniently, these were exactly the events that respondents remembered most vividly. They tended to report these events, while ignoring (not reporting) the many meetings and decisions that resulted in continuations of present funding.

Each MGE project/divisional history, once constructed, contained over 150 events. Material on a few additional events involving general managers was added from the interview notes. All events involving general managers were then identified and analyzed separately. These events were classified into over forty types via a Q-sort. The types were then aggregated, via a second Q-sort, into five overall categories and sixteen subcategories.

The Q-sorts were carried out without reference to any prior analytic framework. The classifications were modified as the analysis proceeded, as inconsistencies and useful additional distinctions were found. The final classification includes forty-nine types, sixteen subcategories, and five categories. The forty-nine types corresponded to forty-nine methods by which general managers could impact on innovation performance.

A Q-sort, for those readers unfamiliar with the technique, is a kind of cluster analysis performed with qualitative rather than quantitative data. The technique used is typically the following. Descriptions of the objects to be sorted (in this case events) are written onto separate sheets of paper. The pieces of paper are then sorted into piles, each pile consisting of a set of nearly identical objects (or events). The piles are then grouped together, similar piles being put into the same group, until the desired level of clustering is achieved. In this case, the first sort produced forty-nine types of intervention. These forty-nine types were then further grouped into sixteen subcategories and five overall categories to complete the sort.

While I did not have project histories from the other companies, the notes from these interviews at ten of these companies were analyzed in a similar fashion. (My contact with USF occurred prior to the beginning of the project. Interviews at USAuto, CementCo, USComputers, AmPro, and EurTel occurred after completion of the initial research project.) Each interview was broken into a series of descriptive statements about the company's management practices and innovation structures. Over 1200 descriptive statements in all were identified. These statements were also classified via a Q-sort method, which revealed a number of management practices that had not been used at MGE. It also highlighted a number of dimensions of structural variation that had not yet been manipulated at MGE. In all, 31 additional methods by which managers could affect innovation performance were identified. These were in addition to the 49 methods already identified in the MGE data.

Once the basic classification work had been carried out, a variety of techniques were used to discern other patterns in the data. Of these, four were used in the analyses reported in this book.

By looking at the MGE events chronologically, it was possible to identify a clear evolution in the types of intervention used by MGE's general managers. The patterns of evolution within the four project histories were compared, a common pattern that fitted all four project histories being found. This pattern provided an explanation of how MGE managers had dealt with the problem of how to change the management systems in which they had been embedded for most or all of their careers. Their method of making simple changes first and then progressing to more complex systems and problems is discussed in Chapters 3 and 5.

It was clear that the eight organizations had evolved differently. Four had focused on developing a greater diversification capacity, the other four on increasing innovation system efficiency. The results of this analysis are presented in Chapter 7.

After looking at how structures and workflows evolved differently at the eight companies, I undertook a more fine-grained analysis of how the management of idea generation, funding, and development had evolved at the primary sites. I identified the optimum systems used by the sample companies, defining 'optimum systems' as those being used by the most effective innovators. Conveniently, the other companies in the sample were beginning to adopt similar systems. Besides describing the optimum systems, I identified the types of management intervention that had been used to create them. The results of this analysis are presented in Chapter 8.

In Chapter 6, I report the results of the last analysis performed as part of the INSEAD research project. As the data collected at MGE were longitudinal, it was possible to observe the effects of all but the most recent interventions. Of the 273 interventions in the database, 93 were subsequently considered to have been deleterious to the company's innovation performance. Forty-two of these 93 involved decisions or policies that were actually reversed. The other 51 comprised decisions that could not be reversed, but that were regretted by the general managers or by the project manager involved in the decision (for example, premature publicity for a project, or too early an entry decision).

I analyzed these data by looking at success and failure by intervention type. I also looked at which level of general manager was making successful and failed interventions. The results of this analysis are presented in Chapter 6.

The analysis in Chapter 9 was developed after the completion of the INSEAD research project. Before developing a comprehensive model of industry variation, I interviewed managers in five additional companies (USAuto, CementCo, USComputers, AmPro, and EurTel). I then compared the notes from these and all previous interviews to identify differences in the industries in which the companies competed. I also identified additional differences in the ways in which these companies managed innovation. A summary of the differences identified is reported in Chapter 9.

Bibliography

Ackoff, R.L. 1978. *The art of problem solving: accompanied by Ackoff's fables.* New York: John Wiley & Sons.

Adler, P.S. 1990. Shared learning. *Management Science,* **36**: 938–57.

Allen, T.J. 1977. *Managing the flow of technology: technology transfer and the dissemination of technological information within the R&D organization.* Halliday.

Anderson, P. and Tushman, M.L. 1990. Technological discontinuities and dominant designs: a cyclical model of technological change. *Administrative Science Quarterly,* **35**: 604–33.

Angle, H.J. 1989. Psychology and organizational innovation. In Van de Ven, A., Angle, H. and Poole, M.S. (eds) *Research on the management of innovation.* New York: Harper & Row, pp. 135–70.

Angle, H.J. and Van de Ven, A.H. 1989. Suggestions for managing the innovation journey. In Van de Ven, A., Angle, H. and Poole, M.S. (eds) *Research on the management of innovation.* New York: Harper & Row, pp. 663–97.

Archibald, R.D. 1992. *Managing high-technology programs and projects,* 2nd edn. New York: John Wiley & Sons.

Ardrey, R. 1970. *The social contract: a personal inquiry into the evolutionary sources of order and disorder.* New York: Atheneum.

Argyris, C. 1985. *Strategy, change, and defensive routines.* Boston: Pitman.

Argyris, C. and Schön, D.A. 1974. *Theory in practice: increasing professional effectiveness.* San Francisco: Jossey-Bass.

Argyris, C., and Schön, D.A. 1978. *Organizational learning: a theory of action perspective.* Reading, MA: Addison-Wesley.

Arnold, J.D. 1992. *The complete problem solver: a total system for competitive decision making.* New York: John Wiley & Sons.

Barr, P.S., Stimpert, J.L. and Huff, A.S. 1992. Cognitive change, strategic action, and organizational renewal. *Strategic Management Journal,* **13**: 15–36.

Bartlett, C.A. and Ghoshal, S. 1989. *Managing across borders: the transnational solution.* Boston: Harvard Business School Press.

Bartlett, C.A. and Ghoshal, S. 1994. Changing the role of top management: beyond strategy to purpose. *Harvard Business Review,* (November–December): 79–88.

Bartlett, C.A. and Ghoshal, S. 1995. Changing the role of top management: beyond systems to people. *Harvard Business Review,* (May–June): 132–42.

Bartlett, C.A. and Mohammed, A. 1994. *3M optical systems: managing corporate entrepreneurship.* Harvard Business School case 9-395-017.

Bartlett, C.A, and Mohammed, A. 1995. *3M: profile of an innovating company.* Harvard Business School case N9-395-016.

Bower, J. 1970. *Managing the resource allocation process.* Homewood, IL: Irwin.

Brown, S.L. and Eisenhardt, K.M. 1998. *Competing on the edge: strategy as structured chaos*. Boston: Harvard Business School Press.

Burgelman, R.A. 1983. A process model of internal corporate venturing in the diversified major firm. *Administrative Science Quarterly*, **28**: 223–44.

Christensen, C.M. 1997. *The innovator's dilemma: when new technologies cause great firms to fail*. Boston: HBS Press.

Christiansen, J.A. 1997. Learning to improve innovation performance: the role of the general manager. Doctoral dissertation, INSEAD.

Clark, K.B. and Fujimoto, T. 1991. *Product development performance: strategy, organization, and management in the world auto industry*. Boston: Harvard Business School Press.

Cohen, W.M. and Levinthal, D.A. 1990. Absorptive capacity: a new perspective on learning and innovation. *Administrative Science Quarterly*, **35**: 128–52.

Czikszentmihalyi, M. 1996. *Creativity: flow and the psychology of discovery and invention*. New York: HarperCollins.

Dierickx, I. and Cool, K. 1989. Asset stock accumulation and the sustainability of competitive advantage. *Management Science*, **35**: 1504–11.

Dougherty, D. 1992. Interpretive barriers to successful product innovation in large firms. *Organization Science*, **3**: 179–202.

Dougherty, D. and Heller, T. 1994. The illegitimacy of successful product innovation in established firms. *Organization Science*, **5**: 200–18.

Eisenhardt, K.M. 1989. Building theories from case study research. *Academy of Management Review*, **14**: 532–50.

Eisenhardt, K.M. and Tabrizi, B.N. 1995. Accelerating adaptive processes: product innovation in the global computer industry. *Administrative Science Quarterly*, **40**: 84–110.

Garud, R. and Van de Ven, A.H. 1992. An empirical evaluation of the internal corporate venturing process. *Strategic Management Journal*, **13**: 93–109.

Ghoshal, S. 1987. Global strategy: an organizing framework. *Strategic Management Journal*, **8**: 425–40.

Ghoshal, S. and Bartlett, C.A. 1995. Changing the role of top management: beyond structure to process. *Harvard Business Review*, (January–February): 86–96.

Ghoshal, S. and Bartlett, C.A. 1998. *The individualized corporation: a fundamentally new approach to management*. London: Heinemann.

Ghoshal, S. and Nohria, N. 1992. Explaining innovation in multinational corporations: reconceptualizing the structure of M-form organizations. In Nohria, N. and Eccles, R.G. (eds) *Networks and organizations: structure, form and action*. Boston, Harvard Business School Press.

Glaser, B.G. and Strauss, A.L. 1967. *The discovery of grounded theory: strategies for qualitative research*. Chicago: Aldine.

Goold, M. and Campbell, A. 1987. *Strategies and styles: the role of the centre in managing diversified corporations*. London: Basil Blackwell.

Grove, A.S. 1996. *Only the paranoid survive*. New York: Currency Doubleday.

Haspeslagh, P. 1985. *Toward a concept of corporate strategy for the diversified firm*. Stanford Business School Research Paper Number 816.

Haspeslagh, P. 1986. *Conceptualizing the strategic process in diversified firms: the role and nature of the corporate influence process.* INSEAD working paper number 86/09.

Hayes, J.R. 1989. *The complete problem solver*, 2nd edn. Hillsdale, NJ: Lawrence Erlbaum Associates.

Henderson, R. and Clark, K.B. 1990. Architectural innovation: the reconfiguration of existing product technologies and the failure of established firms. *Administrative Science Quarterly*, **35**: 9–30.

Henry, J. 1963. *Culture against man.* New York: Random House.

Imai, M. 1986. *Kaizen: the key to Japan's competitive success.* New York: McGraw-Hill.

Itani, J. 1963. Paternal care in wild Japanese monkeys. In Southwick, C.H. (ed.) *Primate social behavior.* New York: Van Nostrand.

Jaikumar, R. and Bohn, R.E. 1992. A dynamic approach to OM: an alternative to static optimization. *International Journal of Production Economics*, **27**: 265–82.

Katz, R. and Allen, T.J. 1982. Investigating the NIH syndrome: a look at the performance, tenure and communication patterns of 50 R&D projects. *R&D Management*, **12**(1): 7–19.

Kawamura, S. 1963. Process of sub-culture propagation among Japanese monkeys. In Southwick, C.H. (ed.) *Primate social behavior*, New York: Van Nostrand.

Kim, W.C. and Mauborgne, R. 1997a. Value innovation: the strategic logic of high growth. *Harvard Business Review,* (January–February): 103–12.

Kim, W.C. and Mauborgne, R. 1997b. Fair process: managing in the knowledge economy. *Harvard Business Review,* (July–August): 65–75.

Kotter, J.P. 1982. *The general managers.* New York: Free Press.

Laing, R.D. 1967. *The politics of experience.* New York: Ballantine.

Leonard-Barton, D. 1992. Core capabilities and core rigidities in new product development. *Strategic Management Journal*, **13**: 111–25.

Leonard-Barton, D. 1995. *Wellsprings of knowledge.* Boston: HBS Press.

Lock, D. 1977. *Project Management*, 2nd edn. Westmead: Gower.

Maidique, M. and Hayes, R.H. 1984. The art of high technology management. *Sloan Management Review*, (Winter): 17–31.

Meyer, C. 1993. *Fast cycle time: how to align purpose, strategy, and structure for speed.* New York: Free Press.

Meyer, C. 1998. *Relentless growth: how Silicon Valley innovation strategies can work in your business.* New York: Free Press.

Miles, M.B. and Huberman, A.M. 1994. *Qualitative data analysis: an expanded source book*, 2nd edn. Thousand Oaks, CA: Sage.

Mintzberg, H. 1973. *The nature of managerial work.* New York: Harper & Row.

Morison, E.E. 1966. Gunfire at sea: a case study of innovation. From *Men, machines and modern times.* Cambridge, MA: MIT Press.

Muzyka, D. 1989. Management practice in large complex projects: lessons from nuclear power plant construction and NASA's shuttle program. Unpublished doctoral dissertation, Harvard Graduate School of Business Administration.

Neill, A.S. 1960. *Summerhill: a radical approach to child rearing.* New York: Hart.

Organization for Economic Cooperation and Development. 1997a. Towards sustainable transportation: Conference organized by the OECD and by the government of Canada, Vancouver, BC, 24–27 March, 1996. Paris: OECD.

Organization for Economic Cooperation and Development. 1997b. *The world in 2020: towards a new global age*. Paris: OECD.

Pearce, J.L. and Page, R.A. 1990. Palace politics: resource allocation in radically innovative firms. *Journal of High Technology Management Research*, **1**: 193–205.

Porter, M.E. 1980. *Competitive strategy: techniques for analyzing industries and competitors*. New York: Free Press.

Prahalad, C.K. and Bettis, R.J. 1986. The dominant logic: a new linkage between diversity and process. *Strategic Management Journal*, **7**: 485–501.

Prahalad, C.K. and Doz, Y.L. 1987. *The multinational mission: balancing local demands and global vision*. New York: Free Press.

Prahalad, C.K. and Hamel, G. 1990. The core competence of the corporation. *Harvard Business Review*, (May–June) 79–93.

Randolph, W.A. and Posner, B.Z. 1992. *Getting the job done! Managing project teams and task forces for success*, rev. edn. Englewood Cliffs, NJ: Prentice-Hall.

Roberts, E.B. and Fusfeld, A.R. 1981. Staffing the innovative, technology-based organization. *Sloan Management Review*, (Spring): 19–34.

Schmidt, R.L. and Freeland, J.R. 1992. Recent progress in modeling R&D project-selection processes. *IEEE Transactions in Engineering Management*, **39**: 189–201.

Schroeder, R.G., Van de Ven, A.H., Scudder, G.D. and Polley, D. 1989. The development of innovation ideas. In Van de Ven, A., Angle, H. and Poole, M.S. (eds) *Research on the management of innovation*. New York: Harper & Row, pp. 107–34.

Sharpe, P. and Keelin, T. 1998. How SmithKline Beecham makes better resource-allocation decisions. *Harvard Business Review*, (March–April): 45–57.

Simon, H.A. 1985. What we know about the creative process. In Kuhn, R.L. (ed.) *Frontiers in creative and innovative management*. Cambridge, MA: Ballinger, pp. 3–20.

Smith, D.K. and Alexander, R.C. 1988. *Fumbling the future: how Xerox invented, then ignored, the personal computer*. New York: W. Morrow.

Spilker, B. 1989. *Multinational drug companies: issues in drug discovery and development*. New York: Raven Press.

Stalk, G. Jr and Hout, T.M. 1990. *Competing against time: how time-based competition is reshaping global markets*. New York: Free Press.

Strauss, A.L. and Corbin, J. 1990. *Basics of qualitative research: grounded theory procedures and techniques*. Newbury Park, CA: Sage.

Tushman, M.L. and Anderson, P. 1986. Technological discontinuities and organizational environments. *Administrative Science Quarterly*, **31**: 439–65.

Utterback, J.M. 1971. The process of technological innovation within the firm. *Academy of Management Journal*, **12**: 75–88.

Van de Ven, A. 1986. Central problems in the management of innovation. *Management Science*, **32**: 590–607.

Van de Ven, A., Angle, H. and Poole, M.S. (eds) 1989. *Research on the management of innovation*. New York: Harper & Row.

Von Hippel, E. 1986. Lead users: a source of novel product concepts. *Management Science*, **32**: 791–805.

Von Hippel, E. 1987. Cooperation between rivals: informal know-how trading. *Research Policy*, **16**: 291–302.

Wheelwright, S.C. and Clark, K.B. 1992. *Revolutionizing product development*. New York: Free Press.

Whyte, W.H. Jr 1956. *The Organization Man*. New York: Simon & Schuster.

Womack, J.P., Jones, D.T. and Roos, D. 1990. *The machine that changed the world*. New York: Macmillan.

Yin, R.K. 1984. *Case study research: design and methods*. Beverly Hills, CA: Sage.

Zuboff, S. 1988. *In the age of the smart machine*. New York: Basic Books.

Index

3M, xiii, 2–3, 8, 9, 94, 95, 233, 273
  company history and change
    programs, 168
  customer information collected, 153–4
  decision-making methods, 156
  development system, 228
  fiscal responsibility, 109
  funding system, 105, 220
  goals, 75–6
  high-uncertainty projects, 234
  idea generation system, 99–101, 159,
    217
  idea types, 236–8, 239–40
  information used in funding decisions,
    113–14
  innovation system evolution, 194, 207,
    208, 209
  laboratory management methods, 158
  mentoring, 160
  project structure, 157
  radical transformations, 252
  regulation, 247
  rotation of personnel, 155

A

abundance of ideas, 236–40
accuracy of funding decisions, 114–16
adaptables, 92, 94
Admin, 9, 10, 273
Advanced Flexible innovation system,
  194–7, 205–11
Advanced Materials, 6–9, 62
  development, 231
  innovation system evolution, 194, 196,
    198, 208
  managers' roles, 181, 182, 186
Advanced Plastics, 182, 183, 186
air transportation industry, 250, 253
aircraft manufacturing industry, 240, 241
airline industry, 250, 253
Alcatel, xii

American Telephone & Telegraph
  (AT&T), 79
AmPro, 9, 10, 272, 275, 277
  young and old at, 88–90
Apple Computers, xii, 146
appliance industry, 240
AT&T, *see* American Telephone &
  Telegraph
automobile companies, 162, 260
  development, 147–8
  diversified activities, 150–1
automobile industry, xii, 96–8, 191, 193,
  202, 209, 233, 234, 240–1, 245, 246
autonomous team structure, 205

B

Bell Laboratories, 79
black box theory of idea generation,
  79–81
breadth of projects funded, 115, 117
business unit managed projects, 205
business unit managers, 265
  role in change program, 172–3, 186–7
business unit personnel's role in change
  program, 173, 187–8

C

cement manufacturing industry, 234,
  236, 253
CementCo, 9, 10, 272, 275, 277
centralized control of projects, 123–4
change process, 4, 11, 12
change program
  communication, 148–50, 152–3, 162,
    163
  company history impact on, 168
  competences, 151–2
  complexity of changes, 160–5
  components of the company, 151–2
  cross-functional coordination, 150
  culture, 144–6, 149, 163–4
  decision-making methods, 155–7

development, 146–8
diversified companies, 148–50
ease of change, 164–5
funding system, 142–3, 162
how to organize, 137–65
idea generation, 150, 159
incentives, 14–16, 149, 163–4
industry differences, 165–7
information collected, 153–4
laboratory management methods,
    158–9
managers' roles, 171–90
mentoring, 160
mobilizing managers, 163
organization structure, 148–50, 162–3
personnel management systems,
    154–5, 163–4
power issues, 168–70
project budgets, 142–3, 160–1
project management methods, 162
project structure, 157–8
rationalizing development, 146–8
risk, 139, 140
sequencing change, 160–5
strategy, 167
training, 162–3
urgency, 167–8
chemical industry 234, 236, 251
Chemical Residues project, 11, 15, 68,
    69, 73, 79, 223, 258, 274
    analysis of story, 53, 56
    delays from funding system, 105
    high-uncertainty project, 228
    history of, 17–52
    information used in funding decisions,
        113
    managers' roles, 176–9, 183, 187
chemistry and radical transformations,
    252–3
children and idea generation, 81–3
children's creativity, 91–2
Cineplex Cinemas, 102
Cisco Systems, xiii, xiv
clothing industry, 250
commodity chemicals, 236
commodity industries, 236
common knowledge, 93

common wisdom, 93
communication systems, 65–7, 265–6
    change program, 148–50, 152–3, 162,
        163
    Chemical Residues project, 26, 37, 45,
        49
    customers, 126–7
    funding system, 221
    idea generation, 217–18
    innovation system evolution, 194, 201,
        204
communications industry, xii
company history
    change programs, 168
    innovation system evolution, 257
company resources and cost of ideas,
    236–40
competence management, 65–8
    change program, 151–2
    Chemical Residues project, 26, 36, 50
    idea generation, 95–7, 214–18
    projects funded, 115, 117
    see also management competence
competitive pressure, 244–6
complex products, 240–1
complexity of changes, 160–5
components of the company, 151–2
computer chip manufacturing, 70, 239
computer industry, 234, 240
Concorde, xiii
ConElec, 9, 10, 273
conformists, 92, 94
consensus decision making, 156
consultants
    Chemical Residues project, 48, 49
    impact on speed of change, 168–9
    use of, 57, 63, 90, 142, 143, 167, 181,
        226, 260–1
    willingness to use, 168–9
consulting to project managers, see
    mentoring
consumer electronics industry, 234
consumer packaged goods industry, 234
consumer products companies, 251
ConsumerCo, 2–3, 8, 9, 69, 95, 233, 273
    customer information collected, 153–4
    decision-making methods, 155–7

goals, 76
idea generation, 159
idea types, 238
innovation system evolution, 294, 208
laboratory management methods,
158–9
project structure, 157
rotation of personnel, 155
young and old at, 87–8
consumers
communicating with, 126–7
in developing countries, 262
in industrialized countries 262
control mechanisms
in companies, 93
in schools, 91
control of projects,
centralized/decentralized, 123–4
core business, innovation in, 4
corporate managers, 265
role in change program, 172, 183–5
cost
development, 120, 125–6
ideas, 236–40
innovation, 75
cost/quality trade-off, 96–8
CR, *see* Chemical Residues project
creativity, 91–5
cross-fertilization of ideas, 213
cross-functional coordination, 150
idea generation, 217
culture, 65, 66, 69, 266
change program, 144–6, 149, 163–4
Chemical Residues project, 27, 33
idea generation, 101
customer information collected, 153–4
customer need
current, 75
development, 120
fit with, 65
future, 75
customer-focused business unit, 207
customers, communication with, 126–7

D

Danone, xiv
data analysis method, 270, 274–7

data collection, 270–3
decentralization, power issues, 169–70
decentralized control of projects, 123–4
decision quality and distance, 108–9
decision-making methods, 65–7
change program, 155–7
Chemical Residues, 27, 33
deregulation and radical transformations,
253
development, 71, 74, 267, 268
cost, 125–6
fit with customer need, 126–7
incentives, 126
rationalizing project plans, 146–8
resources, 124
speed, 124–5
theory of, 119–127
uncertainty, 125, 223
development systems, evolution of,
223–32
diagnosing problems in innovation
system, 127–32
distance between ideas and funds, 103–9
distortion of information, 104
speed, 104
distortion of information in funding
decisions, 104
diversification
number of funding sources, 111
opportunities available, 241–2
see also management interest in
diversification
diversification capacity, 191–2, 200, 212,
261–2
diversified companies
change program, 148–50
managers' roles in change program,
183–8
division managers, 265
role in change program, 172, 185–6

E

ease of making changes, 164–5
Eastman Chemical, 7–9, 95, 273
development, 231
goals, 76
idea generation, 217

innovation system evolution, 194, 196, 198, 208
laboratory management methods, 158
efficiency of innovation system, 191–2, 200–1, 212, 261–2
electronics and radical transformations, 252–3
electronics industry, xii, 234, 239, 241, 245, 253
endorsements from leaders, 87
environment hospitable to creativity, 5
environment, *see* industry environment
environmental limits, 262–3
Ericsson, xiii
EurAuto, 8, 9
  development, 225
  goals, 76
  idea generation, 159, 213
  innovation system evolution, 194, 196, 198, 202, 208
  laboratory management methods, 159
  mentoring, 160
  rotation of personnel, 155
EuroChem, 9, 10, 273
EurTel, 9, 10, 246, 272, 275, 277
event study methodology, 274

F

fairness and idea sharing, 102
fashion-driven industries, 250
filtering ideas, 82
financial services industry, 234
FinCo, 9, 10, 273
fiscal responsibility and funding decisions, 109
fit with customer need and development, 126–7
Flexible innovation system, 194–8, 199, 200, 204–11, 212, 232, 242, 256
  development, 223–4
  funding, 221
  idea generation, 214
focus strategy and number of funding sources, 111
focused companies and managers' roles in change program, 188–90

Focused innovation system, 194–8, 199, 202, 205, 207–11, 212, 232, 242, 256
  development, 223–4
  funding, 221
  idea generation, 214
following the market, 127
food processing industry, 234
foreseeability of tasks, 123
Formula One Hotels, 102
Frye, Art, 94
functional team structure, 198
functions as idea source, 85
funding, initial, 74
funding phase, 71
funding search, 74
funding systems, 64–6, 266–7, 268
  change program, 142–3, 162
  communications, 221
  Chemical Residues, 27, 29, 33, 36, 40, 45, 46
  dimensions of, 103–14
  evolution of, 218–22, 232
  incentives, 105, 114, 221
  information used, 104, 111–14, 221
  new business creation, 257
  number of funding sources, 104, 110–11, 221
  outcomes, 114–18
  theory of, 102–19
  who makes funding decisions, 221

G

General Electric (GE), 3, 164
General Motors (GM), 93
goals, 65, 66, 68, 266
  Chemical Residues project, 21, 33
  development, 77–8, 226
  funding, 77–8
  idea generation, 76–8, 99–100
  innovation system overall, 74–9
government and radical transformations, 253
grounded theory methodology, 270
group managers, 265
  role in change program, 172, 185–6
Grove, Andy, 239

H

health care industry, xii
heavy industrial equipment industry, xii
heavyweight team structure, 202, 205
heroes, impact of designating, 114
Hewlett Packard, xiv
high-quality strategies, 256–7
high-uncertainty projects, 224, 226–31, 233–4
hiring outsiders, 167, 168–9, 181, 226
  Chemical Residues project, 43
  idea generation, 82–5
history, *see* company history

I

IBM, *see* International Business Machines
idea generation defined, 73
idea generation methods, 64–6
  change program, 159
  Chemical Residues project, 24
idea generation phase, 71, 267, 268
idea generation systems
  3M, 99–101
  communications, 150, 217–18
  competence management, 214–18
  complementary theories of, 102
  cross-functional links, 217
  evolution of, 213–18, 232
  new theories of, 95–101
  old theories of, 79–81
  rotation of personnel, 218
  theory of, 79–102
ideas, differences in, 234–44
improvement, finding opportunities for, 131–4
improving innovation performance, *see* change process
incentives, 65–7, 266
  change program, 144–6, 149, 163–4
  Chemical Residues project, 21, 27, 33, 38, 44, 48
  cost of development, 126
  funding systems, 105, 114, 221
  new business creation, 257
independent projects, 205

individualists, 92, 93
individual's impact on innovation system, 170
Industrial Chemicals, 6–9, 11, 59, 63
  Chemical Residues project, 17–52, 55
  change efforts at, 142
  development, 231
  funding system, 106, 113–14, 220
  goals, 75
  incentives, 163–4
  information in funding decisions, 113–14
  innovation system evolution, 194, 196, 198, 199, 200, 207, 208
  managers' roles in change program, 176–9, 180, 182, 186
  power issues, 168–9
  urgency of change, 167–8
industrial machinery industry, 234
industrial products industry, 234, 260
industry differences, 4, 11–13, 259, 261
  change programs, 165–7
  innovation system design, 233–53
industry environment, 244–9
information
  collected on customers, 153–4
  distortion and distance, 108
  funding decisions, 104, 108, 111–14, 221
innovation system efficiency, 191–2, 200–1, 212, 261–2
innovation system, diagnosing problems, 127–32
innovation within existing businesses, 243–4
inter-business networks, 257
interest in innovation, 255–6
International Business Machines (IBM), 93
Internet, xii

J

Japanese automobile companies, 96–8, 245
Jobs, Steve, 146

K

knowledge
  distance and decision quality, 108–9
  funding decisions, 104

L

laboratory chiefs' power, 204
laboratory management methods, 64–7
  change program, 158–9
laboratory-operating unit relations,
  79–81
launch phase, 71, 268
Lawn & Garden, 6–9, 61, 63
  development, 223
  funding, 221
  idea generation, 217
  innovation system evolution, 194, 196,
    198, 202, 208
  managers' roles in change program,
    179–80, 185, 186, 187
  power issues, 170
  project structure, 157–8
LC49 project, 179–80, 185, 186
  project structure, 157–8
leading the market, 127
learning from failed projects, 119
length of projects, 121–2
lightweight team structure, 205
lone inventor, 79, 94, 98, 99
low-cost strategies, 256
low-uncertainty projects, 224–6, 233
Lucent, xiii, xiv

M

MachineCo, 9, 10, 273
machinery industry, 234
mainframe computers, 240
management competence, 253–5
management interest
  in diversification, 256
  in innovation, 255–6
management tools, *see* tools for
  improving innovation performance
Manufacturing Group Europe (MGE), 6,
  7, 11, 63, 167, 168, 194
  change efforts, 142
  Chemical Residues project, 17–52

development, 223, 228, 231
funding, 105, 220
idea generation, 159, 217
laboratory management methods, 159
managers' roles in change program,
  176–88
mentoring, 160
methodology, 270–7
rotation of personnel, 155
strategy, 18, 33–5
market need, 71
  see also customer need
materials technology and radical
  transformations, 252–3
memory chip manufacturing, 70, 239
mentoring
  change program, 160
  Chemical Residues project, 30
Merck, xiv
methodology, 5–6, 264–77
MGE, *see* Manufacturing Group Europe
Minnesota Mining & Manufacturing, *see*
  3M
mobilizing managers for change
  program, 57, 63, 163
monkeys and idea diffusion, xiii, 85–7
Montessori schools, 91
motor vehicle companies, *see* automobile
  companies
Multi-focus innovation system, 194–7,
  202–4, 207–11

N

Netscape search engine, xii
new business creation, 242–3, 257
new feature strategies, 256–7
newcomers and idea generation, 82–5
NIH, *see* Not Invented Here syndrome
Nissan, xii
Northern Pharmaceuticals, 6–9, 60
  change efforts, 142, 143
  development, 223, 226
  goals, 76
  idea generation, 159, 213, 217
  innovation system evolution, 194, 196,
    198–9, 200–1, 202–4, 208
  laboratory management methods, 159

managers' roles in change program,
180–1, 186
power issues, 168–9
urgency of change, 167–8
Not Invented Here syndrome (NIH), 85,
169
nuclear power industry, 250
number of funding sources, 110–11, 221
number of projects funded, 115–16

O

old and young people, relations between,
87–90
older companies, why they stay in
business, 84
operating unit–laboratory relations, 79–81
operational control of projects, 174, 183,
185–6, 187, 188
Chemical Residues project, 42
opportunities for improvement,
identifying, 131–4
opportunities, differences in, 234–44
OptiCo, 9, 10, 273
optics industry, 234
order, mechanisms for keeping
in companies, 93
in schools, 91
organization structure, 65, 66, 68, 265–6
change program, 148–50, 162–3
Chemical Residues project, 36, 49, 50
innovation system evolution, 194, 200,
202–4
new business creation, 257
see also project organization structure
organizations, impact on creativity, 92–3
outcomes of projects, 115, 118
outline of the book, 10–13
outsider hiring, see hiring outsiders
outsiders and idea generation, 82–5

P

Palo Alto Research Center (PARC), xiii,
80, 146
parallel work, 201, 202, 226
PARC, see Palo Alto Research Center
participation in projects, Chemical
Residues, 39

permanent project team, 207
personal accessories industry, 250
personal computer, 80, 93, 146
personnel management systems, 65, 66,
68, 69, 266
change program, 154–5, 163–4
Chemical Residues, 24
idea generation, 101
Pfizer, xiv
pharmaceutical companies, 162, 259–60
development, 146–7
diversified activities, 150–1
fiscal responsibility, 109
pharmaceutical industry, 191, 193, 202,
209, 233, 234, 238, 244, 245
regulation, 247, 248–9
phases of innovation process, 72–4,
267–8
politics and idea generation, 83–4
Post-It™ notes, xiii, 94, 105, 158
post-launch development phase, 71
power and idea generation, 83–4
power issues
change programs, 168–70
laboratory chiefs, 204
predictability of environment and
innovation system, 249–53
pre-idea period, 73
privatizations, 246, 253
problems in innovation system, diagnosis
of, 127–32
process for idea generation, 100–1
process innovation, 256
process of improving innovation
performance, see change process
product innovation (vs process
innovation), 256–7
product launch, 71, 268
product life, length of, 244–6
product-market strategy
innovation system configuration,
256–7
projects funded, 115, 117
project budgets and change program,
142–3, 160–1
project chiefs' role in change program,
173, 187–8

project control, centralized/decentralized, 123–4
project funding systems, *see* funding systems
project management methods, 64–6, 266–7
  change program, 143–4, 162
  Chemical Residues, 29, 30, 40, 42, 44, 45, 46, 50
  idea generation, 101
project organization structure, 46, 48, 64–6
  autonomous team, 205
  change program, 157–8
  functional team, 198
  heavyweight team, 202, 205
  innovation system evolution, 194, 201
  lightweight team, 205
project plans, standard, 127
project set-up, Chemical Residues, 30
project similarity, 122–3
project team members' role in change program, 173, 187–8
projects
  business unit managed, 205
  independent, 205
  length, 121–2
  sequential or parallel work, 201
  size, 121–2

Q

Q-sort method of data analysis, 275–6
quality/cost trade-off, 96–8

R

radical transformations, 249, 251–3
rationalizing development projects, 124–5, 146–8
reflection, 57
regulation
  as a problem, 248–9
  impact on innovation systems, 247–9
Renault, xii
resistance
  to change, 162
  to new ideas, 83–4
resource allocation, *see* funding

resources and development, 124
risk in a change program, 139, 140
risk management in funding, 118–19
risk profile of projects funded, 115, 118
roles of different managers in change program, 171–90
rotation of personnel, 155, 218
Rubbermaid, 238

S

Safety Materials project, 223
  high-uncertainty project, 228
  managers' roles in change program, 182, 183, 186, 187
scarcity of ideas, 236–40
schools, impact on creativity, 91–2
scope of a manager's actions, 55–62, 173–4
separation theory of idea generation, 79–81
sequencing change, 57–63, 160–5
sequential work on projects, 201, 202
Siemens, xiii
signaling need for change, 174, 185
Silicon Valley, 84
similarity of projects, 122–3
similarity of tasks, 123
simple and complex changes, 160–5, 259
simple products, 240–1
size of projects, 121–2
skunk team, xiii
skunk works, 145–6
SmithKline Beecham, 110–11
speculative product development, 127
speed and distance in funding decisions, 105–8, 109
speed in development, 120, 124–5
speed of change, 168–9
speed of funding decisions, 104, 114–16
speed of innovation, 75
spin-off's from failed projects, 119
stability of environment, 249–53
stable and unstable industries, 192–3
standard project plans, 127
stimulating reflection, 57
strategy, 65–7
  change programs, 167

Chemical Residues, 21, 22, 27, 33, 35
  idea generation, 99–100
structure for idea generation, 100–1
Summerhill, 91
supervision system, Chemical Residues
  project, 37, 42, 44

T
task foreseeability, 123
task rationalization, 124–5
task similarity, 123
tasks in development, 120
technical solution, 71
technological revolutions, 82, 249,
  251–3
technological transformations, 82, 249,
  251–3
telecommunications equipment industry,
  234–46
Texas Instruments, xiv
tools for improving innovation
  performance, 3, 53–57, 267
  classification of types, 63–9, 173–4
  managers' roles in change program,
  173–4
Traditional innovation system, 194–209
training and change program, 162–3, 261
trucking industry, 253

U
uncertainty
  development, 125, 223–4
  foreseeable tasks, 123
  industry variation, 192–3
  innovation system variation, 192–3,
    249–53
urgency and change programs, 167–8
US Food Products (USF), 1–4, 9, 10,
  272, 275
USAuto, 9, 10, 272, 275, 277
USComputers, 9, 10, 239, 272, 275, 277
USF, *see* US Food Products

V
Viagra, xii
virtual financial services industry, xii

W
Welch, Jack, 164
Wozniak, Steve, 146

X
Xerox, xiii, 80, 146

Y
young and old people, relations between,
  87–90